The Wanderer's Guide

To

Lucca

The Wanderer's Guide to Lucca

Brian Robert Lindquist

EER
Edward Everett Root, Publishers, Brighton, 2020.

EER
Edward Everett Root, Publishers, Co. Ltd.,
30 New Road, Brighton, Sussex, BN1 1BN, England.
Details of our overseas agents are given on our website.
www.eerpublishing.com

edwardeverettroot@yahoo.co.uk

Brian Robert Lindquist
The Wanderer's Guide to Lucca

© Brian Robert Lindquist 2011, 2020.

First published in England by Edward Everett Root Publishers 2020.

First published in America by Lindquist Historical Guides 2011.

This edition © Edward Everett Root Publishers, 2020.

ISBN: 978-1-913087-23-4

Brian Robert Lindquist has asserted his right to be identified as the owner of the copyright of this Work in accordance with the Copyright, Designs and Patents Act 1988 as the owner of this Work.

All rights reserved. No part of this publication may be reproduced, stored in a retrieval system or transmitted in any form or by any means, electronic, mechanical, photocopying, recording or otherwise, without the prior permission of the copyright owner.

Book production by DW Graphic Arts.

For Wendy

*In memory of
Peter Della Santina*

Acknowledgments

Krishna Ghosh Della Santina, for sharing her home and family during many stays in Lucca.

Silvia Scuoteguazza, Anna Lia Nannipieri, and Antonio Nannipieri, whose friendship and hospitality made the fulfillment of this project possible. Antonio for the photographs of San Matteo.

Giovanni Sinicropi and Andreina Bianchini, for being there from beginning to end and at every turn in the path.

Neil Guy, for enthusiastically sharing his deep knowledge of the architecture of Lucca, and for being the best of wandering companions.

Dott. Marco Paoli, Director of the Biblioteca Statale di Lucca, for his warm welcome, encouragement, and assistance at the inception of this project.

Darcy Witham of DW Graphics, who turned this manuscript into a book.

The people of Lucca, who have been practicing hospitality for two thousand years.

Glenn Magnell, who sent me to Italy for the first time, knowing it would seduce me.

My family, without whose steadfast patience and love this book would never have been conceived nor finished.

"...and so straight to my first fixed aim, Lucca, where I settled my self for ten days—as I supposed. It turned out forty years..."

John Ruskin, recalling his visit in 1845 at the age of twenty-six.

Preface

As John Ruskin discovered, a visit to Lucca can fill a day, or a lifetime. This book should keep you occupied for some period between the two. It is designed to let you wander where you want in Lucca's maze of streets, to help you quickly find out where you are, what you are looking at, and to learn something interesting about it.

It is, first of all, a guide to the **History** of the city, so it starts with a brief review. Many more historical details are woven into the sections which follow.

Lucca is a city of **Churches**—there seems to be one on every corner—and they are the repository of much of its art and history, so the churches are dealt with comprehensively.

The other great buildings, the **Palazzi**, are even more numerous. As many of these as possible have been included.

It is the **Families** who occupied these buildings which were the soul of the town. Their stories are told in their own section.

The number of **Streets** is too large to be dealt with completely, but the most interesting are covered.

Finally, its **Walls** have always defined Lucca, so they receive their own treatment.

~

Author's Note

I got waylaid by Lucca. I hope you do too.

The first time I visited Lucca I knew nothing about it. Wandering around, with my tourist map in hand, I remember feeling constantly lost. Finding my way back to a place I had just been usually proved impossible. As I walked past an endless array of Renaissance palazzi, medieval buildings, and a daunting number of churches filled with art I couldn't identify, my sense of bewilderment deepened.

Standing in front of the Cathedral my frustration peaked. Here was a grand, exuberant structure, as vibrant a building as I had ever seen. When I read that it was started in 1060 and finished about 1200, questions began to plague me. Who were the people who built this? What was going on in this obscure location at such an early time to inspire them to such a feat? Where did the money come from?

Lucca appeared to be an isolated spot, plunked down on a plain between mountains, with no natural defenses, and yet I read that it had always been independent and prosperous. What made its inhabitants so successful? How did they govern themselves? As my awareness grew to encompass the elegant rebuilding of the 1500s and 1600s—and those walls!—my wonder increased.

Having raised these questions I confess that this book barely begins to answer them. Its purpose is more practical: first, how not to get lost; second, to learn something about all those churches and the art within them, about the palazzi and the people who lived in them, and to provide as much of the historical context as possible. But as you wander around, I hope you will keep this question in mind—what accounts for the success of this place? Or, what makes it special? For the longer you wander, the more you look and wonder, the more special I think you will find it.

~

Contents

Introduction 1
Vocabulary and Conventions 3
Things to Look For 4
Chronology 10

History 13

Churches 43
    Former Churches 274

Palazzi 287

Families 321

Streets 351

Walls 357

Index of Artists 365

Maps 371

~

Introduction

*L*ucca is deceptive. It does not begin by overwhelming you, except for those walls. After a one day trip you may leave thinking you have seen it. Stay a few days more and you begin to feel that you haven't seen it at all. Stay a little longer and you may discover, as Ruskin did, that a lifetime has gone by and you are still looking.

The walled city isn't large. It takes twenty minutes to walk across it east-west, at a leisurely but steady pace. This has been true since 1650, when the present set of walls was completed. For about 500 years before that, when the medieval walls defined the city, it took less than fifteen minutes to make the same transit. For more than a thousand years before that, when the Roman walls stood, it took only ten minutes to traverse the city. Most of your visit will take place within the circuits of the Roman and Medieval walls.

Don't expect to maintain a steady pace, however, for if Lucca is not large, it is dense. It has been continuously inhabited for more than two thousand years; it was never abandoned and it was never destroyed. During most of its history Lucca thrived. It survived the Dark Ages intact and by the early Middle Ages it was the capital of Tuscany. In the High Middle Ages it was the silk capital of Europe; its merchants and bankers preceded those of Florence and Siena. During the Renaissance Florence conquered the rest of Tuscany but Lucca never fell. Though it did inevitably succumb to Napoleon, he prized the small Republic sufficiently to bestow it upon his sister, Elisa, to rule as princess.

All of these periods survive today, in layers. When Lucca rebuilt, it always built on what came before. No city better preserves its original Roman street layout. The medieval buildings were erected on Roman foundations, and the Renaissance mansions assembled medieval houses and towers into grand edifices. Peel the plaster off a Renaissance building and you will usually find medieval brick underneath.

If you have only one day in town, you will want to see the Cathedral of San Martino, which is always open, and San Frediano, which closes at noon for a couple of hours. You will want to spend some time in Piazza San Michele, site of the Roman forum, dallying and admiring the façade of the church. If the weather is fine you will certainly want to spend some time walking or bicycling along the walls. If the weather is inclement, the Cathedral museum has an excellent audio tour, which takes about an hour. The Villa Guinigi museum has a precious collection of local art and antiquities, and the Mansi museum allows you to visit one of the grandest palazzi in town, filled with treasures.

Try not to be overly ambitious. A visit to Lucca is often inserted into a hectic tour of must do's and must see's in more famous places, and Lucca is the perfect place to stop and catch your breath. Wander aimlessly a while, have a cappuccino, wander some more. You can't get lost for long. You may get disoriented in the net of narrow medieval streets, but walk a bit in any direction and you'll soon find yourself in some recognizable piazza. Feel free to get lost.

Two or three days is a more appropriate schedule for a visit. You can begin to explore the other churches—San Pietro Somaldi, Santa Maria Forisportam, San Paolino, the excavations in San Giovanni and the Baptistery, San Salvatore—or perhaps the new museum dedicated to comics. Depending on how you feel about heights, you will want to climb the Guinigi tower and the clock tower. There's a good chance you will find a concert worth attending since Lucca is a city of music. And you will have time to explore the streets, where every few paces there is a palazzo with a story behind it, another church, a workshop or store, and an endless supply of cafés. You will begin to absorb the city, not just see it. In one of these cafés you will probably begin to plan your return trip.

~

Vocabulary and Conventions

Lucchese—A noun and an adjective. A *Lucchese*: a citizen of Lucca; *Lucchese* architecture. Lucchesi is plural. Not italicized in the text.

Lucchesia—The territory of Lucca. The accent is on the *i*.

Gonfaloniere—The chief executive officer of the State through much of its history.

Comune (Italian) and commune are used interchangeably. The same is true for *Anziani* and Elders, the ruling body of the Republic.

Monofora, bifora, trifora and *polifora* windows—the Italian words for mullioned windows. A monofora window has a single opening; a bifora has two, separated by a column, and so on. The English term is also used.

Trifora windows. Note putlog holes.

Saints are referred to, somewhat indiscriminately, by both their English or Italian names. The Italian is always used for lesser known saints. Churches are referred to by their Italian names. To distinguish churches from saints, the Italian prefix (San, Santo) is used for churches, the English (Saint) for the person. Thus: San Paolino refers to the church; St. Paolino to the man. (Likewise, San Frediano, St. Frediano; San Michele, St. Michael.)

Italian is used instead of English where it seems more appropriate, or simply more euphonious.

The use of centuries to refer to time periods has generally been avoided. Thus, the thirteenth century is called the 1200s, and so on. The Italian is sometimes used: the 1200s are the Duecento, the 1300s the Trecento, the 1400s the Quattrocento, the 1500s the Cinquecento, the 1600s the Seicento.

~

Things to Look For

Wandering around Lucca you should keep your eyes open for a number of features which you encounter at nearly every turn.

Decorative brick—Lucca has perhaps the finest and most prolific examples of decorative brick of any city in Italy. This is brick which has been sculpted or molded with repetitive designs and is employed as an architectural embellishment. It was most commonly used to enliven the arches of windows, doors, and *oculi* (see below). We can thank the later plastering over of the city for preserving much of this work and as more plaster is removed new examples are sure to be found.

Most decorative brick was made by sculpting the clay before it was baked, though sometimes the design was carved into the finished brick. The use of molds does not seem to have become prevalent until the late 1300s.

The earliest datable examples, about the year 1150, are on the churches of San Tommaso (#1), Sant'Anastasio (#29) and San Giusto (#15). By the mid-1200s its use had become widespread and the technique refined, allowing increasingly complicated designs. In the later 1300s and early 1400s the use of molds became more

Examples of Decorative Brick

common and the bricks could be employed more lavishly. The best examples of this later period are found on the Palazzi Guinigi (#58) and the home of the Knights of Altopascio (on via dell' Altopascio). Many sites of decorative brick are pointed out on the map, but a sharp eye will reveal many more, and there are more still to be uncovered.

Oculi—One of the architectural curiosities of Lucca, these small circular openings below windows are typical of the city, though similar examples are found infrequently in nearby places. Most are now filled in, but originally they were open and had iron bars on them to keep birds from flying in and objects from falling out. Although they became an architectural embellishment—many have lovely examples of decorative brick—they must have had a practical function as well and various theories as to their original use have been proffered. It has been suggested that they were little windows for small children to look out onto the street, but this seems unlikely. They are usually explained as ventilation holes, but if so it is strange that they are at the bottom of the room, since warm air rises and they would provide circulation only if placed near the ceiling. Whatever their origin, they enlivened the facades of many medieval houses.

Iron Lunettes (*Roste*)—These were standard features of Renaissance doorways, filling in the arch above the doors. They are so common that it is easy to pass them by with little notice, but many are exquisite examples of the iron worker's art. They are best viewed from the interior where they form intricate silhouettes against the daylight.

Guelph windows—Another typical feature of Lucchese Renaissance architecture was a window which was divided into three parts by a cross beam about two-thirds of the way up, and a centered vertical post above this, the effect suggesting a cross without the lower part. These have traditionally been referred to as Guelph windows, the supposition being that they identified families which were partisans of the papacy. There may be something to this, since the style appears to derive from examples in Rome, but their use as a symbol of Guelph allegiance is probably too dogmatic an interpretation. A more prudent designation is the "Lucchese cross window" but we will use the more suggestive word.

Whatever its inspiration, the Guelph window was an architectural style that swept through Lucca in the early 1500s. In his study of the Civitali family's architectural heritage Neil Guy makes the case for the introduction of the Guelph window about 1501 in Palazzo Gigli (#39) which was probably designed by Matteo Civitali (who died in 1501) and executed by his son Nicolao. Nicolao then spread the style, making it almost an architectural signature, though it was widely copied. The fashion was spent by about 1540, so where we see evidence of Guelph windows we can safely say that the palazzo was constructed or renovated between 1500 and 1550.

Few originals of these windows remain intact but when they were updated the two stone beams were usually just cut off flush with the jamb, leaving the remaining stubs on the top and sides, so they are easily identified. The more you look for them, the more you will find. Not only are they a clue to the influence of the Civitali family, they are testimony to the renaissance of fortunes which Lucchese merchants were experiencing in the early 1500s. They had a great deal of money to spend on their mansions and the Guelph window was a sign that the family was both fashionable and socially prominent.

Towers—The subject of towers in Lucca is too large to be done justice here; medieval Lucca was often described as a forest of towers. Whether one approached the city along the flat plains or descended from the mountains the first sight of Lucca was memorable. One estimate of the number of medieval towers is 740, which is surely an exaggeration, though medieval drawings of the city make it almost seem plausible. There were certainly hundreds. These towers were exceptionally strong and they lie today behind many a wall.

Taking pride of place, naturally, were the bell towers of the churches. These could be truly massive, as those of the Cathedral and San Frediano. Most, however, were more modest. Many were added onto later; church towers tended to rise as private towers fell.

A few tower remains can be dated to the 700s and 800s; these were probably public fortifications. In the 900s, as feudal lords began moving into the city, private, inhabited towers began to be erected. The Clock Tower on Via Fillungo dates to about the year 1000 and gives a good sense of how solid these mini-fortresses were. They had very few openings, only slit windows and small doors. By the mid-1000s they began to have attached courtyards, wells, orchards, and barns. Another limited but suggestive example from this period can be seen on the northeast corner of Palazzo Mazzarosa (#69).

The early towers were entirely of stone, but in the 1100s brick became the material of choice. The towers became less fortress-like, with larger doors and wider windows which opened up the interiors to sun and street life. They became less important as fortifications and more important as symbols of status. On the outside they frequently had wooden appendages, stairs and balconies, which were supported on the stone corbels you often see on the facades. Though most of these towers have been cut down, they form the backbone of many buildings. Keys to recognizing them are exposed stone bases, exceptionally wide walls, and asymmetric spacing of windows and doorways. Many of the towers were lowered in the 1300s and 1400s, sometimes because of civic regulations restricting competition, but often simply because of age, the cost of upkeep, and the desire for more comfortable and spacious homes. The collapse of the Poggio family tower in 1495 prompted city officials to order the demolition of other decaying survivors.

Arches—This is an extensive subject but it would be remiss to not point out the many examples of the medieval use of non-concentric arches which enliven doorways and windows, especially in churches. We are used to regular arches, which have concentric curves on the inside (intrados) and outside (extrados). The medieval workman seemed determined to distort this classical form. Most churches were rebuilt in the 1100s and 1200s and very often the arches were of this non-concentric type, which has a different center point for the intrados and extrados. This added an exoticism to the form, which was often emphasized by the use of alternating white and green voussoirs, which is generally referred to as a Pistoian motif, rather unfairly to Lucca.

Putlog holes—Putlog is one of those good Anglo-Saxon words which is pronounced like it looks and means what it says. It is a hole in a masonry wall where a log was put to hold up scaffolding. These may seem too mundane a feature to point out, but I always enjoy coming across them. They remind me of the craftsmen who scaled these walls and laid these bricks, stones, and mortar.

One of the enduring fascinations of the great churches is trying to figure out how they were built. There are virtually no good records of the construction techniques; we have little idea how they managed to scale such heights with such heavy material. The putlog holes are one of the clues they left behind.

Scaffolding, then as now, had to be light and easily taken apart and reassembled in a new location. Most scaffolding would have been made of light poles lashed together with rope. Such a framework was adequate to support the workmen and their tools, but not heavy masonry blocks. The putlog holes are square and quite large; they were meant for inserting heavy pieces of oak which would jut out from the wall three or four feet, on which planking could be laid. The beauty of the system was that it was unnecessary to build the scaffolding from the floor up. As the wall rose, the suspended scaffolding could simply be moved to new holes further up. The sturdy beams undoubtedly were also used for attaching pulleys and hoisting up heavy materials.

Putlog Hole–alternative use

Why weren't the holes plugged up after the job was done? The primary reason, builders being practical people, was so inspections and repairs could be easily made; simply reinsert the putlogs and scale the wall. But I doubt that the esthetics escaped them. Putlog holes are found in large unbroken expanses of wall, un-pierced by windows or other ornamental openings. The play of light and dark on flat surfaces is often the only ornamentation on Lucchese Romanesque churches, and putlog holes provided ready-made shadows and relief.

~

Chronology

To get you started.

218 BC	Hannibal invades the Po valley and drives the Roman army across the Apennines to Lucca, a military outpost.
180 BC	Lucca is established as a colony of Rome.
56 BC	Julius Caesar meets in Lucca with Pompey and Crassus to patch up their Triumvirate.

First or second century A.D. The amphitheatre is built.

488 AD	Theodoric, king of the Goths, invades Italy.
553	Lucca becomes the last Goth stronghold to fall to the Byzantine general Narses in his conquest of Italy.
568	The Lombards invade and quickly conquer Italy. Lucca becomes the capital of the Dukedom of Tuscany.
774	Charlemagne conquers the Lombard kingdom; Lucca becomes the capital of the Marquisate of Tuscany.
800	Charlemagne becomes Holy Roman Emperor.
1002	First war between Lucca and Pisa.
1061	Construction of the Cathedral begun by Bishop Anselmo, who two years later becomes Pope Alexander II.
1160	Welf VI of Bavaria, Marquis of Tuscany, sells to the commune of Lucca his rights over it.
1196	Philip, Marquis of Tuscany, renounces all claims to the title; Lucca becomes a republic.
1100s	Construction of new walls. Completed early 1200s.
1222-56	Wars with Pisa.

CHRONOLOGY

1261	Ghibelline League formed against Lucca. First mention of *Anziani* (Town Elders).
1263	Lucca falls to Ghibellines; Guelphs exiled.
1268	Charles of Anjou arrives in Italy, Guelph league revived.
1274-76	Tuscan League defeats Pisa on land.
1284	Genoa defeats Pisan navy at Battle of Meloria.
1301	Blacks (Guelphs) defeat Whites (Ghibellines) and exile their leaders.
1308	New popular Statutes enacted, banning noble families from office; exodus of important citizens ends Lucca's monopoly over the silk trade.
1314	Lucca conquered and sacked by Pisa.
1316	Castruccio Castracani becomes Imperial Vicar and Lord of Lucca.
1328	Castruccio dies. During the next fourteen years Lucca is bought and sold many times.
1331	List of citizens who pledged allegiance to John of Bohemia, an important source of names.
1342	Pisan rule of Lucca begins.
1348	The great plague.
1369	April 11. Lucca regains independence, which it retains until Napoleon.
1399	The processions of the Bianchi (see church #5).
1400	Paolo Guinigi, by means of a coup, becomes Lord of Lucca.
1430	Guinigi overthrown in a popular revolt.
1522	Attempted coup by the Poggio family.
1525	First Lutheran books arrive in Lucca; the city soon becomes the center of the Protestant movement in Italy.
1531	Uprising of the *Straccioni* (workers revolt).

CHRONOLOGY

1542	Fatinelli conspiracy.
1556	Martinian Laws enacted, creating an oligarchy.
1558	Banishment of Lutherans.
1628	*Libro d'Oro* published, the official list of Lucca's nobility, who alone were permitted to rule.
1629	Bankruptcy of the Buonvisi merchant house and the decline of many others.
1630	Plague.
1652	In severe financial straits, the rulers of the city sell a limited number of positions in the nobility.
1796	Josephine, Napoleon's wife, is welcomed to Lucca.
1797-99	Lucca becomes a pawn between France and Austria.
1800-05	Although the French control Tuscany and most of Italy, Lucca is granted special status as an independent republic.
1805	Lucca becomes hereditary possession of Elisa Baciocchi, Napoleon's sister.
1813	British and Austrians occupy Lucca.
1815	Lucca becomes hereditary possession of Maria Luisa Bourbon.
1824	Maria Luisa dies, rule passes to her son Carlo Ludovico.
1847	Lucca absorbed into Grand Duchy of Tuscany.
1865	Lucca joins the Kingdom of Italy.

~

A Short History of Lucca

A Short History of Lucca

Lucca has always been a border town, with the sense of independence and self-identity common to such places, perched as they are between two worlds. It lies on the northern edge of Tuscany, the first town you encounter when you descend the mountains from the north, the last when you leave for the Po valley and northern Europe.

The earliest settlers we know of were the **Etruscans**; Lucca lay precisely on the northern border of their civilization. The settlement was always threatened, and occasionally taken, by the **Ligurians** who controlled the coast and the mountains to the north.

Until recently the origin of the name Lucca was thought to be Ligurian, from their word *luk*, or swampy place, Lucca being at the time (and for long after) surrounded by vast areas of swamp. It is now generally thought that the name derives from the Indo-European root *lewk*, or open, light, space, though this is surprising since place names tend to be the most persistent of words, and neither Ligurian nor Etruscan were Indo-European languages.

Lucca was originally little more than a rocky sandbar, formed by the torrent of the Serchio River when it hit the flat Lucchese plain. The site had few natural defenses other than the swamps which surrounded it, but it held a strategic position on the trade routes up the Serchio valley and along the coast to Genoa.

From the founding until the year 1000

The **Romans** began to exert their influence in the area in the middle of the 3rd century BC but Lucca does not appear on the historical stage until 218 BC. In that year Hannibal crossed the Alps and defeated the Romans in the Po valley at the battle of Trebbia. The Romans retreated south across the Apennines to Lucca which must have already been a defensible place. Hannibal followed, although there is no record of his attacking the outpost. He apparently bypassed it along the foothills to the north and then headed south across the great swamp of Bietina towards Florence. His army barely made it through the pestilential area and Hannibal, riding his only surviving elephant, contracted a fever which cost him the sight of one eye.

While the Romans spent the next fifteen years battling Hannibal in southern Italy they continued their war against the Ligurians in the Apuan Alps. In 193 BC these Ligurians were strong enough to lay siege to Pisa, Rome's most northerly port, and in 182 BC the Senate decided to build a fortified *castrum* at Lucca as protection against further attacks. According to the Roman historian Livy the fortifications were completed in **180 BC**, the same year the Apuan Ligurians were finally defeated and exiled en masse to southern Italy.

Lucca was the last of the old-style Roman colonies to be established. The colonists were granted land but not the full rights of Roman citizens, unlike the colonists of nearby Luni when that city was founded three years later. Lucca was primarily a defensive settlement.

This city on a sandbar was laid out in the traditional fashion. A surveyor set up a stake in what was to be the center of the future town, in this case at the highest point of the island (and what remains today the high point). He took a sighting at the rising of the sun, then at the setting. This enabled him to orient himself due east-west and to lay out the road called the Decumanus Maximus. Today this is the line of streets called Via San Paolino, Via Roma, and Via Santa Croce. The surveyor then set out a perpendicular (north-south) street, the Cardus Maximus—today called Via Fillungo. Once these main streets were established parallel streets could be laid out, creating the grid which still defines the center of the city today.

After the boundaries and streets were established the walls were constructed. They were rectangular, or nearly so: 2,170 feet on the north and south, 1,750 feet on the east and west, enclosing an area of 90 acres. The walls were 8 feet wide and 23 feet high. If not originally, then very early on, a bulge appeared on the northwest corner of the city to accommodate a theatre, the remains of which can still be seen outside the church of Sant'Agostino.

Lucca disappears from view until **56 BC**, when it was the site of one of the most important meetings of the classical world. Three years earlier Julius Caesar had made a political alliance with Crassus and Pompey, known to history as the First Triumvirate, although Livy preferred to call it "a conspiracy against the State by its three leading citizens." Caesar was made governor of

180 BC—1000 AD

Transalpine Gaul (France) and Cisalpine Gaul (northern Italy). By the year 56 the three potentates needed to confer on future action. Caesar was not permitted to cross into Roman territory with his army and dared not do so without it, so he arranged a meeting at the city nearest to Rome within his province of Cisalpine Gaul, Lucca. Plutarch tells us that besides the Triumvirs the meeting was attended by 200 Senators, 120 lictors, the governor of Sardinia, and the proconsul of Spain. This great assemblage walked many of the same thoroughfares the visitor does today, though the pavement the Romans trod is about eight feet beneath the present. I often walk down Via San Paolino thinking of Caesar's footsteps underneath my own.

After this meeting Lucca fades for a long time from the historical record, though the colony must have thrived. In the first or second century AD an amphitheatre was built just outside the city walls. Here great spectacles would take place, while the theatre was used for dramatic performances. There has been little opportunity in Lucca for archaeological excavations which would expose what of Rome remains underground but those in the basement of San Giovanni (Church #20) have revealed finely tiled floors, a hydraulic system, and baths; the site is well worth a visit.

In **376** Germanic tribes, the Goths, began their assault on the Italian peninsula and eventually wrested it entirely from the Roman emperor in Byzantium. In **535** Emperor Justinian determined to drive the Goths out and reunify the empire, unleashing the Gothic Wars which ravaged Italy. In 551 the eunuch general Narses took control of the Byzantine forces. He swept victoriously up the peninsula until he found himself before the walls of Lucca, where he was brought to a halt. The walls must have been in good repair since the inhabitants refused to surrender. They managed to hold out for three months and finally capitulated, in **553**, only when Narses agreed to spare the town and its inhabitants. He appointed Tuscany's first Duke, Buono, who ruled from Lucca.

Narses himself ruled Italy until 567, by which time he was almost ninety years old. The next year came the cataclysm. The **Lombard** tribes, which had fought with Narses in his final campaigns but were expelled from Italy when they were no longer needed, returned and quickly overwhelmed the Byzantine regime. By **570** they had taken Lucca. The Lombards ruled Italy until

774 and their descendants remained to influence it for centuries after, in few places more so than in Lucca, in its architecture, its economy, and its social structure.

The first years of Lombard rule were ones of destruction, famine, and natural disaster. The Lombards were Arian Christians, heretics in the eyes of Rome, so they began their reign by destroying Catholic churches. In Lucca they drove Bishop Frediano from his Episcopal seat, which was located where San Giovanni is now. He was allowed, however, to build a new church outside the city walls, where San Frediano now stands. The Lombards themselves gradually embraced Catholicism and began building churches with the fervor of converts. Many of the churches we see in Lucca today were founded in the Lombard period.

The Lombards rarely achieved political unity, their territories being ruled by semi-independent Dukes. Lucca was the capital of the Duchy of Tuscany, chosen because it was the most thriving, strategically placed, and defensible city of the region. When the Lombards arrived, Lucca must have been little changed since Roman times; its location made it too important to let it fall into decay. Its stand against Narses had proven the strength of its walls, and he had spared both its buildings and its populace.

During the 600s the Lombards solidified their rule. It is a period of obscurity, but we know that in the 640s King Rotharis (who still clung to the Arian faith though his wife was a Catholic) mounted a campaign against the remaining Byzantine holdings in Liguria, just west of Lucca. He defeated Genoa and the ancient colony of Luni, where he razed its walls and enslaved its inhabitants. Lucca must have been the staging ground for these attacks.

In **742** the unique crucifix known as **Volto Santo** (The Holy Face) arrived in Lucca. The statue would become the city's main object of pilgrimage and its symbol abroad throughout the Middle Ages.

In **774** Charlemagne conquered the Lombard kingdom but he did not make extensive political changes at the local level. A handful of Franks were given land and titles but most of the Lombard nobility remained in positions of influence. Charlemagne renamed the domain as the Marquisate of Tuscany and made Lucca its capital. In the 800s the rulers of Lucca expanded their power and became virtually independent. They mounted a

180 BC—1000 AD

campaign against the Saracens in which they liberated Corsica and made safe the coast of Tuscany. In 877 the Duke of Lucca, Adalberto I, made a military alliance with the Duke of Spoleto; Lucca provided 4,000 troops. Together the two rulers occupied Rome and imprisoned the Pope. They also took the city of Narni, from which Adalberto absconded with the relics of Saints Fausto and Cassio. He brought them to Lucca and placed them in Saint Frediano's church. Their altars are still there.

Adalberto's son, **Adalberto II**, ruled from **886 to 915**. He bore the epithet "The Rich" which was well-deserved. When the Emperor visited Lucca in 901 he took offense at the grandeur of Adalberto's court, considering it more appropriate for the Emperor himself than for one of his vassals. When Adalberto II died his redoubtable wife Berta, whose ambitions and abilities more than equaled her husband's, assumed the rule of Lucca and Tuscany. Both she and her husband were buried in the cathedral of San Martino. When this was rebuilt in the 1060s their tomb slabs, with epitaphs extolling their achievements, were placed in the new cathedral, where they remain today for you to read of their glories. (See the Cathedral, Interior, for the epitaphs.)

The 900s were a time of turmoil and contested control of Italy. The century has been called the dark age of the papacy, as the holy office sank into an abyss of immorality, incompetence, and political intrigue. In Lucca there was a dramatic halt in the building of churches and many which had been the personal property of Lombard nobility were transferred to the Bishop when their upkeep became a burden. In mid-century the resurgent German monarchs began their invasions, first proclaiming themselves King of the Lombards and then, in **963**, Holy Roman Emperor. They never remained long enough to establish effective rule, however, and the Lombard nobles were able to maintain their own fiefdoms. The lack of any centralized authority created a breeding ground for the independent city-states which would flourish in the following century.

The greatest changes during the final years of the first millennium were the development of the merchant class and the rise of pilgrimages. Lucca was well positioned to take advantage of both these movements as they grew in importance over the next several hundred years.

The Middle Ages
1000-1300

At the turn of the millennium the city-states made their appearance, having been nurtured in the central power vacuum of the 900s and the weakening of the local nobility. The citizens of Lucca, thrown back on their own resources, turned to trade and hospitality, making themselves a center of business and pilgrimage.

They announced the new order in the year 1002 by engaging in their first war with Pisa, establishing a rivalry which would continue for centuries. Pisa was Lucca's most convenient port but, fearing Pisan control over their shipping, Lucca aligned itself with Genoa for the bulk of its sea born transport. Lucchesi merchants were allowed to set up shop in Genoa on the same terms as the seaport's own citizens, a rare exception to Genoese xenophobia.

War with Pisa became endemic, personal, and often vicious. It culminated, in 1314, in the sack of Lucca by the Pisans. Then, from 1342-1369, Pisa ruled the city. This was Lucca's most humiliating hour, what is still referred to in town (rather inappropriately, since the Lucchesi were not exiled) as its Babylonian captivity.

The Revival of the Church

In the mid-1000s the Church emerged from the depths it had reached in the previous century. The reforms of Pope Gregory VII (1073-1085), the greatest pope of the Middle Ages, were set in motion by his predecessor and ally Alexander II who was Bishop of Lucca when he was elected Pope in 1061. In that same year Alexander II began building Lucca's Cathedral of San Martino. He was also responsible for building San Michele and for enlarging his namesake church, Sant'Alessandro, the oldest and most intriguing jewel of Lucchese architecture.

Not content with reforming the Church, Alexander II was also an early champion of the laboring classes, the populace—*il popolo*—the group which would redefine the political structures of the medieval world. When he had formerly been the Bishop of Milan he had supported the *patarini* (literally "the scrap dealers") as they mounted one of the first challenges to the established secular order.

1000—1300

Alexander II was not only holy and industrious, he was also militant. He conferred the papal banner on several military adventures, most notably on William the Conqueror's invasion of England in 1066.

Despite this early auspicious alliance with Rome, Lucca's later relations with the Papacy were often turbulent. Indeed, Alexander's successor as bishop, his nephew the learned Anselmo II, was driven out of the city by factions which found clerical reform not to their advantage.

An epigraph on the front porch of the Cathedral, dated 1070, records Alexander as its builder. A nearby inscription, dated 1111, proclaims the oath of all those "money changers and dealers in spices" who plied their trades in the piazza in front of the Cathedral. They were to "commit no theft nor trick nor falsification within the court of St. Martin, nor in those houses in which men are given hospitality." Just to be sure, the prudent Lucchesi added "there are officials who always guard this court and who see to it that any wrong that may have been done shall be amended...Let everyone who comes here peruse this inscription, and place trust in it, and fear nothing for himself." It is an oath which the Lucchesi took to heart and have scrupulously upheld to the present day. In the 21st century, as in the 11th, one can depend on the probity of Lucca's merchants.

Political Independence

Along with the other rising city-states, Lucca became increasingly self-ruled. In 1081 the Emperor proclaimed his nominal control over the town but this Imperial protection only strengthened the local powers. They were granted privileges and immunities guaranteeing their self-governance and Lucchesi merchants were exempted from market tolls as far away as Pavia and Rome as well as from the port fees of Pisa.

In 1155 Emperor Frederick I declared that any merchants from beyond the Alps "must spend eight days in Lucca and make payments for all their purchases there before they would be permitted to proceed to Pisa."

In 1160 the last vestiges of Lucca's feudal status were virtually extinguished when Welf VI of Bavaria, Marquis of Tuscany, sold to the town his hereditary rights over it. Lucca officially became what it already had been in practice, a self-governing commune. In 1180 peace was arranged with Pisa, which lasted 40 years. Pisa even promised to stop counterfeiting Lucchesi coins. Lucca had housed an independent mint since the days of the Lombards and its coins were a guarantee of value as well as the badge of the city abroad. In the Middle Ages the symbol on the coins was Volto Santo, who became recognized internationally. It was a shrewd bit of marketing, the coins spreading the familiarity of Lucca's pilgrimage icon. Everyone knew Volto Santo. The king of England swore by him, though in French, "Saint Voult de Luques." Although it is an unresolved debate, it appears that the present image of Volto Santo was carved in the mid-1100s, even though its presence is attested much earlier. If the present image is a substitution for a previous one, the original must have been no longer adequate for its fame and potency.

The Commercial Revolution

In the 1100s and 1200s Lucca became the center of silk production in Europe. The earliest mention of its product is in an early Romance, written about 1030, in which the German hero is described as wearing stockings held in place by silk garters made in Lucca. (On the garters were sown little bells.)

By this time Lucca already had merchants in the Middle East, particularly in Syria, and it relied on this network to provide the raw materials for its silk trade. All production took place in town—dyeing, weaving, and the finishing into sumptuous fabrics. Lucca provided the finest vestments to the Pope, thick with gold and silver, and the most expensive brocades to the richest courts of Europe. By the late 1200s there would be more Lucchese silk in the papal treasury than from any other source.

Lucca became a hive of independent workshops and busy workers, a breeding ground of entrepreneurs. Their success depended on foreign trade so the town's merchants began opening permanent offices in the capitals and fairs of Europe. They became masters of money changing and transport, making Lucca one of the first banking centers of the Middle Ages. By the 1200s their mastery of foreign exchange led to *de facto* private banks which began floating some of the largest loans in Europe. In the late 1200s it was Lucchesi paymasters who traveled with and paid the armies of Edward I as he conquered Wales. Many of the Lucchese palazzi which would be built in the 1600s bore the names of merchant families which had emerged in the years 1000 to 1300.

The wealth of Lucca depended not only on its control of silk and foreign trade but on the town's location, which brought a steady stream of travelers. It sat astride the Via Francigena, the route of choice for many centuries between Rome and Western Europe, hence its name, the "French Road." It wound its way north from San Gimignano through the flatlands to Lucca, passing between (and missing both) Florence and Pisa. Lucca was the last stop on the road before the mountains, the last chance for provisions and penitence before the dangerous crossing. For those who had just completed the passage from the north, Lucca provided a well-earned respite.

As Lucca became an essential stop along the pilgrimage and trade route accommodating the travelers required a substantial infrastructure. There was the church of San Pellegrino, St. Pilgrim, to welcome them to the town; it had sister churches at the high pass over the Apuan Alps and at their northern base in Modena, along the shortest route between Tuscany and the Po Valley. There was also a network of "hospitals," traveler's refuges, maintained by benevolent orders. Pilgrims as well as merchants had to be fed, provisioned and sheltered; fortunately for Lucca, most of them were able to pay. With this combination of international commerce and pilgrimage Lucca became a very busy and prosperous place.

The Transformation of the Physical City

Lucca was almost entirely rebuilt in the 1100s and 1200s. In 1100 the Roman walls still stood but they were severely compromised as military defense. Suburbs of workshops and houses clustered just outside the wall; churches and other buildings utilized it for one side of their structure. Several of the suburbs were building their own haphazard walls and the temptation to remove and reuse the well hewn Roman blocks often proved irresistible, despite regulations prohibiting it. In the 1100s work on new walls began in earnest and the job was finished by the early 1200s. The new walls were high and turreted, with grand gates, proclaiming Lucca's independence and wealth. Almost nothing of the Roman wall was left above ground, except for what would become the western side of the exquisite little church of Santa Maria della Rosa, the only place where it can still be seen.

Even before the new walls were finished, the city was undergoing a more radical transformation—being raised above flood level. The entire city—every street, house, and church—rose in elevation about 8 feet. It was a complete reconstruction, carried out systematically under the watchful eyes of the authorities. The street plan did not change; buildings rose up on existing foundations, and the public ways were carefully preserved against encroachments. The grading was tightly controlled, so that water would run off gently in all directions from the high point in the center.

The medieval walls enclosed an area of 180 acres, twice the size of the Roman city. They incorporated into the town proper the tanning district of *pelleria* on the northwest, the extensive *borgo* of San Frediano on the north, and the old neighborhoods around San Pietro Somaldi and Santa Maria Forisportam on the east. The river Serchio still lapped at the northern wall and threatened the city, though the raising of streets and buildings (and the resultant capability of laying subterranean sewers) ameliorated this problem. The north wall along the river was particularly stout, as can still be seen where it was incorporated into the Renaissance wall.

Within this redefined space construction went on at a feverish pace. Virtually every church in town was rebuilt. Despite later tinkerings, these are the churches you see today. For some the transformation was total. San Frediano, begun in 1110, was rotated 180 degrees and doubled in size, creating a great Romanesque basilica. Santa Maria Forisportam, which had stood outside the Roman gates (hence its sobriquet) was similarly transformed into a great church. San Michele was finished by the 1160s (the upper loggias of the façade were added in the 1200s and 1300s). Virtually every other church was also thoroughly renovated between 1100 and 1300, resulting in the lush corpus of Lucchese Romanesque architecture which confronts us at almost every turn. (Many of the architectural elements are too often cavalierly categorized as

Pisan or Pistoian.)

The city was being rebuilt in brick. Much of this is still evident; the rest underlies the gentrification of the 1500s and 1600s. The upper stories of the new medieval houses looked onto the street through graceful mullioned windows, with slender columns and gothic arches. Most of these windows have been filled in but many are still apparent.

Beginning about 1150 Lucca developed the specialty craft of decorative brick, the molding of bricks with designs in relief. Such bricks were usually employed on the arches of doors and windows, providing a typically restrained Lucchese embellishment. These graceful ornaments are often exposed when plaster is removed, so their number will certainly increase. The dating of these remnants is another pleasant pastime afoot. They reached their most accomplished expression on the Palazzo Guinigi in the early 1400s. (The lovely ones on the Deutsche Bank on Via Fillungo are modern, though faithful, reconstructions.)

Along with the rise of the merchants and the Church, the social fabric of the town was transformed by the influx of landed nobility who had ruled their fiefdoms in the surrounding hills but who increasingly took up residence in town. Abandoning their ancestral castles they erected constrained substitutes, towers, urban keeps into which they could retreat during a siege. The height of the tower reflected the prestige of its owner and the competition resulted in a forest of little skyscrapers. The numbers given for towers in the Middle Ages are barely credible, 740 is one estimate, but illustrations of the 1300s make it seem almost true. The greatest of these were pillars of large stone blocks, true little fortresses. There are few towers left today but their remains can be found everywhere. The proliferation of towers reflected, of course, the development of urban wealth, which was now concentrated in the city instead of dispersed about the countryside.

The common residence of the urban gentry in the 1100s and 1200s was the house-tower (*casa-torre*) which included the requisite tower, increasingly built of brick, with living quarters attached to it. Two or three stories high, these new buildings were built on the foundations of the previous Roman and Lombard structures. The ground level of the city was a honeycomb of interlocking vaulted areas, a semi-public space open to the street through large archways. In towers these arches were often passageways into interior courts. In the other buildings they housed workshops, stables, or storage. It is common to find the remains of these archways today and easy to envision the medieval streets. On the floor above lived the families. Here the buildings would often encroach upon the public air space, by the addition of wooden structures—porches, a bit of extra room space, exterior walkways—which were supported on numerous stone corbels, many of which can still be seen on the front of the medieval buildings. With this overhanging canopy the view of the sky and exposure to the elements was severely limited on the streets below.

The Development of Self-Government

During the 1100s there was apparently too much money being made for political and social factionalism to get in the way. By the 1200s new social classes were coalescing and new political solutions were needed. The first *podestà* appears in **1187**. He was the chief magistrate, who held office for a limited period and was always a foreigner (from another city) so he would presumably be fair in his decisions.

In **1196** the last Marquis of Tuscany renounced all claims to his title and Lucca officially became an independent Republic. The next year saw the formation of the "Society of the Army of the People" which served notice that the established families could no longer rule by dictate. The dominion of the old nobility was over though the families, of course, remained.

Government in the 1200s was the competition and accommodation between the *magnati* and the *popolo*. The *magnati* were primarily the descendents of landed gentry, nobility who traced their roots to Lombard Lords. They had long held political power by right, tradition, and wealth. The *popolo* was a broad mix of everyone else, the newly rich merchants and the extensive workforce they employed and represented. This broad swath of the population had moved from being fiefs of the nobility to being free workers.

This societal division reflected the broader conflict of the Guelphs and the Ghibellines. The shifting of allegiances between these two factions is one of the deepest conundrums of Italian history but, essentially: the Guelphs were the party of the Pope and the *popolo*, the party of reform; the Ghibellines were the party of the Emperor and the nobility. All politics is local, however, and the relations between Lucca, the Papacy, and the Empire always depended on each actor's self-interest at the time.

The 1200s were truly the century of the merchants, who became the managers of the city. They were united into a college (*collegio*) which had its own courts with widespread jurisdiction. Subgroups of the merchant community had their own organizations. The guild of dyers had 86 Masters, each of whom sat atop a pyramid of many workers. The number for the weaver's guild is lost, but it was undoubtedly larger. In a city of perhaps 10,000-15,000 people, these groups exercised practical control.

Popular government did not put a stop to the problems with Pisa. From the 1220s to the 1250s the two cities were generally at war. Pisa was one of the most steadfastly Ghibelline of all cities, always placing its hopes in the Emperor for help against its arch-enemy, Guelph Florence. In 1261 Pisa joined a Ghibelline League which was able to drive the Guelphs of Lucca into exile, but they soon returned and reorganized. In 1284 Genoa delivered a devastating defeat upon the Pisan navy which strengthened Lucca's hand and the influence of the Guelphs. Guelphs soon became known as the Blacks (*neri*), while the Ghibelline sympathizers became the Whites (*bianchi*).

By the end of the 1200s, the *popolo* were the dominant political group. In 1301 the Blacks drove the Whites from the city. In **1308** the popular rulers wrote extensive new Statutes, which amounted to a new constitution. The democratic forces thought they were ushering in a new era of public improvement and good government but the vision would come crashing down only six years later.

In the Statutes of 1308 the old nobility was forbidden to hold any office of significance. The Statutes also laid out an ambitious vision of civic reform and planning, organizing the city on progressive and practical bourgeois principles. The popular government closed down the most fetid tanning areas in town and concentrated them in the main *pelleria* in the northwest. This allowed the authorities to cover over some of the open sewers which traversed the city, making them into proper streets. The merchants, of course, looked out for their own; they retained the right to shut down production in order to limit surpluses and support prices.

Although the revolution of 1308 (for such it was at heart) signaled a change in power, it did not substantially alter the form of government which already operated within a republican structure. The Lucchesi had learned how to govern themselves and although the arrangements would be modified over the centuries the essentials of proper and organized civic behavior had been established very early on.

The city was governed by deliberative councils. By the early 1200s there were two of these: the *consiglio generale del comune* and the *consiglio del popolo*. By mid-century, at the latest, there was an executive body, the *Anziani*, or Elders, who administered the day to day affairs of the State. The *Anziani* was always filled from the ranks of the leading families. The institution would survive until the end of the Republic in 1799.

1300s—Disaster and recovery

For Lucca the 1300s were certainly the calamitous century, though it proved ultimately regenerative. A simple recounting of events conveys the turmoil.

1301—The Blacks (Guelphs) defeat the Whites (Ghibellines) and exile their leaders, including the family of Castruccio Castracani.

1308—Victory of the *popolo*, the great families banned from office, reformist Statutes enacted, urban renewal undertaken.

1314—Pisa, leading a Ghibelline revival, attacks, conquers, and sacks Lucca. The Pisans choose Castruccio Castracani, one of the exiled Whites, to be their Viscount.

1316-1328—Castruccio exercises dictatorial rule. Lucca becomes a militant State which subjugates most of northern Tuscany, up to the walls of Florence.

1328-1342—Lucca is in utter turmoil, bought and sold by mercenary troops, sacked and burned again and again, the King of Bavaria giving it to the king of France to pay for a dowry, sold to Genoese merchants, attacked by Florence. In 1335, completely out of money and with no means to defend the city, the Anziani gives

1300s

Lucca over to the Lordship of Verona, which was preferable to being conquered by Florence.

1342-1369—Lucca suffers the ultimate indignity of being ruled by Pisa. Their rule is relatively benign, however, order is restored, trade and prosperity begin to return.

1348—The Black Death appears; it returns in 1363.

1369—Lucca buys its independence; it is once again a free Republic.

The final years of the century would be spent reorganizing the government, fighting with Pisa, reviving trade, and preparing for another dictatorship.

Considering the upheaval of the 1300s, it is remarkable how much of life went on. The merchants were never out of business for long, though their fortunes could swing wildly. Churches were attended and attended to. Even in the disastrous 1330s the Busdraghi were doing well enough to establish the church of San Nicolao, with an attached school and hospital. It was during the Pisan domination that the façade of San Michele was finished. The chaotic years had only strengthened Lucca's ability to govern itself as the local authorities, under the most difficult circumstances, had scrambled to collect taxes, pay mercenaries, construct defenses, and maintain public order. Most importantly, the humiliation of Pisan dominance cemented Lucca's determination to never again fall under someone else's yoke.

When the city regained its independence in 1369 the Gonfaloniere became the chief executive officer and commander in chief. He was elected for a two month term by the nine Elders, who served for two years, and by the Council of 36. There was also a General Council of 180, composed of sixty members from each of the three sections of the city.

Castruccio Castracani—Mary Shelley's second book, after *Frankenstein,* was the utterly romanticized and a-historical story of Castruccio, entitled *Valperga: Lord of Lucca*. It did little to revive his reputation (or strengthen hers) which is a pity since he was such a dominant figure in his day. Under Castruccio Lucca's boundaries and political influence grew to their greatest extent. A member of the ancient and noble Antelminelli family, he was exiled from Lucca with the other Whites in 1301. His family moved to London where he spent his hell-bent youth in the company of the King's dissolute son. Fleeing from a murder charge, Castruccio became a soldier of fortune and eventually found employment with Ghibelline Pisa. When Pisa conquered Lucca Castruccio was made governor but he soon took control for himself. In the southwest corner of town he built his great fortress, the **Augusta**. It would be the symbol and means for control of Lucca until the Republic dismantled it in 1370. Almost nothing remains of the Augusta except for stones and bricks which were reused in other structures.

As Lord, Castruccio brought Lucca back with a vengeance. In 1325 he defeated the Florentines at the battle of Altopascio, occupied the territory as far as Pistoia, and brought his army up to walls of Florence. He celebrated his victory over the Florentines by running three triumphal races around their town, the final one conducted by the camp prostitutes. After his death in 1328 his family became marginalized almost immediately. Machiavelli also wrote a biography of Castruccio, but he used it as an occasion more for invention than for history.

The century was brought to a fitting close by the remarkable and poignant penitential movement of the Bianchi whose goals were peace and mercy. (See church #5, Crocifisso dei Bianchi, for their story and legacy.)

1400s—Tyranny and Renaissance

In 1400 Paolo Guinigi took control of Lucca. He abolished its representative government and ruled as Lord until 1430 when he was overthrown. His father had paved the way, gaining increasing influence and wealth in the early days of the restored Republic. Although Guinigi could be ruthless, he also understood the needs of his peers, the wealthy merchants; he stayed in power by attending to their interests. His family built two great palazzi, one with the famous tree-topped tower. He also built a villa (so-called because it was outside the walls) which is today the National Museum. His most precious legacy is the tomb of Ilaria del Carretto, his beloved wife who died at age 23. It is the sublime work of Jacopo Della Quercia and can be seen today in the Cathedral, for a small charge.

The leading families, feeling Guinigi's weight, finally deposed him and established an exceptionally stable civic rule. They retained the essential political structures created in the 1200s. Nine Anziani, elected from the elite families, would be the actual decision-makers of the Republic. At their head was the Gonfaloniere, the most prestigious position in the State. The rolls of the Gonfalonieri provide a clear list of the leading citizens through the centuries. The influence of the most democratic body, the *Consiglio Generale*, would wane as the Republic increasingly became an oligarchy but in the 1400s the support of the laboring classes was still essential for the revival of the city's fortunes.

And revive they did. The dreams of military grandeur à la Castruccio were abandoned, but Lucca resolutely fought for control of its surrounding area, the plains to the east and west, and to the north the precious foothills, site of their villas and the valley of the Serchio, the Garfagnana. To fully appreciate Lucca, a visit to these areas is essential.

Controlled by merchants, Lucca was governed conservatively and efficiently. Though it no longer had a monopoly on silk, its products still had cachet. The merchants still went abroad, applying themselves to whatever could turn a profit, especially cloth and loans. In town the ruling group competed among itself in claiming the most ancient ancestors though the defining qualification for membership in the elite was, of course, wealth and wealth came primarily from trade. By the end of the 1400s the upper strata of society was solidifying into the group of families which would rule Lucca until the end of the Republic—the Buonvisi, Cenami, Arnolfini, Burlamacchi, Busdraghi, and others.

In the later 1400s Lucca underwent its own artistic renaissance, which was dominated by the superb sculptor Matteo Civitali (1436-1501). His relative obscurity is usually explained by the fact that almost all his work was confined to Lucca and most of that in the Cathedral. Henry James called him the "greatest of Lucchesi... the wisest, sanest, homeliest, kindest of Quattro-cento sculptors, to whose works the Duomo serves almost as a museum." James spent little time in Lucca; he found the city so enchanting he was afraid to return and perhaps suffer disillusionment. He need not have worried.

An unwelcome characteristic of the century was the rise of Florence. Lucca would never challenge Florence again, but neither would it ever submit. Florence went on to conquer the rest of Tuscany, but it would never conquer Lucca.

1500s—The nobility consolidates power

The 1500s saw Lucca turn into a true oligarchy. Wealth became increasingly tied to banking and loans. The artisan and laboring community, the *popolo*, began to feel the pinch. They were represented, on the face of it quite adequately, by a pyramid of elected officials, but the decisions were always made by the small group of citizens at the top.

In **1531** the popolo demanded their rights in what was called the *Sollevazione degli Straccioni,* literally, the uprising of the ragmen. It turned out to be the last gasp of the working class, whose future had looked so bright in 1308. In **1556,** with the passage of the Martinian Laws, named after Martino Bernardini, Lucca officially became an oligarchy. Membership in the nobility was closed, accessible only by marriage or extraordinary dispensation.

The Martinian Laws resolved the two main political problems: the relationship between ruler and ruled, and the distribution of power within the ruling class. Competing interests among the elite threatened to tear them apart, and perhaps bring back one-family rule. In **1522** a Di Poggio assassinated the Gonfaloniere, which led to the entire family being expelled from their traditional neighborhood (the area of Puccini's house). In **1542** some of the Fatinelli plotted their own conspiracy. Lucca could not afford such troubles. A pact was reached among the dominant families to rule jointly, as benevolently and prosperously as possible. They established a private democracy which would govern Lucca for more than two hundred years, generally admirably fulfilling its mandate.

Another threat to the independence of the Republic arose when Francesco Burlamacchi, one of the leading citizens (he had been Gonfaloniere twice), conceived the idea of a Tuscan Union with Pisa and Siena. The main opponent of such a Union was Florence, but Lucca's ruling families, fearful of losing their independence, found common cause with the Medici and were

1500s

instrumental in having Burlamacchi beheaded, by order of the Emperor, in **1548**. Embraced long after his death as a forerunner of Italian nationalism, Francesco Burlamacchi's statue today holds court in the most prestigious site in town, the piazza of San Michele.

Their dominance assured, the regime prospered, and the city and countryside of the Republic generally prospered with it. In the 1500s a new wave of palazzo building began to transform Lucca into the streetscapes we see today. Virtually all of the new palazzi were built by joining several medieval buildings into one by unifying the exteriors and rationalizing the interiors. The medieval palazzi provided excellent raw material, foundations dating to the Romans, massive towers, and high vaulted ground floors which proved as useful for carriages and courtyards as they had been for shops. Above this was the *piano nobile*, a grand floor of brick arches and solid beams. The Lucchesi generally shied away from ostentation, so the exteriors portray a restrained dignity, but within his castle the Lucchese merchant was free to indulge his worldly success. The palazzi which were not remodeled in this century would be in the next.

The most enduring monument to the ruling class which took power in the mid-1500s was the new town wall, a massive undertaking of audacious ambition backed by complete determination. The need for new walls had been made clear in 1492 when the King of France invaded Italy, bringing with him cannon which could quickly dispatch any high, narrow, medieval wall. Lucca, being a very diplomatic city, was never seriously threatened but the lesson of siege artillery for the future was clear. By the time the French were no longer a threat the Medici were and Lucca's medieval wall had become a charade as defense. The city fathers were too practical to do nothing about it.

By 1525 plans for the new civic endeavor were being made. It was a daunting project. The walls would be earthen structures one hundred feet thick, impervious to an eternity of cannon shots. They would be shaped by the latest principles of fortification, allowing a comprehensive field of fire in any direction. They would be encased in brick, with sally ports, guard towers, and bastions large enough for a host of troops and artillery. Within the bastions there would be cavernous storage rooms, kitchens, armories, and stables. Most dramatically, everything outside the wall was to be leveled—every hut, church, house, tree—for several hundred yards, the length of a cannon shot. This *tagliata* (cut-down zone) sloped away from the walls so that approaching infantry would have to advance up through raking fire. Just outside the walls was another band of earthen and brick fortifications, platforms for snipers and pickets. These can now be seen only on old maps (where they give a starburst effect in plan) though the remains of two outworks on the north side give sufficient fuel for the imagination to restore the rest; you can see them from the walls between Baluardo San Frediano and Santa Croce.

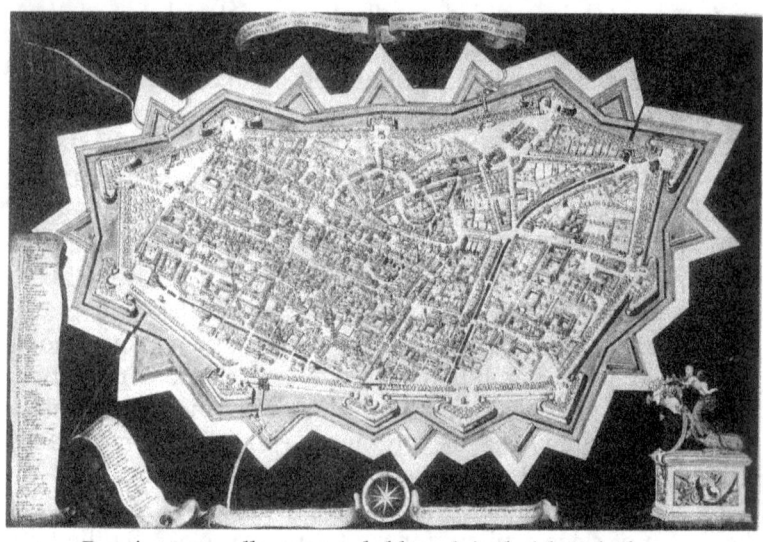

Renaissance walls surrounded by original picket platforms.

Construction of the walls began in 1550 and would take 100 years to complete. Every citizen of the Republic of Lucca was compelled to contribute, which for many meant using a shovel and wheelbarrow to move a load of dirt from here to there for a week or more every year. The walls of Lucca truly belonged to every citizen.

The greatest crisis which the rulers of Lucca had to confront in the 1500s was the Protestant revolution. The stage had been set with the death of Savonarola in 1498, when many of his followers settled in Lucca after being driven from Florence. Their distrust of Rome and of moral turpitude found fertile ground among the burghers of Lucca, a group with close ties to northern Europe. Almost as soon as reform broke out in the north it appeared in Lucca; indeed, it looked as if Lucca would become the center of the Protestant take-over of Italy. The church of San Frediano became the domain of one of the most influential of the reformers, Peter Martyr. The Pope eventually threatened to send in the Inquisition but the city fathers, who resented outside interference both secular and sacred, decided to resolve the issue themselves. Protestants would have no rights in town. Any who left would have to leave their wealth behind, any who remained would have their homes confiscated. Quite a few Protestant sympathizers moved abroad, not infrequently to prosper. For their relatives who stayed the decline was severe, but those who remained faithful were able to work their way back into positions of security.

The building boom of the 1500s included not only the palazzi but the churches, although only one new church, San Paolino, would be erected in that century, when the previous church of the patron saint of the town was demolished to make way for the new walls. The exteriors of the other churches were changed little but the frescoed interiors were plastered over, crypts were filled in, artwork was replaced, and most of the medieval embellishments were destroyed. The art would be increasingly influenced by the Counter Reformation and the need for so many new canvases encouraged the development of a thriving, if somewhat provincial, artistic community in Lucca. A number of these local artists would find fortune in Rome and abroad. Wealthy Lucchesi patrons could afford to commission works by the best Italian artists but much of the art remained indigenous and in the deep shadow of Florence.

1600s

In the 1600s Lucca began to retreat into itself. Florence was too dominant and other foreign merchants too numerous for the Republic to aspire to international influence, but neither would it idly suffer threats. The new walls were finished in 1650, at a time when the Medici were conspiring to finally pluck the rich plum of Lucca. The city still ruled over a substantial territory, including the mountainous Garfagnana which, though poor, was essential to the city's self-sufficiency and security. The city began the century by fighting a war with Modena for control of the mountains and it would spend much of the following decades preserving this patrimony by battle and diplomacy. Outside of its domain Lucca sought accommodation, freedom to trade, and the occasional opportunity to make an exorbitant loan to a destitute monarch.

In **1628** the patricians of Lucca established their political dominance with finality. The Martinian Laws of 1558 had given them control but now their nobility was certified by their inclusion in the *Book of the Noble Families of the Republic of Lucca*, commonly known as the *Libro d'Oro*, the Gold Book. It listed the recognized noble families and it was closed to new entries. 243 families made the cut. The Senate decreed that government offices could only be held by families who had served during the preceding 70 years (since 1558). The governing class of Lucca became a closed club.

No doubt these chosen few foresaw a protected future but they were shaken from their self-contentedness the next year, 1629, when the merchant house of the Buonvisi declared bankruptcy. The entire merchant and ruling class, though it showed remarkable resiliency, never fully recovered. The following year, 1630, plague reduced the population of the city by a third.

By the 1650s the town coffers were so bare that the ultimate indignity was suffered. Titles were sold to the nouveau riche, which Lucca was still able to produce. A few families were added to the list of nobles, paying dearly for the privilege.

Palazzi continued to be built, in the space opened up by the new walls which had increased the area of the city by one hundred acres.

Two new churches were built in this century. One of them, Suffragio (#30) was erected on the site of mass burials during the plague. The transformation of most of the rest of church interiors was completed with the installation of marble altars and art work in accordance with the dictates of the Council of Trent. In the 1640s Lucca again asserted its independence from the Pope and again suffered interdiction.

By the end of the 1600s the Republic was settling into genteel, slowly dwindling prosperity. The nobility grew ever more jealous of their status but they were generally benevolent and efficient rulers, so the populace enjoyed at least the comfort of stability and the pride of independence as a nation.

1700s

1700s—Decline of the Old Order

Lucca was well positioned to slip into the twilight of European nobility which ended with Napoleon. It was small enough to not present a threat to other regimes, shrewd enough to not become embroiled in their alliances, and still rich enough to buy its way out of trouble.

Nonetheless, the pact made among the nobility was a pact of their own denouement. Without new blood their numbers dwindled. When families bound for extinction sought ways to perpetuate themselves a law was passed in 1711 prohibiting noblemen from marrying not only women of a lesser class but even elderly rich widows and spinsters, which was seen as an unseemly attempt at self preservation and as a way to rob the bride's family of their anticipated inheritance.

By 1720 it was necessary to reduce the number of men needed for a quorum to govern. By 1786 of the original 243 families in the *Libro d'Oro* less than a hundred remained and the group able to hold office had been reduced to that of a small club. To reaffirm their status, as the stirrings of democracy and revolution percolated even here, in 1787 the nobility updated the *Libro d'Oro* to reflect the current "Original Families and Noble Individuals of the Republic."

Less than a decade later Napoleon would invade Italy, with his own ideas about nobility. On August 4, 1796 Lucca and Napoleon had their first contact when his wife Josephine appeared in town. She had been with her husband in the Po valley but his situation had turned critical when the Austrians tried to drive him out. On August 5 he would fight the battle of Castiglione, which would by the closest of victories leave him in control of the field. The outcome yet unknown, it was prudent for his wife to escape to sanctuary; Lucca, on the other side of the Apennines, was the first place she deemed a safe refuge. She was not disappointed. When she arrived unannounced in front of the gates at 5 o'clock in the morning the town fathers roused themselves and quickly devised a suitable welcome for so notable a visitor, arranging the most gracious accommodations as possible. Considering that Napoleon's future eminence was still not certain, it was the traditional Lucchese custom of cultivating all possible alliances which accounted for Josephine's warm welcome. Her own past, certainly, fell short of Lucca's standards of propriety.

Despite some who were reluctant to embrace this socially questionable wife of an upstart general, Josephine was given an almost regal reception and was taken under the wing of Eleonara Bernardini (*nee* De Nobili) with whom she formed an enduring friendship. By such a chance event the patricians of Lucca forged a personal relationship with Napoleon, which would serve them well when he became all powerful.

In March 1797 Lucca sent two ambassadors, a Garzoni and a Mazzarosa, to meet with Bonaparte. They returned with a letter proclaiming his friendship and solicitude. In October the French army passed by Lucca without threatening it, although a troop of 2,500 did file though the *tagliata*, watched by the citizens from the walls. The soldiers were given food and wine, of course. The patrician fathers must have spent endless hours in discussion. They had made a deal with the devil and the payments would one day come due. Could they afford it? Early in 1798 they sent an embassy to Paris where Talleyrand extracted the first installment, a million lire to guarantee Lucca's independence. The extortionists were just testing the waters but the payment bought some relief when Napoleon's navy soon after docked at Livorno.

The last two years of the century were a see-saw of fate between the new order and the old. In January 1799 the French finally did enter Lucca with soldiers and began extracting money from the nobility. Jacobins were readmitted to town and the structure of government was revised. Considering the excesses of the French Revolution, however, the transition was remarkably civil. Of course, the Martinian Laws of 1556 and the *Libro d'Oro* were repealed; Lucca no longer had a nobility. In February the new government began to make reforms, which included the ending of torture and censorship. In June 1799 the French left and the Austrians entered. They brought back the Gonfaloniere and the Anziani but they made Lucca a regency, visited stern justice on the reformers, and extorted as much money as possible.

1800s—The end of the Republic

In June 1800 Napoleon defeated the Austrians at the battle of Marengo and in July the French reoccupied Lucca. They were now even more desperate for money and this time they did not receive as warm a welcome. They stayed only two months, however, and in September the Austrians were back; they lasted a month and in October Napoleon returned to become the final arbiter of Lucca's fate.

He looked benevolently on the place. He made his sister Elisa and her husband sovereigns of Tuscany, but he exempted Lucca, which was guaranteed its independence. It seemed that the negotiations of the Lucchese patricians had paid off. Of course there would be a French advisor and the government would be reformed on more democratic principles. A new Constitution was written and on January 1, 1802 the new government took its seat. It would be a reasonable adaptation of old forms to new realities. The patricians were recognized as experienced governors and were granted half of the important positions. There would be a *Consiglio Generale* of 300 members, open to all respectable citizens. They would choose 12 Anziani and these would rotate as Gonfaloniere. The administration was rationalized into departments of health, finance, justice, foreign affairs, and public improvements. For the first time administrators were to be paid, rather than to serve out of noblesse oblige. Lucca was now a democratic republic with a privileged class. Considering the turmoil which ravaged Europe, the small state had survived with remarkable aplomb.

But as Napoleon's grasp increased, Lucca could not expect to retain its independence. In December of 1804 he had himself crowned King of Italy, with the Iron Crown of the Lombards. The following June, acquiescing in the inevitable, the *Consiglio Generale* requested the Emperor to accept their small domain as a principality of his esteemed house. On June 24 Lucca became the hereditary possession of Felice Baciocchi, husband of Napoleon's sister Elisa. It was a gift to Elisa and it was she who truly ruled. She took pride in her possession, enjoyed it to its full, and made many plans for its "improvement." She began a program of urban renewal which was not entirely welcome in a town quite content with the way it was. She cleared a large area in front of her palace, creating Piazza Napoleone. She did the unthinkable and opened a new gate in the walls on the Florence side, but then Florence was no longer a threat. She planned a grand esplanade between this gate and her palace which would have been a scar running across town, but fortunately she was deterred. A daughter of the enlightenment, if an imperfect one, Elisa was attentive to civic and social reform and sought guidance among the patricians of Lucca. Indeed, the Lucchesi could feel quite good about how they had emerged from the whirlwind. An indication of their privileged status was the fact that citizens of Lucca were exempt from inscription into the French Army. Lucca was still an independent State, albeit with a foreign ruler, and it hosted one of the most glittering courts of Europe. Elisa entertained in a manner befitting a princess. Her musical director, Niccolo Paganini, dazzled her guests and wrote some of his most sublime pieces during his stay here. The remnants of the nobility must have felt quite at home, and reassured.

In 1809, however, Napoleon restored the Grand Duchy of Tuscany and Elisa moved into the Pitti Palace in Florence as Grand Duchess. The effect on Lucca's social life was immediate, though she did enjoy returning to her villa in the hills near town.

By 1813 Napoleon's fortunes had reversed and so his sister's. The British briefly occupied Lucca, and then the Austrians returned. After Waterloo, the Congress of Vienna granted Lucca to Maria Luisa Borbone as a hereditary duchy. Lucca was to be her personal possession until her death, when it was to be absorbed into Tuscany. Lucca still clung to the vestiges of independence.

Maria Luisa's rule was benevolent and appreciated. It is her statue which dominates Piazza Napoleone today. When she died in 1824 her son Ludovico became Duke. He was not a worthy successor; he had insatiable appetites and was constantly in debt. Fortunately, he was more interested in the trappings of rule (he acquired a formidable art collection) than in its exercise, and he left most of the operations of the State to able overseers drawn from the patricians, most eminently Ascanio Mansi who managed to make the period one of well regulated progressiveness. In 1826 Mansi revived the *Libro d'Oro*, though its numbers were by now greatly reduced.

In 1847, as revolution was again brewing in Europe, Carlo Ludovico's reactionary impulses and financial excesses became intolerable. His ministers resigned, the town was in ferment, and he was forced to sign a new constitution which resulted in Lucca finally being absorbed into the Grand Duchy of Tuscany. This was the end of Lucca's independence and grandeur. It had, after so many centuries, become a province. In **1865** it formally joined the new Italian State.

The Modern Period

Though deprived of political independence, the mentality of separateness was too ingrained in the Lucchesi for them to surrender their identity. Behind their walls they continued on their way. Always the practical burghers, the townsfolk did their best to take advantage of changing times. The city once famous for silk became famous for cigars and olive oil. There was still enough private money for private banking to survive, as it does, discreetly, today. Later in the 19th century Lucca would bask in the reflected glory of its son Giacomo Puccini. Nonetheless life was hard, especially in the countryside, and many Lucchesi emigrated to the Americas, primarily to the United States and Argentina. Even then they kept their identity, many returning after having made sufficient fortunes, and today they return every year en masse for the festival of Santa Croce (Volto Santo), the famous *luminara* when the entire town is lit with candlelight and the groups from New York, Chicago, Los Angeles, and Buenos Aires process through the streets behind the icon which has symbolized their city since the Middle Ages. (If you plan on going to this wonderful festival, book your rooms early.)

In World War II Lucca was relatively spared, though plaques dot the streets commemorating where partisans died in the final firefights. The city experienced a slow revival after the war as it struggled to find the resources to maintain its extensive architectural heritage. The city spilled well beyond its walls, which were fortunately too imposing to dismantle. It resisted, as it had under Elisa, the more drastic improvements. The plan to build a bridge over the walls from the autostrada into Piazza Napoleone was thankfully allowed to remain on the drawing boards, as many of Elisa's plans had been.

By the mid-1990s, when I first saw it, Lucca was a quiet oasis of gentility, its buildings peeling away and no apparent urgency to repaint them. The economic resurgence in recent years has been dramatic. Church after church has been cleaned and repaired—major undertakings. There is little peeling paint today. There are cranes everywhere, as old palazzi are renovated into apartments and hotels. The work is being carried on with the pride in its past which has preserved Lucca since the Roman surveyor first laid out the streets. Every year more of the medieval city is revealed as old plaster is removed; Renaissance palazzi are rescued as they are transformed within; frescoes are discovered beneath whitewash and paper; thirteenth century beams and arches and vaults are exposed.

The city maintains the unique identity it has protected for more than two thousand years. It nourishes a rich cultural life, particularly in music. Its artistic heritage is receiving overdue attention and a surprising specialty, comic books, is now celebrated in its own museum. The hills overlooking the town are still charming and peaceful, with many villas which should be visited to appreciate the stature of the Lucchesi patricians. The town remains what it has long been, a welcome rest for the traveler and a restorative site of pilgrimage.

~

The Churches of Lucca

Crucifix, 1300s, in San Paolino

Churches

1. San Tommaso in Pelleria
2. San Pellegrino
3. Waldensian
4. San Matteo
5. Crocifisso dei Bianchi
6. Santa Caterina
7. San Paolino
8. Oratorio of San Pierino
9. San Romano
10. Sant'Agostino
11. Santa Maria Corteorlandini
12. Sant'Alessandro
13. San Salvatore
14. San Michele
15. San Giusto
16. San Girolamo
17. San Frediano
18. Sant'Andrea
19. San Cristoforo
20. San Giovanni and Reparata (Baptistery)
21. San Martino (Cathedral)
22. San Leonardo
23. Combonian Fathers
24. Benedettine del SS. Sacro
25. San Pietro Somaldi
26. Santi Simone and Giuda
27. Oratorio of the Angeli Custodi
28. San Nicolao
29. Sant'Anastasio
30. Suffragio
31. Santa Giulia
32. San Benedetto in Gottella
33. Santa Maria dei Servi
34. Oratorio of San Lorenzo dei Servi
35. Oratorio of San Giuseppe
36. Santa Maria della Rosa
37. Santa Maria Forisportam
38. Santissima Trinità
39. San Micheletto
40. San Francesco
41. San Ponziano

The Churches of Lucca

Every Lucchese knows that at one time there were precisely one hundred churches in town. It is a somewhat mythical number (in fact, the official web site calls it "the city of ninety-nine churches") but in the Middle Ages it was not far from the truth, if we count every oratorio, chapel, and those churches which lay just outside the walls. Though diminished, the number is still impressive today. In the following section forty-one churches are identified as "existing." This includes virtually every church where the building is still identifiable as such. Many of these are no longer open and some have been adapted to other purposes. Another thirty-seven churches have been identified as "former." Most of these have been demolished, while a few others have been so radically altered that their earlier incarnation is completely lost.

We have records of at least forty churches in the 700s, most of which were established by the Lombards beginning in the 600s, though some, such as San Giovanni, had their origin as early as the 300s. There was a drastic drop off in church construction in the 800s and 900s but by the year 1000 more than fifty were recorded. These early churches provided the model for later Lucchese architecture. All of the churches in town were drastically reconstructed in the 1100s and 1300s, as were all other buildings in conjunction with the raising of the streets. Most of the churches we see today have remained relatively unchanged since that time although almost all lost their medieval interior by the 1500s. In the 1600s, in accordance with the tenets of the Counter Reformation, the interiors were regularized with new marble altars and didactic paintings.

The most pervasive influence on the local architecture was Lombard. The best way to get a sense of this influence is to drive around the foothills of Lucca searching out or stumbling upon those churches which date to the 700s, 800s, and 900s and are little changed since that time. The vision behind them can easily be translated to the churches in town. One of their most enduring features was the non-concentric arch, in which the arch swells over the top and narrows at the ends, giving it a somewhat exotic appearance, very different from the regularity of Classical and Renaissance arches. The jambs of the doors are also an important feature—they are massive vertical stones, which often don't match. The same is true of the lintels, also massive and which, if there is more than one door, are rarely uniform, perhaps not even at the same level. Windows are often off-center, or spaced irregularly. Materials change whimsically according to the availability of supply. Given these precedents it is not surprising that the Lucchesi could put a new facade on the cathedral and not be bothered that one end was precipitously cut off and the portico scrunched in.

~

1. San Tommaso in Pelleria
St. Thomas in the tanning district

San Tommaso is off the beaten track so it would be easy to miss, which would be a shame. Not only does it contain notable art, the building itself is a chronicle in brick and stone of almost a thousand years of Lucchese history. When you visit the church you should stroll down Via Pelleria, which preserves its medieval atmosphere as well as any street in town, and has some early examples of decorative brick.

The first record we have of San Tommaso is dated 758. The building referred to in that document was probably built some decades earlier, during the great wave of Lombard church construction in the early 700s. San Tommaso may, however, have been founded centuries earlier when the leatherworkers were first converted to Christianity. It has certainly always been their church, as its toponym makes clear.

The *pelleria* was the tanning district. Because of the foul nature of that trade it was placed outside the Roman walls, along the Serchio river which flushed away the fetid waste. There were other *pellerie* inside the town but the main tanning center was always here. From an early date the district was surrounded by its own wall, to protect it from the river as much as from marauders. By 950 the neighborhood was an official parish which allowed its priest to perform the sacraments.

In the early 1100s the church was entirely rebuilt and its floor level was raised several feet to accommodate the general raising of the city streets which was being undertaken at the time. Construction was finished about 1150, the date of an inscription found on a window sill. The church benefited from the growing pilgrim traffic of the time. The nearby *Via delle Conce* (Tanning Street) during the Middle Ages was called *Via dei Pellegrini* (Pilgrim Street) because the pilgrims would enter the city by this route and proceed on to the church of San Pellegrino. In the 1200s, when the new city walls were built, the *pelleria* was integrated into the city proper, and about the same time a new limestone façade was placed on the church.

In the 1600s and 1700s the church must have been flourishing since the interior was completely transformed, the roof raised, new altars installed, windows blocked up. The best local painters were commissioned to supply the art, much of which remains today.

The church is erratically open.

Exterior

The history of San Tommaso is written on the north wall, in the seams where the building was lengthened or raised, in the different shades of brick where windows and doors have been filled in and new designs superimposed on the old, in the odd placement of a window, a door, an oculus, or a corbel, or where some detail was spared the restorer's zeal in homage to his predecessors.

The most notable of these remains is the side door which is sunk below street grade. The level of the Roman streets, and therefore the ground floor of buildings, was about eight feet below the present; this level had not changed much for over a thousand years. This door must be a relic of the earlier building and indicates the level of the Lombard church. The doorway was obviously "improved" in the 1100s, however, because decorative brick, here a band of diamond shapes, did not appear until that time. Thanks to the dating on the rear window sill we can be quite certain that this is one of the earliest examples of decorative brick in the city. (An example around the corner on Via Pelleria is  from the same period.) The side portions of this brick frieze are original; the center section has been restored. The "bird's beak" capitals atop both jambs are also recent reconstructions (note the date 1956) but they recreate the original work. The non-concentric arch is typical of the early medieval period.

The renovations over the years can be read in the seams and color changes of the brick. The narrow monofora window by the

1. San Tommaso

rear door is where the date 1150 was inscribed; you can still discern "Anni…." This window sill, with busts on either side almost entirely  worn away, was probably reused from the original Lombard structure; the wreath design it bears is a style of a century or two before the millennium.

The three monofora windows on the upper wall are original, but the decorative brick on only the middle one is original, the ones to its sides being faithful reproductions. On the same level as these ancient windows the lighter rectangular brick sections show where larger windows were later inserted, only to be walled up again when the roof was raised. This raising is made clear by the upper plastered portion with new windows (two of them later blocked up).

The front of the church had its façade of white limestone put on during the prosperous 1200s. The main door, with its massive plain white jambs and lintel and an arch of alternating green and white stone is typical of the period throughout northern Tuscany. The tympanum, which originally housed a fresco, now has a bronze bas-relief of **Doubting Thomas** from the 1950s. Above the closed rose window is a medieval lion's head, a remnant rescued from the original Lombard church.

Interior

The interior retains the appearance of the 1600s, when it was renovated in the style of the Catholic Reformation, with large main and side altars, and the pulpit removed. The church, unfortunately, is usually dark, the windows on the south being blocked by adjoining buildings. It is still an active church, serving the *pelleria* neighborhood as it has for well over a thousand years, though today it must be the rare tanner who worships here.

San Tommaso is a good opportunity to see the collaborative work of Coli and Gherardi. **Giovanni Coli** (1636-1681) and **Filippo Gherardi** (1643-1704) were inseparable in life and remain so in death. They first appear as students of the eminent Lucchese artist Pietro Paolini. As young men they went together to Rome and then to Venice, where they collaborated on a number of works. Returning to Rome in 1669 they had an active joint career in oils and frescoes, working at times for the Lucchese community there. In 1678 they returned to Lucca where they frescoed the vault of San Giovanetto (former church #18, on Via Fillungo) and did frescoes in Santa Maria Corteorlandini. At the height of their joint career they were commissioned to fresco the cupola of the Cathedral, but Coli died soon after they started and Gherardi was left to finish it alone. He went on to do the lower frescoes in the apse of San Paolino. In the work they did together it is almost impossible to distinguish their respective roles. They are buried together in the same vault in San Cristoforo.

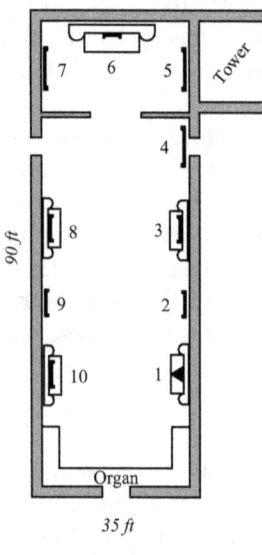

San Tommaso

1. (Altar) Statuary *Crucifixion Scene*, behind glass, anonymous.

2. *Doubting Thomas*, anonymous.

3. (Altar) *Child Mary Being Instructed*, anonymous.

4. (Over door) *Immaculate Conception* by **Coli and Gherardi**.

5. *Martyrdom of St. Thomas* by **Coli and Gherardi**.

6. The high altar dominates the rear wall. Its extravagant gilt and cherubim-laden sunburst holds a small painting of the *Madonna of the Miracles*, dwarfed by the altar and the large vibrant paintings of Coli & Gherardi to its sides. It is a copy with baroque embellishments of the original fresco *Madonna dei Miracoli*, a particularly revered and peripatetic Lucchese icon, which rested finally in San Romano.

7. *Doubting of St. Thomas* by **Coli and Gherardi**.

8. (Altar) *St. Francesco Saverio Preaching* by **Antonio Franchi** (1638-1709), restored 2000. Franchi, called "the Lucchese," was a contemporary of Coli & Gherardi and developed in the same

1. SAN TOMMASO

milieu. One of the main painters of late Tuscan Baroque, Franchi spent most of his working life in Florence, where he became the official portrait painter of the Grand Duchess.

9. *Madonna on Throne*. A charming painting, the intricacy of the tapestry accentuating the simplicity of the figure, who is identified only by a white lily at her feet and a halo unobtrusively woven into the fabric behind her.

10. (Altar) ***St. Anthony of Padua***, mid-1650s, by **Giovan Domenico Ferrucci** (ca.1619-1669). Ferrucci had a flourishing practice in Lucca and is well represented in its churches. He was a student of Cesare Dandini, as was Antonio Franchi.

~

Note: After the above section was written and about to go to print I had the chance to look at San Tommaso one more time. The exterior had recently undergone a thorough cleaning. Looking at the window sill where the date 1150 was reported to be inscribed I was able for the first time to read it clearly. It is MCLXXIIII, 1174, not 1150. The earlier date was first reported in 1907 so even then centuries of grime had rendered it unreadable.

The four I's at the end are scrunched under a flower, with the nonchalance typical of such inscriptions in the 1100s.

Annunciating Angel, ca. 1400, in San Paolino

2. San Pellegrino
St. Pilgrim

A few steps from the Palazzo Mansi museum is what remains of the church of San Pellegrino, now reduced to workshop and storage space. In its day it was one of the busiest churches in Lucca, the first stop for pilgrims who had just crossed the Apennine Alps. San Pellegrino has two sister churches. One is at the crest of the Apennines, at the pass of San Pellegrino in Alpe, where the body of St. Pellegrino can still be seen inside a marble sarcophagus built by Matteo Civitali. The other is in Reggio, at the start of the route from the Po valley. A pilgrim beginning his journey would pray for safekeeping in Reggio. Reaching the high pass midway he would gives thanks and rest in the hospice. Arriving in Lucca he would enter through a gate in the wall surrounding the leather district, and make his way down Via Pellegrino (today called Via delle Conce, Tanning Street) to this church where—with much relief—he would gives thanks for the successful completion of his journey.

The Via Francigena carried the bulk of merchants and pilgrims to Lucca but the shortest route to the Po valley was up the Serchio River to Castelnuova in the Garfagnana, then due north, and almost straight up, to the pass at San Pellegrino (4900 ft, 1525 m). The traveller could then descend either to Modena or, passing by the castle of Canossa, to Reggio. The control of this latter road was the source of wealth for the Lords of Canossa, the house of the "Great Countess" Matilda. (Her castle was where the Holy Roman Emperor stood three days in the snow in supplication before the Pope, in 1077). In the Middle Ages this road was crucial to Lucca, and control of

Crest of San Pellegrino

it was a constant concern of the commune's foreign policy.

The church in Reggio is known by the late 800s. The church in Lucca is first recorded in 1078 and the one at the pass in 1110 but they both probably originated in the 800s. The relics of the saint were in place by 1200; they were reassembled and dressed in the 1600s, by the same restorer who put Saint Frediano back together again.

Remarkably little of these origins clings to the building in Lucca. The pilgrims dwindled away, though the cult of San Pellegrino persisted. In the 1600s the interior was renovated and its paintings included a **Marracci** and a **Ligozzi**. Eventually the church was adopted by the Mansi family, who maintained it and made it their preferred burial site. The exterior was refaced completely in the 1800s, hiding whatever remained of the Middle Ages.

~

3. Evangelica Valdese
The Church of the Waldensians

The Waldensians (*Valdese* in Italian) are a reformist sect from the pre-Protestant era. They trace their origin to Peter Valdes, a wealthy French merchant who about 1170 left his wife, gave away his money, and embarked on a path of spreading the Word. He acquired a following and, despite his reformist message, was granted Papal approval in 1179—provided that his followers preach only when authorized by the official local clergy. This commandment the Waldensians found themselves unable to follow, leading to centuries of persecution which they met with remarkable fortitude.

In 1184, at the Council of Verona, Valdes was condemned as a heretic together with the Cathars, the Humiliati, and others. This decree of excommunication (issued by Lucius III, the only pope born in Lucca) has been called the charter of the Inquisition. Prepared in collaboration with Emperor Frederick Barbarossa, it outlawed heretics by both Church and State, leaving the outcasts nowhere to turn for protection.

The Waldensians hid out in the Alps. With the rise of the Lutherans, who published the Waldensian confession in 1538, many Waldensians were absorbed into the new movement but holdouts persisted in Savoy territory in the eastern Alps. At times they were able to defend themselves from the persecutions of the Duke of Savoy's army, but a massacre in 1655 was so infamous that Oliver Cromwell intervened in the matter and relief funds were raised in England on their behalf. Thirty years later the Duke tried again, with limited success, to drive them from their valleys. In 1848 they were finally given the right to practice their religion openly in Italy and gradually established small communities throughout the world, including the town of Valdese in North Carolina.

This is the only non-Catholic church within the walls.

~

San Matteo

4. San Matteo
St. Matthew

We learn of San Matteo just before the year 900. At that time it was called San Matteo *in fossa Natale* because it lay along one of the main sewerage canals (*fosse*) which ran through the city. The church was rebuilt about 1290 (the date on an epigraph found inside). As the last example of classic Lucchese Romanesque church architecture it warrants attention.

Typical of the genre which we call Lombard is a style which shows either a lack of concern for the symmetrical or a delight in the erratic (there is always a question as to what is happenstance and what is design). In San Matteo, for instance, the doors are asymmetrically spaced along the front, probably adapting to pre-existing walls. The two side doors are each treated differently—different heights, different widths. The door jambs have an ornamental function but their aesthetic was subservient to the materials at hand—two large pieces of white marble served the purpose; they did not have to be identical, or even finely worked. The right hand door is lower than the left, which usually means it is older. Might it be a remnant of the earlier building, perhaps the entrance to a much smaller church? This door originally had a lintel, which must have been removed to gain head-height when the floor levels were raised in conjunction with the elevation of the street in the 1100s. The left hand door is not only higher, the jambs are more balanced and the lintel intact, all indications that it was built later than its mate.

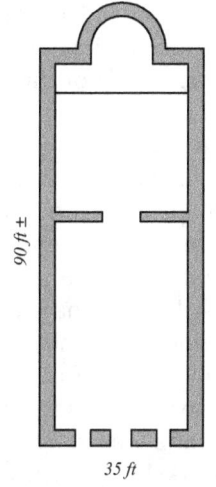

San Matteo

The central door is imposing. It has the same elements as those on its sides, but is more classical. Even here the width of the jambs is different, contributing to the slightly jarring quality of the front. The arches over all three doors are non-concentric, that is, the interior arc (intrados) has a shorter radius than the exterior arc (extrados). The side door arches suggest bichromia, within the limitations of sandstone, but the main door embraces it, using alternating green and white marble voussoirs, the dominant motif of northern Tuscany.

During the 1300s the church received its fair share of bequests. In 1383 one Giovanni Luporino requested to be buried "in front of the figure of Our Lord Jesus Christ which is painted on the wall to the left as you enter." In the same year one Nicolao Folchini, a baker, promised that if he was unable before he died to have a painting done for San Matteo, he would leave 4 gold florins to see that it was accomplished after his death. Perhaps this fairly modest painting of "**Mary and Child, with St. John on one side and St. Peter on the other**" still exists somewhere. Among those for whom San Matteo became a burial ground was one of Lucca's greatest citizens, the historian and writer Giovanni Sercambi (1345-1424).

San Matteo is a substantial church, but from the street it appears diminished, squeezed in between adjoining buildings. Maybe it was the *chi* of this positioning which destined it to be neglected. In any case the church has fallen into unjustified obscurity and decay. Walking past it you realize how commonplace a 700 year old church is in Lucca. Yet it is well wrought, an excellent snapshot of Lucchese architectural style at the end of the 1200s. San Matteo's reputation may have suffered from its coming at the end of an architectural period and so, rather than being regarded as the culmination of a style, it is seen as being just more of the same. A recent judgment dismissed the main door as repeating "in a fairly tired and repetitive manner the scheme of Guidetto's doors, with lions jutting out on the side of the architrave." That is one way to look at it. Another is to see it as the product of a workshop which had honed its skills to mastery. In either case, the church is a guidepost to the architectural development of the city and we can only hope that salvation will once again bless San Matteo.

It has been closed for almost a century.

~

5. Crocifisso dei Bianchi
Crucifix of the Bianchi

*I*t is unfortunate that this church is closed because it memorializes one of the most important events in Lucca's history, the Bianchi penitential movement of 1399.

When we first we hear of it, in 941, the church on this site was named San Benedetto. To distinguish it from San Benedetto *in gottella* (#32) it was given the toponym *in palazzo* because it served the suburban palace of the Marquis of Tuscany. This palace was just outside the Roman walls and provided a respite from the more formal State palace in the center of town.

In 1410 San Benedetto was chosen to house the Crucifix of the Bianchi and was renamed in honor of the precious possession. This crucifix, which the processions of the Bianchi had carried through Tuscany a decade earlier was (after Volto Santo) the most revered icon in the city.

There is nothing evident left of San Benedetto. It underwent extensive renovations in the early 1500s and in 1760 a complete reconstruction was undertaken by the architect **Francesco Pini** who twenty years earlier had designed Santa Caterina, just down the street. Crocifisso was his last work. The interior was frescoed by the local painter **Lorenzo Castellotti**, a protégé of Pini.

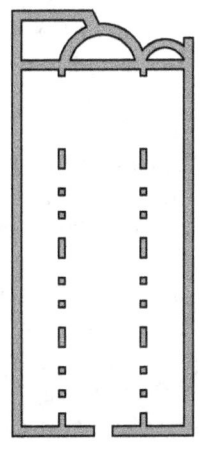

Crocifisso dei Bianchi

To enclose the crucifix on the main altar the eminent Lucchese silver worker **Giovanni Vambré** created an elaborate cherubim-laden sunburst. On a large copper panel the Lucchese **Giovanni Marracci** painted *The Procession of the Bianchi*.

What had been intended as the rebirth of the church turned out to be its last hurrah. Napoleon stripped it bare, leaving only the crucifix. The side altars were shipped to neighboring towns and the paintings were dispersed.

At last sight the building was boarded up and badly peeling.

The Crucifix of the Bianchi

Until provisions are made for its display, this crucifix will remain one of the hidden treasures of Lucca. The church built to host it is closed but the sculpture retains its sacred status so it would be inappropriate to house it in a museum. The only solution appears to be for a benefactor to renovate the cross's proper home.

The crucifix is a remarkably well preserved specimen from the early 1300s. Safe in its sanctuary and, for the last three hundred years, protected from the curious by the screen painted by Giovanni Marracci, the crucifix was allowed to age gracefully, free from intervention except for an occasional oiling. It also managed to escape the eyes of scholars. It was only in the 1990s, resurrected for a major exhibition of early Lucchese wood sculpture, that it was appreciated for the unique treasure it is.

The restoration for the exhibition entailed only removing the layers of oil which had preserved but darkened the work. Almost uniquely among similar works it had never been repainted. In the words of its restorer: "Of course the process of aging has left some traces. The dark green of the trunk and arms of the cross were originally bright green; the interior of the perizoma, painted with azurite, was once a more luminous sky blue...[But aside from this] we have here the rare fortune to see a medieval sculpture in almost the identical state in which it left, 650 years ago, the artist's workshop."

The statue, "with relaxed facial expression, the eyes quietly closed as if in sleep" was not made for the procession of the Bianchi; until they appropriated it it had been in San Romano. Its artistic origins are unknown but it has similarities to the work of Giovanni Pisano about the year 1300. If not done by him, the crucifix derives from his influence.

The Bianchi Movement of 1399

In early July 1399 there appeared at the gates of Genoa a group of several thousand people dressed in white hooded robes, carrying a crucifix and chanting in unison "peace, peace, peace, mercy, mercy, mercy" (*pace, misericordia*). They had been inspired by a local peasant's vision of the Virgin Mary in which she told him

5. Crocifisso dei Bianchi

that the only way to prevent the complete destruction of mankind was for all people to become penitents and to go from town to town making peace among enemies. They were to dress in white linen robes with a red cross sewn on and to go on procession for nine days, carrying a crucifix before them, fasting and chanting. They were not to sleep in a walled town or remove their robes or sleep in a bed. Each day they were to enter a new town, take mass and hear sermons, and to leave by nightfall. These Bianchi, as they were called from their white robes, swept through the Po valley and Tuscany, becoming the last great penitential movement of the Middle Ages.

In each town they came to a new group would form and depart; in this way ever more processions spread across the countryside. On August 10 a group from Pietrasanta entered Lucca. They visited Volto Santo and the major churches before leaving at nightfall. The chronicler Giovanni Sercambi, who witnessed the events, wrote that so many Lucchesi determined to join the pilgrimage that the town fathers, fearing an economic disaster, forbade them to leave. Nonetheless, about a thousand inspired souls managed to get out before the gates were closed, carrying with them the crucifix from San Romano.

To placate those left behind the Elders organized their own nine day processions within the city, with special masses every day. This contrived celebration only fueled the spiritual fires. At last the Elders agreed to let groups leave the city, but only in stages. On August 23rd almost two thousand penitents, carrying the crucifix from San Frediano, departed on their pilgrimage toward—what more appropriate place than the ancient enemy?—Pisa, and then along the Lucchese plain. As soon as they returned a second group went out, towards Florence, with the crucifix from San Pietro Somaldi. This group of pilgrims returned to Lucca on September 13th, the eve of the city's most important annual festival, the Luminara (still celebrated today). One observer of that year's celebration wrote that "it is certain that in more than fifty years there have not been so many people in Lucca on a single day." Sercambi estimated the crowd at 25,000.

While these events were taking place the plague appeared in Lucca. It would rage for the next year, killing up to 150 people a day. The plague had already devastated Genoa, and indeed was probably the true inspiration for the Bianchi movement, which sought to prevent the imminent destruction of mankind. Unfortunately, the plague spread with the pilgrims; the Bianchi were unwittingly propagating the very scourge they set out to prevent.

Their movement, one of the most spontaneous, hopeful, and benign episodes of the Middle Ages, simply evaporated. Within the year Lucca would suffer mass death. It would also see the liberty won only a generation earlier collapse into the dictatorial rule of Paolo Guinigi. Only the Cross remained to remind the Lucchesi of this brief period of *pace* and *misericordia*.

~

6. Santa Caterina
Saint Catherine

The unpretentious neo-classic façade of this small church, only the size of an oratorio or a chapel, gives no suggestion of its sumptuous interior nor its unusual oval floor plan. As an exquisite expression of late Baroque in Lucca, it is a shame it is not more frequently open for visits.

The original church was built in 1575 but it was entirely renovated and reconsecrated in 1748 under the direction of the Lucchese architect **Francesco Pini**. He later designed the nearby Crocifisso dei Bianchi.

Among the artists who worked on the adornments were the sculptors **Giovanni Lazzoni** and **Giovanni Cybei** from Carrara, to whom are attributed the statues of *Charity and Purity* on the side of the main altar. The illusionist decoration of the cupola is probably the work of **Bartolomeo De Santi**; he may have been assisted by **Lorenzo Castellotti**, who also did the painting of Pius V on the left of the high altar. The *Holy Family* is by **Domenico Brugieri**, an eminent Lucchese artist of the early 1700s, better known for his work in Santa Maria Corteorlandini. **Pompeo Batoni**, the preeminent Lucchese artist of the 1700s, painted a large *Ecstasty of Saint Catherine* for the main altar; it is today in the Palazzo Mansi museum.

Santa Caterina

~

7. Santi Paolino e Donato
St. Paolino and St. Donato

San Paolino, as it is commonly called, built to honor the saints who watch over Lucca, is a serious church with no hint of frivolity about it. It is somber, grey, and imposing. In my mind's eye I always see it in the rain (though this may simply be the residue of visiting it too often in February). When it was built in the early 1500s the Lucchese architectural aesthetic was a far cry from that of the 1200s. Compare the facade of San Paolino with that of San Michele just down the road. San Paolino is dark and severe, San Michele white and playful. San Michele was conceived and built during Lucca's most prosperous and optimistic period, the 1100s and 1200s, and expresses an almost giddy relief after the tribulations of the preceding age. When San Paolino was built the social and religious sensibility was far different: the church reflects the influence of Savonarola, the dour Florentine preacher who was burned at the stake in 1498. After his death many of his followers fled to Lucca where his puritanical approach found considerable favor. The first published biography of Savonarola was by a Lucchese, Filippo Burlamacchi, who lived across the street from San Paolino. The church's architect, **Baccio da Montelupo**, was a follower of Savonarola and one of Burlamacchi's sources for his biography.

In 1513 the town fathers began making plans for a new set of city walls. The first step was to demolish buildings and clear the outlying area. One of the first buildings to be destroyed was the ancient basilica of San Donato, located where Baluardo San Donato is today. (San Donato was an Irish monk who became bishop of Fiesole; he died about 876.) The decision was made to build an entirely new church dedicated jointly to Donato and to the town's patron saint, Paolino—thus the full name of the church.

Via San Paolino follows the track of the Roman *Decumanus Maximus*, the main east-west road in the city, the pavement of which lies about eight feet below the present street level. As a holy site San Paolino can trace its genealogy further back than perhaps any church in Lucca, there being evidence of a pagan temple beneath the present building. The first documentary evidence we have of a church in this location is dated 738 when the church was named San Giorgio *in Pisticoro*, the somewhat obscure toponym perhaps referring to the bakers' district. By the 1000s the church had been rededicated to St. Antonio. When, in 1261, the lost remains of St. Paolino were discovered in the basement the church was again rededicated to Saints Paolino and Antonio. Columns from this medieval church are preserved in Villa Guinigi.

In 1515 Baccio da Montelupo was chosen as architect for the new church. When he died in 1535 the building was not quite finished; interior and decorative work went on for another hundred years.

The importance of the church to the civic life of the town, plus its structural soundness, spared it from the Napoleonic suppressions which in fact enriched it, since it became a repository for works from less fortunate churches.

Saint Paolino

Dispatched by St. Peter to evangelize the area around Lucca during the persecutions of Nero, Paolino successfully converted the area but he was then seized by the Imperial forces and martyred about the year 68. Condemned and buried with him were Saverio, a deacon of Lucca, and Teobaldo, a converted soldier. The cult of Saint Paolino did not originate until the fortuitous discovery of his remains in 1261. A list of the bishops of Lucca compiled less than a century earlier does not include Paolino.

Baccio da Montelupo

Baccio's name is not well-known today, but during his life he was one of the most highly regarded sculptors in Florence, chosen to supply the statue of Saint John the Evangelist for the exterior of Orsanmichele.

Although born into a poor family in Montelupo, a small town near Florence, his talent was obvious enough for him to be admitted to Lornezo the Magnificent's school of art in San Marco. It has been said that he was the only student who was not rich, not noble, not Florentine, and without influential friends. Among his fellow students was Michelangelo, with whom he became a good

7. SAN PAOLINO

friend and collaborator. Indeed, it now seems likely that the four statues for the Piccolomini altar in the Cathedral of Siena, always attributed to Michelangelo, were actually executed, at least in large part, by Baccio. At about the same time Baccio and Michelangelo traveled together to Carrara to select blocks of marble.

Baccio was a follower of Savonarola and undoubtedly due to the influence of the friar devoted himself to religious works, particularly the crucifixes for which he and his workshop were most famous.

What led Baccio to forsake Florence for Lucca is uncertain but it was most likely the more congenial religious climate in Lucca after the fall of Savonarola. Vasari rather fatuously wrote that "being bored with Florence, he went to Lucca, where he did some sculptures." It is unlikely that boredom was sufficient cause for him to uproot his workshop and family and move to Lucca.

When it was decided to build San Paolino requests for designs were made to two non-architects, Baccio and Donato Benti. Deciding between them seems to have been difficult so in 1519 Martino Bernadini wrote to Michelangelo, a friend of both artists, asking him for help in deciding between the two. Michelangelo's response is not known but Baccio got the job.

Interior

1. St. Paolino, attributed to **Pompeo Pinotti**, 1606. A boyish San Paolino holds Lucca in his hand; it is still encompassed by its medieval walls. On the other side of the main door is a companion painting, *St. Donato* (#19). Both of these paintings were originally covers for the reliquary niches behind the main altar; both have been cut down in size.

Pinotti is an almost completely obscure Lucchese artist, represented only by his work in this church. Yet the hand in both these paintings is that of an accomplished painter and, particularly in the San Donato, an unusually sympathetic portraitist. Judging by these works Pinotti should have had a successful career, yet he remains undocumented. He also did a painting of *Sts. Tiberio, Valeriano, and Massimo* (1588) which was originally on the first right hand altar but is now in storage.

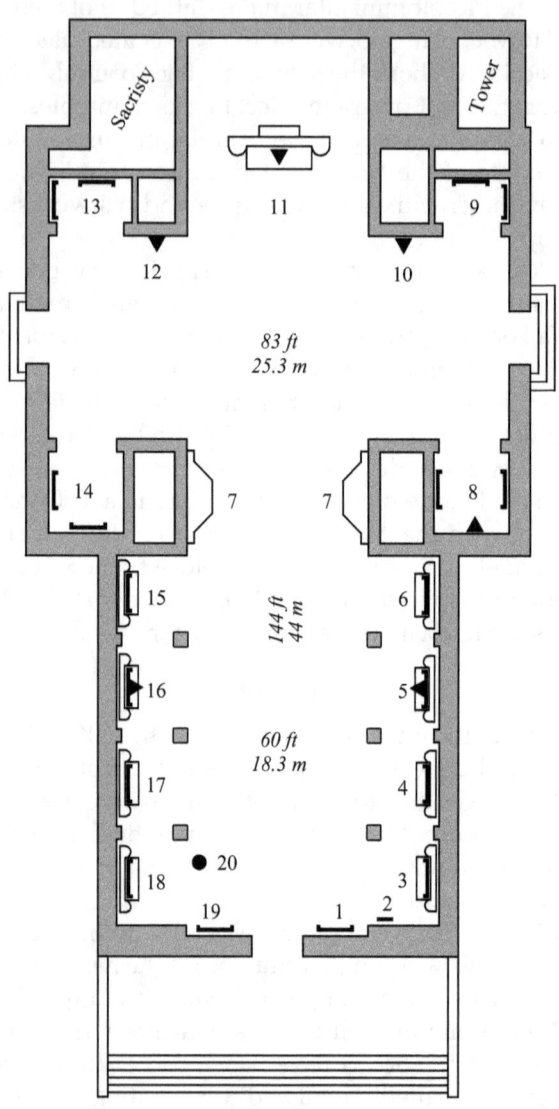

San Paolino

7. San Paolino

2. Plaque. A stone epigraph (ca. 18" x 48") preserved from the earlier church of Sant'Antonio. It bears the date "MCCPrimo" (1201) and commemorates the discovery in that year of the remains of St. Antonio.

The discovery of relics conferred legitimacy on a church and fame on their finder. Such discoveries could be remarkably timely, as was the case with this one, which came at a crucial moment for Lucca. In 1196 Emperor Henry IV had freed Lucca from feudal subjugation and granted it the status of an independent Republic. When the Emperor visited Lucca in 1197 he and the bishop had the good fortune to discover a paleochristian sarcophagus in the church basement. But what was needed were the relics of a saint, and in 1201 the bishop managed to find those of one Antonio, along with the remains of several other martyrs. It was an important spiritual and political event for the city, but the discovery was altogether too opportune and its legitimacy is now discounted. The sarcophagus and relics are now located behind the main altar, where they can be viewed.

3. (Altar, dated 1691) *The Trinity* by **Bartolomeo Neroni,** called **Il Riccio** ("curly haired"), 1566. The Sienese Neroni, who was a student of Sodoma and married to Sodoma's daughter, is barely represented in Lucca. At the bottom is his signature and date, with the inscription "Don't remember the sins of my youth." He was 66 at the time, and returned to Siena the following year.

4. (Altar) *Mary and Child with Sts. Anthony the Abbot, John the Baptist, Nicholas of Tolentino and Sebastian* by **Alessandro Ardenti**. Signed and dated 1565. Restored 1996. Ardenti (1505?-1595) was quite active around Lucca at this period in his life, before he moved to Turin in 1572 where he worked at the Savoy court.

5. *St. Ansano,* wood sculpture by **Francesco di Valdambrino**, 1414. This treasure of early painted wood sculpture is set, rather distractingly, into a painting of *St. Barbara and St. Bartholomew* (anon). Valdambrino was a Sienese, a friend and collaborator of Jacopo della Quercia, who was famously active in Lucca at this time. The statue was originally done for the church of Santa Maria Filicorbi (also known as Sant'Ansano), which was destroyed in

1812 for urban redevelopment.

Lucca is rich in early wood sculpture, an opus which has recently received overdue scholarly attention.

The small plaque (6"X18") to the left of the altar is from the previous church and records the discoveries of 1201.

6. (Altar) ***St. Theodore, Bishop of Lucca*** by **Pietro Testa**. Testa (1612-1650) was born in Lucca and is called *Il Lucchesino*, but he spent little time in his birthplace. This is one of the few paintings by him in Lucca, though he is well represented in foreign museums.

7. ***Marble Organ Lofts*** by **Nicolao and Vincenzo Civitali**, 1500s. The one on the right incorporates a superb grotesque mask, possibly Roman. The small organ of the 1800s was often played by Giacomo Puccini, who was a parishioner of the church.

8. Chapel.

Tucked away in this little alcove is what is perhaps the finest Lucchese panel painting of the 1300s, depicting the ***Burial of St. Paolino***. It was originally either an altar piece (a *paliotto* or *dossale*) or perhaps a panel for the urn which held the remains of the saint.

The inscription reads: "Here is the uncorrupted body of Paolino, whom the blessed Peter made the first bishop of Lucca. He was martyred in Pisa under Nero. Also the bodies of the priest Severo, the soldier Teobaldo, and a deacon of Lucca, all martyred under the same emperor. They were placed here by their companion, the hermit Antonio; he also met his death under Nero."

Antonio, whose remains were supposedly found in the church in 1201, is the monk in dark clothes holding the head of Paolino. The identity of the others has been debated. They were commonly thought to be St. Peter on the right, and on the left Christ with St. Paul behind him, but it seems more likely that they are, on the right, St. Valerio, who succeeded Paolino as Bishop and, on the left, two Lucchesi who were the patrons of the painting; on the sides of the sarcophagus are their family crest, the Massei

7. SAN PAOLINO

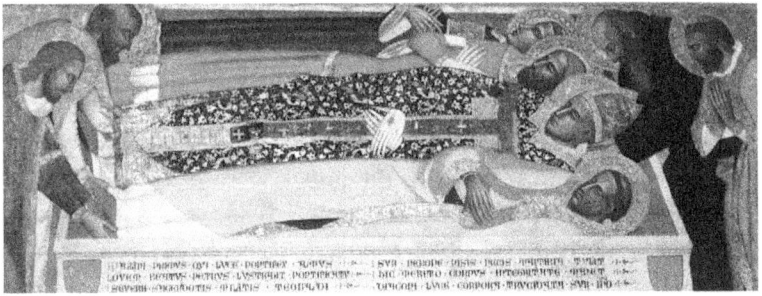

degli Aitanti, who lived not far from the church.

The artist is unknown. **Angelo Puccinelli** has been suggested, as has **Paolo di Lazzarino**. They were the two most important painters working in Lucca in the mid to late 1300s. Lazzarino is an especially elusive artist, well documented in the archives but with no certain paintings attributable to him.

The work has considerable civic importance. The best hypothesis, by Marco Paoli, is that it was done to commemorate the liberation of Lucca from Pisan domination in 1369. In June of that year Emperor Charles IV (who had just freed Lucca after being paid 100,000 florins) participated with the Bishop and the town elders in the solemn opening of the urn of St. Paolino; the painting was quite possibly commissioned on that occasion.

On the opposite wall is a painting of *Mary and Child with two Bishops*. It is un-attributed and I am not aware of any literature regarding it, but the style, particularly the sympathetic treatment of the Bishop's faces, suggest Pompeo Pinotti, who painted the San Paolino and San Donato [#1 and #19].

On the rear wall is a *Crucifix*. This superb work of the early 1300s has been in the church since it was built. The torso is emaciated, cadaverous, almost skeletal, with every rib clearly defined, yet the face is full and forceful. It is generally thought to show Germanic influences, and was perhaps brought to Lucca from abroad (though to me this northern origin seems unduly hypothetical).

The statue has a cavity cut out in the

rear of the torso to keep the wood from splitting as it dried. The head is attached separately, and may have been reworked. The cross itself seems to be original. Its use of tree limbs covered with sprouts suggests that this vehicle of death is in fact the tree of life. The extravagant sunburst which now serves as a backdrop is a diminishing addition, as if the image were inadequate to the message. The figure had been repainted numerous times, but was effectively restored about 1990, which resulted in a dramatic lightening of the work.

9. Chapel

On the rear wall: *Miracle of St. Paolino*. This painting had traditionally been attributed to **Girolamo Scaglia** (1620-1686) but in the 1990s it became generally accepted as by **Giovan Domenico Lombardi** (1682-1751). The event it commemorates took place on July 12, 1664, during the festival of San Paolino. One of the cannons which were being fired from the wall in celebration inadvertently sent a live shell directly into the crowd, but by the miraculous intervention of St. Paolino the injuries were insignificant. The painting is an elaborately detailed portrayal of the event and rewards a close examination of the costumes and fortifications of the time.

Right wall: *Mary and Child with Sts. John the Evangelist and Lodovico* by **Lorenzo Zacchia**, signed and dated 1585. Known as Zacchia the Younger (he was a student of Zacchia the Elder, who was perhaps the main painter in Lucca in the 1500s), Lorenzo (1524-1587) was born and worked in Lucca but few of his works survive.

10. *Annunciating Angel*, painted wood sculpture. Traditionally attributed to **Pietro d'Angelo di Guarnerio**, father of Jacopo della Quercia, though it seems more likely that it is by an unknown artist working under the same influences. It can fairly safely be dated about 1400. Stylistically it is very similar to a work by Pietro, dated 1394, in Bagni di Lucca. The angel was restored in the early 1990s, resulting in a dramatic change in the color of the drapery, which had been over-painted in dark purple, and is now white with remains of the original decoration. The face, which had turned a

7. SAN PAOLINO

ghastly gray has been restored to its original luminous color.

11. High altar area.

The altar was consecrated in 1580.

Behind the altar (you can walk up and look) is an early Christian sarcophagus (300s-400s) with a relief of the Good Shepherd. This sarcophagus was discovered in 1197 in the crypt of the then existing church of San Giorgio. Set on top of the sarcophagus is an urn with an inscription which identifies the relics as St. Paolino, Severus, Valerius (considered by the faithful, if not by historians, to be the second bishop of Lucca) and St. Antonio, the reputed third Bishop.

The choir stalls along the side walls are by **Salimbene Magni**, 1563.

The walls and vault are frescoed with scenes from the life of St. Paolino:

Lower right wall: *Miracle of San Paolino* by **Filippo Gherardi** (1643-1704) with a view of the city walls and of Porta San Donato. (This is the same event painted by Lombardi in chapel #9).

Lower left wall: *Martyrdom of San Paolino*, also by **Gherardi**. Both frescoes were done in the late 1600s, after the death of Gherardi's partner Giovanni Coli.

Martyrdom of St. Paolino by Filippo Gerardi

Upper walls and vault are by **fra' Stefano Cassiani, called Il Certosino** (died 1714). On the right: *St. Paolino Preaching*, which includes a portrait of the work's benefactor. On the left: *St. Paolino Baptizing*, with a self-portrait of the artist. On the rear wall: *Glorification of St. Paolino*.

Lower on the rear wall is a painting of *St. Paolino* by **Michele Marcucci**, done in 1901. To its sides are exquisite wood reliquaries by a local artisan, 1605. These were originally covered by Pinotti's paintings [#1& #19].

12. *Saintly Bishop*, painted wood sculpture. This elaborately painted statue of a very youthful blond bishop was universally considered to be of St. Paolino. A recent restoration revealed, however, that the model of Lucca which he holds in his right hand replaces an original unknown object and that the statue probably did not originally represent St. Paolino. The restoration in the early 1990s was entirely salutary, revealing rather than repainting the original. The work apparently dates from the late 1300s and shows signs, stylistically and technically, of a Germanic origin. The restoration provided an opportunity to remove and examine the supposedly precious "jewels of St. Paolino," a set of 23 brooches which studded the hat and vestments and which appeared to be diamonds and other gems in gold settings. It quickly became evident that the settings were  brass and the jewels were paste glass. Perhaps these replaced original priceless stones; the existing ones were placed in the statue sometime in the 1600s.

Historians' demands satisfied, the statue has returned to its holy function as St. Paolino, once again holding Lucca in his hand and apparently resplendent with jewels.

13. Chapel

Rear wall: ***The Coronation of the Virgin, with a view of Lucca***, tempera on panel, one of the best and most intriguing Renaissance paintings in Lucca. On the left is St. Paolino, kneeling, in a robe of sumptuous gold filigree. On the right is St. Sebastian, dressed

7. SAN PAOLINO

as a young nobleman, identifiable only by the arrow he holds in his hand. Though the central figure of the Virgin dominates the work, it is the portraits of the surrounding assemblage which show the hand of a master. St. Peter, with key and book, has the most memorable visage. The faces of others in the crowd may well include portraits of eminent Lucchesi of the day. I suspect there is a self-portrait of the artist looking out at us in the dark haired man to the right of the mandorla. It is a painting which rewards leisurely perusal.

Its authorship is an intriguing question. Long considered anonymous, it has now been associated with **Baldassare di Biagio** (first recorded 1455, dead by 1484). He was formerly known only as "Master of the Bennabio Tryptych" until that work was shown to be his by the discovery of its commission, dated 1469. The definition of his oeuvre is one of the hottest topics in Lucchese art. Hesitations about ascribing this painting to him have recently surfaced, demoting it to a work by a "Friend of Baldassare." Despite these uncertainties, the painting is datable to about 1470.

This painting is also a good chance to observe Italian restoration techniques. From normal viewing distance it appears to be whole, but if you look closely you can see that the central vertical portion has been repainted using the technique of *tratteggio*, short brush strokes of varying colors which merge together to provide the illusion of an integrated surface.

On the left wall: *St. Barbara with Sts. Bartholomew and Emilio* by the important Lucchese **Agostino Marti** (1482-1540). St. Barbara holds the tower of her captivity, Bartholomew the skinning knife with which he was flayed alive. Emilio is in his bishop garb. This painting was originally over altar #3, which is dedicated to St. Emilio.

14. Chapel

Rear wall: *St. Joseph and Child with St. Carlo Borromeo and St. Anthony of Padua* by **Lorenzo Castellotti**. Castellotti was born in Lucca in 1718. He worked under Pini in the churches Crocifisso dei Bianchi and Santa Caterina.

Right wall: *Madonna with Infants Jesus and John the Baptist and two Saints*, oil on wood, anon., early 1500s. The infant John the Baptist is known as San Giovannino (Little John). The two saints are presumably the two fathers.

15. (Altar) *Martyrdom of St. Valerio* by **Giacinto Gimignani**, signed and dated 1650. Until recently this painting was generally attributed to the more famous Paolo Guidotti (died 1630). St. Valerio succeeded Paolino as Bishop of Lucca (see #8 and #11).

16. (Altar) *Mary and Child*, early 1400s. This sculpture is Germanic in inspiration and perhaps origin, as we have seen with other works in the church—an indication of the close commercial and cultural ties the city had with the lands beyond the Alps. It was moved to San Paolino from the defunct church of Santa Maria Filicorbi. It is set into an unremarkable painting of *Sts. Anna and Gioacchino* by **Giulia Merli**, signed and dated 1828.

17. (Altar) *Virgin with Child and Saints* by **Francesco Vanni**, ca. 1600. There is a study for this painting in the Louvre. Vanni (ca. 1560-1610), was one of the most admired and successful artists of the early Tridentine (Catholic Reformation) period, with numerous commissions in Siena, Rome and abroad. By the 1590s he was the leading figure in the artistic life of Siena, and aspired to its nobility.

18. (Altar) *Deposition* or *Pietà* by **Giovan Domenico Lombardi** (1682-1751), one of the most successful Lucchese artists of the early 1700s. He was the first teacher of Pompeo Batoni.

19. *St. Donato* (see #1).

20. *Acquasantiere* by **Nicolao Civitali** (1482-1560).

~

8. Oratorio of San Pierino

This small church is documented as early as 1048, when it was known as San Pietro in Vincoli. In the 1300s it was the home of the Confraternity of Silk Spinners, and was called San Pierino Siricaiolo. The present building is from the 1500s; the interior was renovated in the 1600s and 1700s. Today it is the home of the Capella Musicale della Basilica di San Paolino.

~

9. San Romano
St. Romanus

This great Dominican church was central to the religious life of Lucca for almost 700 years. For much of that time it served as the civic church of the town and was connected by an elevated walkway to the offices of the Elders, which were located where Palazzo Ducale now stands.

As early as 792 a small oratorio was recorded near the site. With the rise of the Dominican Order, founded in 1215, a new church was built and consecrated in 1281. In 1316 Castruccio Castracani became Lord of Lucca and built his fortress, the Augusta, in the area surrounding San Romano. After his death in 1328 the Augusta was used by the subsequent owners of Lucca (the town being bought and sold numerous times during the next fifteen years) and then by the Pisans during their occupation. When Lucca regained its freedom in 1369 the despised fortress was dismantled and its materials were used in new building projects, including the church of San Romano which was turned into the massive brick structure we see today.

In 1375 Catherine of Siena was welcomed here while on her Papal mission to secure the loyalty of Lucca during the Great Schism. In 1399 the procession of the Bianchi set off from San Romano, carrying before them the church's crucifix. (The church of *Crocifisso dei Bianchi* was later built to house this miraculous cross.) A few years later Paolo Guinigi celebrated his marriage to Ilaria del Carretto in San Romano. In 1498 many followers of Savonarola fled to San Romano from Florence after the execution of their leader; they found in Lucca sympathy for the severe, moralistic Savonarolan ethic. Blessed Angelo Orsucci, the first Italian martyr in Japan (1622), departed from the monastery of San Romano.

During the 1400s and 1500s the interior underwent frequent alterations. In 1660 it was completely renovated, producing the interior we see today. The work was directed by Giovanni Buonvisi and the architect Francesco Buonamici. The massive brick structure has always been high maintenance. It was closed for many years but finally reopened in 2003 as an auditorium.

The exterior gains its power from the mass of brick, not from adornments. The façade is prepared to accept stone facing but this is no longer likely to happen.

Interior

1. Altar of Santa Rosa da Lima, consecrated 1698. **Sts. Ludovico and Rosa**, 1675, by **Camillo Ciai**. St. Rosa died in 1617 and was canonized in 1671.

2. Bust. *St. Antoninus Archipiscum*.

3. Carminati Chapel. Altar of St. Vincent Ferrer. ***St. Antonino of Florence with St. Peter Martyr*** by **Giovan Domenico Ferruci**, 1668. Previously here was *San Vincenzo Ferrer* by Borghese di Pietro Borghese, now in the Villa Guinigi Museum.

4. Marble monument honoring Sante Pagnini (1470-1536). Born in Lucca, a follower of Savonarola, Pagnini became the most important orientalist of his time. His Latin version of the Bible was used by Martin Luther for his translation into the German. Pagnini was also one of the theologians who supported the annulment of Henry VIII's marriage to Catherine of Aragon.

9. SAN ROMANO

5. Bottini Chapel. Altar of St. Stanislao, 1635. *Miracle of St. Stanislao* by **Domenico Viola**.

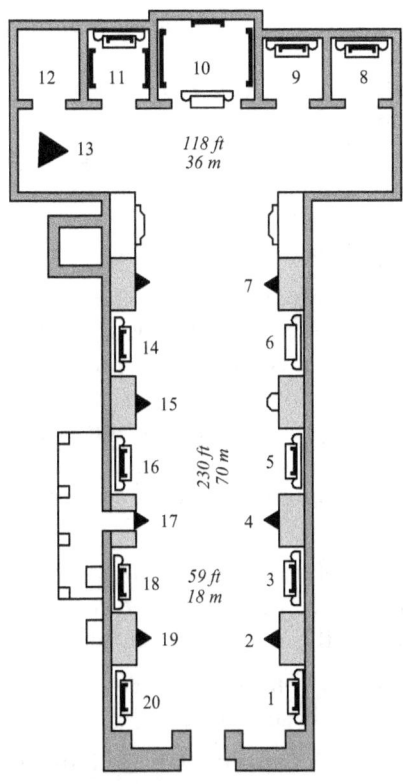

San Romano

6. Altar of the Madonna of the Miracles, formerly Altar of the Rosary. *Madonna of the Rosary*, 1563, by **F. del Brina** was formerly here. The altar was sumptuously reconstructed in 1635 by the Republic of Lucca in thanksgiving for surviving the pestilence of 1630, attributed to the intercession of the Virgin of the Rosary. (The plague of 1630 was devastating; anyone who survived had been blessed.) When the large church of San Pier Maggiore was torn down in 1813 the fresco *Madonna dei Miracoli* was moved here.

7. Pagnius Lucordium.

8. Sesti Chapel. Altar of St. Raymond of Pennafort. *Saint Raimondo* by **Pietro Paolini**. A late workshop painting by Paolini, who died in 1681. Raymond of Pennafort (1180-1275) was Master-General of the Dominicans and a notable writer. His collection of canon law was the standard for almost 700 years. He was canonized in 1601. The chapel decoration is by **Bartolomeo de Santi**, 1754.

9. Bottini Chapel. Altar of St. Agnes of Montepulciano. *Mary offering the Infant to St. Agnes of Montepulciano*, 1610, by **Paolo Guidotti**. St. Agnes (1268-1317) was a Dominican nun. The chapel was decorated by **Bartolomeo De Santi** and **Francesco Cecchi**.

10. A chapel of elaborate stucco. The high altar contains the relics of St. Romano, placed here in 1626 after various other translations (as such movements of relics are called) in 1197, 1490 and 1556. Behind the main altar is what remains of the *Sarcophagus of San Romano*, 1490, by **Matteo Civitali.**

On the rear wall, *Decapitation of St. Romano*, 1719, by **G. Domenico Lombardi**. On the side walls are two other paintings by Lombardi, moved here in 1873 from San Ponziano, depicting the *Miracles of Blessed Bernardo Tolomei*, 1721. They have been called the best works of this Lucchese artist.

The intarsia choir stalls are by **Giuseppe Gigli**, 1511.

11. Chapel of the Name of Jesus. On the rear wall: *Circumcision*, 1636, by **Rutilio Manetti** (1571-1639), commissioned by the Arnolfini family. Manetti was a student of Francesco Vanni and one of the best Caravaggians. On the side walls are two paintings by **Lombardi**: *St. Peter Cures the Cripple* and *Institution of the Congregation of the Name of Jesus*.

The chapel decoration is by **Bartolomeo De Santi** and **Lorenzo Castellotti.**

12. Montecatini Chapel, or Chapel of the *Madonna della Misericordia*, so-called for the work by **Fra Bartolomeo** commissioned for this site, which today is in the Villa Guinigi Museum.

13. Funeral monument of *Archbishops Vincenzo and Sebastian of the Portico*, 1590. Both men were Lucchese Bishops.

14. Bernardini Chapel. Altar of San Domenico, 1636. *Madonna, Child and Saints with St. Domenic* by **Pietro Testa.**

15. Statue of the Lucchese *Paolino Bernardini* (1517-1585), a Dominican theologian; anonymous work of the 1600s.

16. Ori Chapel. Altar of San Giacinto, 1637. *San Giacinto Revives a Young Man* by **Domenico Cresti,** who was called **Il Passignano.** Giacinto was a Polish Dominican missionary who was canonized in 1594.

17. (over door) Bust of *St. Romano*.

18. Marchiò Chapel. Altar of St. Thomas Aquinas. *The Crucifix talks to St. Thomas Aquinas*, 1602, by **Francesco Vanni** (1536-1619). The gray stone is from the 1500s chapel. This painting by

9. SAN ROMANO

the stunningly prolific Vanni was highly regarded in the 1700s.

19. Statue of *Albertus Magnus*.

20. Burlamacchi Chapel. Altar of the Holy Spirit, 1639. ***Descent of the Holy Spirit*** by **G. Andrea Coppola** (1597-1659). Originally in Sant'Agostino. Formerly the altar was dedicated to St. Catherine and held *Eternal Father with St. Catherine and Mary Magdalene*, 1509, by **Fra Bartolomeo**, now in the Villa Guinigi Museum. The Coppola painting was given to the church by the State in exchange for the Fra Bartolomeo.

Organs.

The marble choir lofts, 1713 and 1719, are by **Vincenzo Saminiati**, a friar. The organ on the left is from the 1600s; that on the right was rebuilt in the 1800s by the Tronci of Pistoia. Both are superb mechanical organs.

~

10. Sant'Agostino
St. Augustine

Sant'Agostino lies on the site of an earlier church, of the 700s, called San Salvatore *in muro*. The toponym differentiated it from a number of other San Salvatores by indicating that it was built up against the town wall (*muro*). This was the Roman wall, where it bulged out on the north side to accommodate the theatre. As Christianity grew and theatre declined, San Salvatore was built in the space between the rear of the theatre and the town wall, precisely the site of the present church of Sant'Agostino.

Inside Sant'Agostino you can see part of the wall of the Roman theatre. Outside, in front of the bell tower and chapel, are the remains of two brick archways. Through those arches the Roman audience entered to find their seats. If you stand in Piazza Sant' Agostino so you can see these arches, you are standing in the center of the stage. The bell tower incorporates remnants of the upper galleries of the theatre.

Sant'Agostino was built in the 1300s. This great brick structure was part of the mendicant movement which needed spacious halls to house the growing audiences for their orations. You see similar structures in San Francesco, built by the Franciscans, and in San Romano, by the Dominicans.

Sant'Agostino was built, of course, by the Augustinians. By the early 1300s they oversaw a monastery in the area which had been opened up by the expansion of the city walls. By 1380 they had erected the large church cum meeting hall which you see today. The emphasis, as with the other mendicant churches, was on functionality, not ornamentation.

Arches of the Roman Theatre

It must surely be more than coincidence that it was in 1369, the year of liberation from Pisa, that a small chapel was consecrated, dedicated to the miraculous fresco of *Madonna del Sasso* (Madonna of the Stone). It was built against the outside of Sant'Agostino, utilizing part of the Roman theatre. The fresco was already ancient and revered. Long ago a sinner had thrown a stone at the image, which would have struck the infant Jesus. The child moved miraculously from Mary's right arm to her left and avoided the blow. The earth immediately opened and the sinner fell into the pits of hell. It was a fitting evocation of the local populace's mood when they expelled their own defilers, the despised Pisans. The hole into which the sinner disappeared is still visible.

Work on the church continued through the 1400s with a new sacristy and a cloister on the north side, which you can enter through the little door just left of the church. A refinement of the front was started, a classic Lucchese white limestone façade embellished only by pilasters and colored horizontal bands, but work stopped at the height of the entrance. The building's presence depends on its brick mass, the front given texture by jutting horizontal rows, and a plain rose window.

Interior

In the mid-1600s the Tucci family paid for a complete

10. Sant'Agostino

renovation but few signs of it remain today. Considering the church's later history, we are fortunate that anything remains. Seen through secular eyes the cavernous building was good for nothing but a warehouse, and after the suppression of the Orders by the new Italian government in 1866 the church was acquired by the State and given to the Italian military for use as an armory. The altars were dismantled, the artworks dispersed and lost, and the church became a shell. Emerging from World War II as a decaying profane structure, it was given in 1946 to the Sisters of the Santa Zita Institute who occupied the adjoining building. (They are the *Suore Oblate dello Spirito Santo*—Sisters of the Holy Spirit.) After 10 years of repair Sant'Agostino was re-consecrated and opened for services.

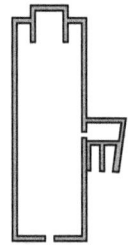

Sant' Agostino

Although almost entirely denuded inside, the vast and unusually daylit space recaptures the sense of the original grand hall and makes one feel how essential to its fulfillment is a large assembly of people.

Since the church is watched over by the Sisters, you will likely encounter one or two of them tending to their spiritual and earthly housekeeping duties. Being a nursing order, they are open and helpful, welcoming the chance to explain (in Italian) the history of the church and to extol the virtues of their Blessed founder, Elena Guerra, whose body lies in the illuminated glass sarcophagus below the main altar. She was a teacher of St. Gemma Galgani.

Sparse as it is, the interior enables us to concentrate on its particular treasures. Halfway down on the right side is an exposed portion of stone wall, remnants of the Roman theatre. Just beyond it is the entrance to the **Chapel of Madonna del Sasso**. This is the chapel constructed in 1369 against the exterior of the church. During the reconstruction of the 1600s it was incorporated into the church proper by opening the wall and it was given an entirely new setting as a Baroque shrine.

In the plainness of the church, this Baroque jewel with its miraculous medieval fresco is the sort of unannounced surprise which, stumbled across, makes us love Italy. The shrine is carefully maintained by the good Sisters.

The frescoes in the chapel are by **Giacinto Gimignani**. On the wall to the right is *Christ Pointing to Madonna del Sasso, with Sts. Peter, Augustine, Andrew, Nicholas of Tolentino and Francis of Assisi*. On the left wall is the *Story of the Miracle and the Descent of the Sinner*. A cavity in the floor is what remains of where the earth opened into hell.

Statues of the four virtues frame the side walls. Numerous plaques attest to the patronage of the Boccelli family. A modern bronze bas-relief records the procession of 1949 when the image, considered with some justice to be the oldest miraculous fresco in Lucca, was displayed throughout the Diocese.

Gimignani also did the chapel to the left of the main altar, paid for by the Barsotti family. The chapel to the right of the altar was rebuilt at the same time by the Franciotti family, which has their sepulchers there. It today houses a portrait of St. Gemma Galgani.

The high altar area of the church formerly housed splendid wood choir seats, donated in the 1400s by the powerful Bernardini family. They are now in the church of San Francesco.

On the right wall there has recently been placed a picture of the *Madonna del Rosario, with St. Dominic and St. Antonio*, anonymous, 1700s. It comes from the private chapel of the Guerra family.

The picture over the main door commemorates the beatification of Elena Guerra in 1959.

The marble sepulcher stones, some from the 1400s, mark clerical and lay graves.

Formerly in the church:

Madonna and Child with Sts. Augustine, Monica, Nicola Torentino, and Girolamo, 1492, by **Michelangelo di Pietro Membrini** (formerly known as **Maestro del Tondo Lathrop**), suggesting the quality of the church's Renaissance works. It is now in the Villa Guinigi Museum.

After the renovations of the mid-1600s the altars held works by Vanni, Zacchia il Vecchio, Paolini and other notable artists.

~

11. Santa Maria Corteorlandini
St. Mary Corteorlandini

Santa Maria Corteorlandini is a medieval church with a baroque and rococo interior. It also holds a perfect replica of the house in which Jesus was born. The toponym *Corteorlandini* is derived from the church's location, facing the courtyard of the Rolandinghi family.

Although there was an earlier church on the site, the present structure was built in 1188, as is recorded in an inscription in the church:

> "In 1187 the perfidious Saracens, under the reign of the warrior Saladin, seized the tomb, temple and cross of Christ. The following year, on August 2nd, began the reconstruction on its foundations of this church which praises our Lord Christ son of the blessed Mary, Vito, Biagio, Concordio, Cerbonio and Alessio. Master Guido built this work."

The only remains of this twelfth century church are the two small apses and the exterior south wall with its original door. In 1580 the church became home to the new order of the Canons Regular of the Mother of God, founded by Giovanni Leonardi, and an extensive project of reconstruction was initiated. In the 1600s and 1700s the church was given a stunning baroque interior, which has been preserved.

Exterior

The front of the church overlooks a space so small it is only a *corte*, not even a *piazzetta*. The present façade dates to the early 1600s. It is a bit of a hodgepodge, reflecting the various stages of construction. The south wall, however, survives in its original form with a row of white pilasters on a brown wall, topped by a band of small hanging arches, typical of the period around 1200. On the corbel of the last arch to the rear the builders incorporated a bust from the earlier structure—the type of small detail you will frequently find in Lucca if you look carefully. The side door is also typical of the period with its plain, heavy jambs, its non-concentric arch of alternating light and dark voussoirs and foliated border, flanked by lions. On the lions and the frieze drill holes were used to provide texture, a technique you see throughout the medieval city. The lengthy inscription on the architrave commemorates the consecration of three altars installed in 1313:

> "In 1313, the 4th of November, the altars of this church were consecrated. They were done by Bishop Filippo of Aquila, under the authority of the Supreme Pontiff, and indulgence was granted to those who visited the church. On the day of consecration there were granted 120 days of indulgence, which is to say, 40 for each altar, and moreover, for the eight days following the consecration. There was granted in perpetuity the same indulgence on the annual anniversary of the eight days of consecration. Vanni Bolpelli, Ghiddino Tepe, Puccinello Barellie were the workers who did this."

In the rear of the church only two small original apses have been preserved, but they show the integrity of the original design, which carried the hanging arches around the perimeter.

Before you enter through the side door don't neglect to turn around and appreciate the superb arches of decorated brick on Palazzo Diodati. They were saved by layers of plaster which, their unintended role of preservation having been fulfilled, have thankfully been allowed to flake off.

Interior

St. John Leonardi began reconstruction in 1580, modernizing the medieval church according to the dictates of the Council of Trent, which integrated the congregation into the performance of the mass. Before this remodeling the choir area took up almost a third of the church. It extended as far forward as the side doors, was elevated several feet above the main floor and was separated from the congregation by an ornate wood choir screen. Leonardi

11. Santa Maria Corteorlandini

leveled the floor and removed the screen, increasing the area available for the congregants and bringing them more intimately into the service. The complete transformation of the interior included replacing the original stone pillars with marble columns. In 1583 the tribunal was frescoed, though these were painted over in 1667 when the new marble altar was installed. It was renovated again in 1719 and there are no traces left of the original medieval structure.

The church is a rare example of Baroque Lucchese architecture. The vault was embellished by stucco and frescoes about 1715 by **Pietro Scorsini**. In the central nave the paintings representing the ancestors of Mary are by **Dom Brugieri**, done before 1721.

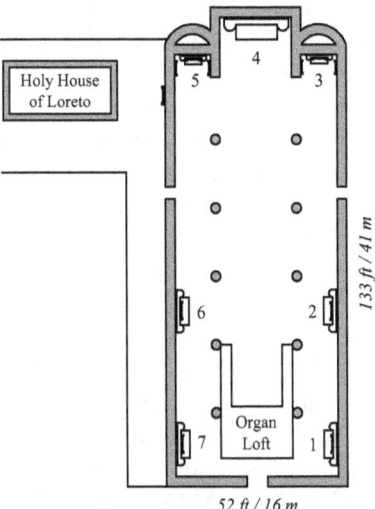

Santa Maria Corteorlandini

1. Altar of San Carlo. *Mary and Child with St. Carlo Borromeo and Blessed Giovanni Buonvisi* by **Antiveduto Grammatica** (formerly attributed to Matteo Rosselli). The altar was dedicated in 1611, one year after the canonization of Charles Borromeo (1538-1584). Borromeo was instrumental in organizing the Counter Reformation, a main figure at the Council of Trent, and a tireless reformer at a time when the church was desperately in need of renewal.

An inscription on the left side of the altar records that it was donated by members of the Buonvisi family. Originally of gilded wood, it was rebuilt in marble in 1660.

2. Altar of St. John. *St. Giovanni Leonardi* by **Enrico Chiari**. This painting was donated by Pope Pius IX on the occasion of Leonardi's beatification in 1861. The face is based on an unfinished portrait done by Paolo Guidotti as Leonardi lay dying. In Chiari's painting the saint, with his right hand, consigns to his followers the Constitution of his Order. With his left he delivers to the heathen nations a book inscribed "Rules of the Congregation of Propaganda Fide…1605." Formerly on the altar was *St. John the Baptist* (1636) by Paolini.

St. John Leonardi was a prophet not entirely without honor in his own country, Lucca, but the rulers of the state saw to it that he spent most of his life in exile. He was born in 1542 at Diecimo, a few miles outside of town. Despite his desire to become a priest his father had him apprenticed to an apothecary in the city, where he subjected himself to a regimen of religious study in his off hours, and finally at the age of 30 was ordained a priest. A passionate advocate of the Counter Reformation he began, in 1574 from his base in the church of Santa Maria della Rosa, to gather about him lay disciples dedicated to charitable work in prisons and hospitals, the purification of the church, and a general "reform of manners." The city fathers were opposed to the creation of any new orders in Lucca, regarding them as attempts to establish the Inquisition in the Republic, a fate they relentlessly avoided. Their fears were reinforced when a Papal emissary visited the city in 1574 and demanded the arrest of three members of the government and their trial in Rome by the Inquisition. The timing could not have been worse for Leonardi, who found himself banished. He would return to Lucca only rarely when granted special permission by the government, which succumbed occasionally to papal insistence.

Nonetheless, Leonardi managed in 1580 to take possession of Santa Maria Corteorlandini (at the time commonly known as Santa Maria Nera) and to establish there his order, which in time became known as the Clerks Regular of the Mother of God of Lucca. It is the primary church of the order to this day. Bishop Guidiccioni approved the order in 1583 and the Pope confirmed this in 1595. Soon afterwards the Pope appointed Leonardi to reform several orders of wayward monks outside of Lucca. In 1601 his order acquired the church of Santa Maria in Portico in Rome, where he was buried in 1609 after dying of the plague, contracted while ministering to the stricken. His relics were moved to Santa Maria in Campitelli in 1662.

Leonardi was close friends with the other reformers of his time, particularly St. Philip Neri. He was offered the control of many churches in his lifetime, but refused most of them, primarily

11. Santa Maria Corteorlandini

out of fear of alarming the authorities in Lucca with his growing influence. His order has never had more than 7 churches at one time and has virtually no presence outside of Italy. He was one of the founders of the Congregation of Propaganda Fide (Propagation of the Faith) which provided us with the word propaganda. (In 1988 it was renamed Congregation for the Evangelization of the Nations.)

John Leonardi was declared a saint in 1938.

3. Altar of the Crucifixion. Copy of *Crucifixion with Sts. Catherine and Giulio* by **Guido Reni**. The original is in Villa Guinigi.

Left wall: *St. Lorenzo* by **Gaspare Mannucci**.

Right wall: *St. Concordio* (possibly St. Lamberto) by **Gaspare Mannucci**.

4. High altar area.

The altar was installed in 1667. On its left it bears the coat of arms of the Buonvisi, on the right of the Arnolfini. The exquisite ciborium is by **Giovanni Vambré** senior, 1673. The bas-relief of the central panel shows Christ at Emmaus as he breaks bread and reveals his resurrection to the disciples. The statuettes to the sides are of Moses and Aron, recalling the Passover which presaged Easter and the Resurrection. In the panel above is a relief of a Pelican, believed to feed its newborn with its own blood, a symbol of Christ's sacrifice in communion. The figure to the right is the Good Samaritan and on the left is Mary Magadalene, arms outstretched, at the moment of exclaiming "I have seen my Lord!" Surmounting the ciborium is a small tabernacle displaying the chalice and host of communion.

The epigraph behind the altar records that here are the remains of "Sts. Giulio, Ludovico, Plinio and Elia...transported to Lucca, to the joy of the whole city, in 1644."

The painting of the *Assumption* is by **Michele Marcucci**. It is a reproduction of the original by **Luca Giordano** which was destroyed by fire in 1916. The frescoes are by **Michelangelo Colonna**.

5. Altar of the Madonna of the Snows. 1800s copy of *Madonna with Sts. Lucy and Magdalene* by Guido Reni (the original is today in the Uffizi).

Left wall: **St. Richard** and **St. Richard Crosses the Sea on his Cloak** by **Francesco Vanni**. This is the Saint Richard, "King of the English," who died in Lucca during a pilgrimage in 722 and whose relics are in the church of San Frediano. The portrait shows him as a pilgrim (with staff and shell on his cloak) trampling on his crown.

Right wall: **St. Bartholomew** and **Martyrdom of St. Bartholomew** by **Francesco Vanni**.

Below the archway are three paintings, also by Vanni, recalling the story of the Madonna of the Snows, including **The Dream of Pope Liberio** and **The Foundation of Santa Maria Maggiore**.

These paintings were traditionally attributed to Ventura Salimbeni but have recently been persuasively given to the eminent Sienese, Vanni. They recall the event of an August night about the year 360 when Mary appeared in dreams to both Pope Liberius and a rich patrician of Rome, telling them to build a church on the site where the next morning they would find snow. Despite the Roman summer snow was indeed found on the Esquiline hill, into which the Pope traced the outline for the church of Santa Maria Maggiore.

6. Altar, rebuilt in marble in 1696. **Nativity of the Virgin** by **Francesco Vanni**, 1602. Signed and dated on the book held by St. Joachim. This was an important commission for which Vanni made many preliminary sketches. The lovely tapestry *paliotto* below the altar table was commissioned in 1662 by Cipriano Mansi.

7. Altar of St. Filippo Neri. **Madonna and Child** (commonly called *Queen of the Angels*), fresco, early 1300s, set in a painting of St. Filippo Neri adoring the image, mid-1600s. The fresco, recently restored, was originally on one of the pillars of the church before the 1600s renovations which substituted columns. The oil painting is closely based on one by Reni in St. Peter's, Rome.

Neri was the founder of the order called Oratorians which gave their name to the musical form the oratorio because it developed out of the *laudi spiritualis* of their services.

Above the main door is a large fresco of **Christ Driving the Moneychangers from the Temple**, ca. 1698, by **Giovanni Marracci**.

In the early 1700s new windows were opened. The walls surrounding the windows and the ceiling vaults were then

11. Santa Maria Corteorlandini

frescoed by **Pietro Paolo Scorsini**. To the sides of the windows are the figures of the Apostles. On the central vault is the *Assumption of Mary*.

In the roughly triangular spaces above the columns, between the arches, are paintings (ca. 1717) by **Domenico Brugieri** depicting the forebears of Mary: Abraham, Isaiah, David, St. Anne, Zaccharias, St. Elizabeth, John the Baptist, St. Joseph.

The Holy House of Loreto

If you pass through the door on the north side of the church you can visit a remarkable edifice, a replica of the house in which Mary and Joseph lived in Nazareth. This is the house in which the Angel Gabriel annunciated Mary, and where the Holy Family lived after Christ's birth. If it seems strange to encounter this building hidden away in Lucca, it is less so given its miraculous and peripatetic history.

In 1291, to preserve the small house from the ravages of the Saracens, angels transported it first to Dalmatia and then, four years later, to the town of Loreto on the east coast of Italy. The first historical mention, however, is about 1470 and the first papal bull regarding it is in 1507. Since that time the house has been a revered site for pilgrimages and miraculous cures. It was particularly favored by St. John Leonardi, which led his followers to replicate it in Lucca in 1662. The interior is a precise duplication, brick by precisely measured brick, of the 14 ft. X 21 ft. structure; the fresco remnants are as they appear in the original. In a niche on the north wall is a duplicate of the small dark figure of Mary, in cedar wood, purportedly sculpted by St. Luke and likewise translated miraculously to Loreto; the original statue at Loreto was consumed in a fire in 1921.

On the south wall of the corridor outside the house is a large, typically vibrant, painting by **Giovanni Coli** and **Filippo Gherardi** depicting the miraculous moving of the house to Loreto. The painting was apparently done between June 1680 and November 1681. As Coli died in February 1681 this would be one of the last paintings of their famous collaboration.

~

12. Sant'Alessandro
St. Alexander

Sant'Alessandro is at once the plainest and most enigmatic church in Lucca. It is often called the purest example of Lucchese architecture and yet it lacks many of the typical aspects of Lucchese Romanesque. Except for the use of white limestone, what could be more different from Sant'Alessandro than San Michele or the Cathedral? Indeed, no other church in town really looks like it. And yet Sant'Alessandro does seem to best capture not only the architecture but the soul of Lucca, with its restraint, its solidity, its doggedness in resisting the onslaught of time.

In recent years the church has been the subject of careful investigations and analyses, which have gone a long way to deciphering its history but have also raised new and intriguing questions. At the core of these is the dating of the building's parts—what was built when? This is a question we encounter often in the churches of Lucca, but nowhere do the hypotheses vary more than in Sant'Alessandro.

Sant'Alessandro is the oldest church in Lucca. This seems a safe statement, though age can be an evasive concept when dealing with structures which have undergone such prolonged attention. But by whatever standards we employ, Sant'Alessandro retains its primogeniture.

Perhaps the best way to get a grip on its age is to work backwards in time.

The building's fourth and final phase of structural work, the raising of the roof, was completed about 1175. Since that time the building has retained its appearance, except for some minor details. No other church has been spared so completely the renovations of later generations. In this respect, certainly, Sant'Alessandro qualifies as the oldest church in Lucca.

The third phase began earlier in the same century, about 1110, and was a continuation of work which had been abandoned in medias res. After 1073, with the death of Pope Alexander II, the Church in Lucca found itself racked by battles between reformers and conservatives. The legitimate bishop, a nephew of Pope Alexander II, had a tumultuous career and eventually departed the city in fear and despair, ending his days in his birth town of Mantua, where he is the patron saint. With the appointment in 1097 of a new bishop a dramatic religious, economic, and political revival began which would transform Lucca over the next two centuries. The work on Sant'Alessandro resumed. The apse was completed, attaining its final height (anticipating the raising of the roof). In the interior the final colonnaded arches were added, on the end towards the apse.

The second phase of Sant'Alessandro's construction coincided with the birth of Lucca's medieval greatness. In 1057 Anselmo da Baggio of Milan was appointed bishop of Lucca. He was a central figure in the reform movement which was about to transform the western Church. He had already been active in Milan on the part of the reformers, overzealously so in the view of Milan's Archbishop, and so was sent to Lucca to get him out of the way. Soon after his appointment he was given title to the church of Sant'Alessandro Maggiore in Lucca. When he took possession, Sant'Alessandro was already an important church; it was under the control not of the bishop, or of canons, or a family, or a monastery, but of

12. Sant'Alessandro

the Pope himself. Saint Alexander had been a Pope, and although his cult was not widespread there were two churches dedicated to him in Lucca, the other being Sant'Alessandro Minore (which was transferred from the Papacy to the canons of the Cathedral in 1045). The granting of Sant'Alessandro Maggiore to Bishop Anselmo emphasized the papal imprimatur of the new bishop. In 1058 Anselmo presented to the Marquis of Tuscany proof that he had acquired possession of the church, and to confirm this the Marquis decreed that a substantial fine would be levied on anyone who attempted to deprive the bishop of his new possession. To give further weight to the grant the Pope then gave Anselmo the relics of Saint Alexander, which had been a papal possession for two hundred years.

Saint Alexander

Alexander, the fourth successor to Saint Peter as Bishop of Rome, was martyred about the year 110. In the 300s his remains were re-interred, by the noblewoman Sabina, in a crypt along a road near Rome. About 820 Pope Pasquale I took possession of the relics and had them more appropriately settled in the basilica of San Presede. In 1060 they finally came to rest in Lucca. These relics acquired by Anselmo did not include the head of the saint, but they did include the chain with which he was bound. The relics are today in the main altar of the church.

Unfortunately there is no good reason to believe that Pope Alexander I, a shadowy figure, was martyred at all; he apparently became confused with another Alexander who was martyred and buried on the Via Nomentana, seven miles outside of Rome.

Having come into possession of such precious items—a papal church and relics with which to consecrate it—Bishop Anselmo immediately set to work renovating the building. He was an ambitious builder. In 1060 he began reconstruction of the Cathedral and of San Michele. The following year he was elected Pope and took the name Alexander II. His identification with his namesake was obviously personal.

It is at this point that the question of the age of the building becomes intriguing. What did Bishop Anselmo inherit in 1060 and what did he do with it?

After Anselmo/Pope Alexander II started the process of rebuilding, virtually every church in Lucca was rebuilt over the next 200 years. But what does "rebuilt" mean? In some cases, as with San Frediano, it meant tearing down the original and rebuilding it from scratch. But it must often have been true that structurally sound components, certainly foundations but also walls and columns, would have been preserved or reused in the process of expanding or refurbishing. In most cases it is assumed that there is little remaining of the original building, which was often founded during the Lombard period. In Sant'Alessandro what, if anything, remains of the building which Anselmo inherited in 1060? It seems a good deal.

The exposed, southern, side of the church at first appears to be of uniform execution. The only obvious anomaly is the presence of two doors: a simple one, now closed, near the apse, placed where we expect to find such a side entrance, and; a second one, more elaborate, placed in the center of the wall. On closer examination other discrepancies appear. The eight simple windows are not as uniform as they seem. The first five from the front are identical in design and execution, with proper jambs topped by capitals surmounted by symmetrical arches. But in the three windows towards the apse irregularities creep in. The limestone blocks are simply cut as they meet the window; there are no jambs. There are no true capitals, only a simple cornice giving the sense of one. And the arches have been subtly transformed from classic concentric semi-circles to the slightly bulging non-concentric arch which so entranced medieval Lucca. This new form seems to have become so natural—it looked right to the medieval eye—that it was irresistible to the carvers, even though they could have easily mimicked the earlier examples to their left.

Mimicked because it is evident that the first five windows from the front are earlier than the three towards the apse. This means that the rear part of the church—windows 6, 7 and 8 (and in the interior, columns 7,8,9) as well as the lower part of the apse—is phase 2, or Pope Alexander's contribution (built between 1060 and 1070). Which in turn means that the front half of Sant'Alessandro must have been constructed before, and probably well before, 1060. This would certainly make Sant'Alessandro the oldest church in Lucca, given that not only remnants are extant, but the

12. Sant'Alessandro

original structure itself. Put another way, when we are looking at the front part of Sant'Alessandro we are looking at phase one. The question then presents itself, when was this part, the original Sant'Alessandro, built?

The Original Church

The exterior of Sant'Alessandro could not be plainer. The surface has no relief; most notably, it is not broken up by blind arcades, which would become *de rigueur* in the 1100s. The "decoration" of this flat surface is almost all horizontal: the lip at the plinth, the sills and capitals of the side windows. The alternating horizontal rows of light and darker colored stone, a motif recapitulated for centuries, is present but extremely subtle, the effect depending as much on the sizing of the stone as in their color contrast.

The front of the church has a single startlingly classical door, which looks more like the entrance to a temple than to a church. Since the mid-1100s, when the roof was raised, the facade has risen to a gabled "frame" giving the front a nearly identical form to San Frediano, which was built at the same time. The original church was about 8 feet lower; the side aisle roofs began to slope down from the bottom cornice of the frame, and their peak was slightly above the high point of the present side roofs. The cornice is as high as the side roofs would have risen originally.

The stonework is more remarkable than it at first appears. The quality of the masonry is not only fine, it seems almost impossibly so for a work of its time. It has been said that the only comparable quality is to be found in the baptistery of Florence. What appear to be solid blocks of stone are in fact facing stones about 4-7 inches thick. They imitate in appearance, though not in function, a form of Roman architecture prevalent in the first and second centuries, known as *pseudisodormo*. In this method of construction rectangular facing stones of equal height would be laid in rows on the inside and outside of a rubble core. These would then be capped with a cross stone laid on top of them, tying together the exterior and interior facings. This process would be repeated upwards row by row, giving an appearance just like the rows of Sant'Alessandro. But in Sant'Alessandro there is only the appearance: the thinner rows, which appear to be cross pieces, are simply narrower facing stones. This is proven by the fact that the rows of the interior wall, done in the same way, do not coincide with the exterior. So Sant'Alessandro was built in conscious imitation of classical forms, with a skill more appropriate to imperial Rome than to the early Middle Ages.

The front door is also self-consciously classical, its triangular tympanum unique in Lucchese architecture. Moreover, the frieze of the border was common in classical Roman architecture, not in medieval. Similar examples have, however, been identified from the time of Charlemagne (about 800).

Close examination of the right side of the church shows the different handwork between the original and the later extension (phase 2). The working of the front part, as on the façade, is exceptionally fine, but beyond the fifth window it deteriorates, a sure sign that the evident seam does not represent simply a pause in construction but the intervention of many years. It was possible to duplicate the stone, because it comes from the nearby Pisan mountains, but it was not possible to duplicate the workmanship.

The interior of the church confirms what is suggested by the exterior. Up to the same seam the workmanship is impeccable. The first five columns and capitals are Roman spolia and are exceptionally fine.

This front part of the church is almost undoubtedly what was granted to Bishop Anselmo in 1058. This building probably had an apse and a crypt, though we lack the excavations to prove so. The dimensions of the original church can be fairly precisely hypothesized. As Carrai has pointed out, the floor plan followed a very classical form, a rectangle of the proportion 1 X the square root of 3. This is the dimension which

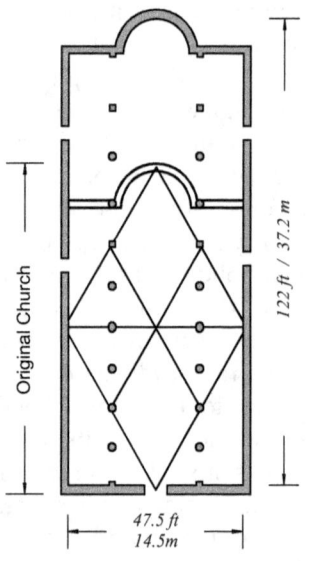

Sant' Alessandro

12. Sant'Alessandro

results from stacking two equilateral triangles, a form which ruled the plan of Christian churches since the paleochristian age, presumably because it replicated the form of St. Andrew's cross, an X. (See the diagram of the church.) A more prosaic reason, but of great importance to the original builders, is that this is one of the simplest ways to lay out a building.

So at last we ask, what was the date of the building Bishop Anselmo inherited? Though this is likely to remain the subject of much discussion, a plausible period is the early to mid-800s, during the revival of the cult of St. Alexander. Pope Leo III, who crowned Charlemagne Emperor on Christmas Day 800, gave to the new Emperor some relics of Alexander to found a church. Pope Pasquale I (817-824) rescued other relics of St. Alexander and encouraged the cult of the saint. It is quite likely that he also distributed parts of these relics (and associated relics, those which had come into contact with the holy bones) to found new churches. Such relics were necessary: in 787 the Fifth Council of Nicea had forbidden, under pain of excommunication, the consecration of a church without the attendant sanctifying relics.

The construction of such a building required a very wealthy patron. This may well have been the Marquis of Tuscany, whose capital was Lucca. This line became increasingly wealthy during the 800s; by the end of the century Adalberto II (his sepulcher epigraph is in San Martino) was distinguished by the epithet *il ricco*—Adalberto The Rich. Indeed, when the Emperor visited Lucca he took offense at the lavishness of Adalberto's court as more appropriate for an Emperor than a mere Marquis.

There is however, the intriguing possibility that the original church was even older. This is suggested by the excessive classicism of the design, but even more so by the quality of the workmanship, which is of a level one could expect of Imperial Rome but which is reasonably thought to have not survived the terrible centuries of the 500s and 600s. One difficulty with this hypothesis is that Roman Lucca was about 8 feet lower than the medieval city. If the original church was so early it must have been perched high atop a flight of steps. Of course this would also have been so, though to a lesser degree, if the church dates to the 800s.

To recapitulate. Phase 1 of the construction of Sant'Alessandro, datable probably to the 800s, comprised roughly the front half, ending just to the rear of the central side door. It may have had an apse and a crypt below the main altar. Phase 2, undertaken about 1060, extended the church to the rear by dismantling the rear wall, crypt, and apse. A new crypt, to house the newly acquired relics of St. Alexander was built below where the main altar is today. The side walls were extended and a new apse was started. The work came to a halt, to be picked up again in the early 1100s, phase 3, when the apse was finished and the new columns and archways built, setting the stage for the fourth and final phase, the raising of the roof. It helps to keep this progression in mind when looking at the church.

Interior

The church has been closed for years, but such an important monument is sure to reopen. Inside it is a classic, refined basilica, suggesting a reduced San Frediano, with fine round columns and especially well wrought capitals. They are so fine because, as in San Frediano, they are spolia, produced about the 200s or 300s.

The capital on the first column on the right has iconography relating to the cult of the Egyptian god Isis. The second on the left has an intriguing design of headless figures, representing the four seasons, of which a twin has been located in Rome. The different origins of the columns is evident: the fourth pair is Hellenistic—ellipsoidal, not round—with vertical bands on two sides. Here the spolia buyer was lucky enough to find a matching pair.

The fifth pair are rectangular pillars, constructed of blocks, and are the last of the original structure. Along their rear base you can see where the workmen did not trouble themselves to finish the surface, leaving it rough. This is evidence that they were the last pillars, butting up against the presbytery: this side would have been covered by steps, not exposed to view.

The original rear wall would have been where the 7th pair of columns is today (originally there would have been a pilaster here). It is conjectural, but likely, that the original crypt would have been located between the 6th pair of pillars and the apse. Again one wishes for archaeological help.

If you look up at the clerestory walls, there are cornices, another horizontal design of the original church. At their ends

12. Sant'Alessandro

are two heads, iconic but also portraits. On the left (north) side is a bishop with trimmed beard and considerable presence, on the right a pudgy faced cleric. The bishop can reasonably be assumed to be Anselmo. (Remember that sculpture was generally painted; traces of red paint are found in the bishop's hat.) The cleric could well be his rector, the man responsible for getting the work done. Together they mark precisely where the new work began; the original wall extended up to this point. Look at the arches below these heads. The columns from here to the front are of one height; those to the rear are higher. The higher pillar of this arch would originally have been the rear pilaster of the church, and its capital would have been the same height as the first six. When the expansion took place it was necessary to raise the arches because the floor below was raised over the crypt. The arch itself shows that the remodeling started here; it starts as one curve and melds into another, ending several inches higher.

It is difficult to see, but on the upper clerestory wall, just above the corbel between the 2nd and 3rd windows, there is the outline of part of the window of the original church. The tops of the original windows would have been where the ceiling groins start today.

The superficial aspects of the interior have been modernized over the centuries. The Counter Reformation of the 1600s saw the establishment of new altars, three to a side, donated by local families, with paintings by notable local artists. The interior was last significantly tampered with in 1840 by the eminent Lucchese engineer Nottolini at the behest of Charles Louis, Duke of Lucca. Nottolini reduced the number of altars to two per side, and he also designed the new balustrade for the presbytery. The basin of the apse was decorated in encaustic by **Michele Ridolfi**.

~

San Salvatore

13. San Salvatore
Our Savior's

Despite its historic and artistic importance San Salvatore can too easily be bypassed though it is still one of the most active churches in town. With its central location, just around the corner from San Michele, but free from the constant flow of tourists into that church, San Salvatore is the preferred destination for the local faithful.

The traditional name of the church is San Salvatore *in Mustolio* (or *Mustiolo*), but the derivation seems impossibly obscure, ranging from "the perfumer's district" to yet another "tanning district" to the "oil district." The toponym was originally needed to distinguish it from several other San Salvatores in town, but they have all disappeared, so today simply San Salvatore is sufficient.

The first document which mentions the church is dated 1009 but it was certainly founded before that, probably by the monastery of the same name which is recorded in the year 800. With the demise of the monastery about 1100, the church became an orphan, and it has ever since led an orphan's difficult life.

During the early 1100s San Salvatore was a source of conflict between the churches of San Frediano and San Michele. At that time the canons of San Frediano were becoming a powerful group. They built a magnificent new church and began acquiring widespread property, in the process alienating not only the officers of other churches but at times the Bishop and even the Pope. At the same time San Salvatore was available and had acquired sufficient wealth to be worth a takeover. It was located between San Frediano and San Michele, but closer to the latter and, therefore, the Canons of San Michele saw themselves as the rightful proprietors. In the traditional method of negotiating such disputes, street fights broke out between the two claimants. Stones were thrown, holy services disrupted. The dispute went on for years. In 1140, his patience at an end, the Pope issued a bull granting the church to the monastery of San Frediano. Popes come and go, but grudges live on. The dispute drew the censure of successive popes, until it was finally settled in favor of San

Frediano, which had established firm ties at the Vatican; the prior of San Frediano would soon after be appointed a Cardinal.

Surprisingly, it was during this dispute that the church was rebuilt, being finished by about 1180, the date of the lintel over the side door. Most likely it was the wealth of San Frediano which paid for the construction, establishing its claim. (And yet the name Rolando on Biduino's lintel may be that of a prior of San Michele in 1167.)

By the later 1300s the church seems to have fallen into such disrepair that it required a complete makeover. A papal bull of 1410 recounts that Simone Boccella, finding the church more like a hovel, had paid to repair it and "make it like a new church." It also recounts that he took such interest in it because his ancestors had built it. Simone Boccella was one of the most successful merchants of the time, having lent money for Lucca to buy its freedom in 1369. In 1370 he represented Lucca in an embassy to the Pope in Avignon.

In 1780 the Monastery of San Frediano was suppressed and San Salvatore was once again orphaned to a succession of squabbling directors, leading one priest to say that "this parish is small, but the most troublesome which one could find." Finally the church was closed and its parishioners assigned to San Michele, which at last won a long awaited victory over San Frediano. In 1818 the archbishop granted the church to the Fraternity of Christian Charity, which began restoration work. This fraternal order later merged with the *Confraternita di Misericordia* (Fraternity of Mercy) and assumed dominion over the church, which it retains to the present. They have proven worthy guardians. It is their ambulances you see garaged nearby. San Salvatore is finally a peaceful parish, except when the sirens go off, as they frequently do. The ambulance service is provided free of charge.

1180 is the generally accepted date for completion of the medieval church, but as is so often the case the question of exactly how old certain parts are is frustratingly elusive. Biduino's lintel may be datable about 1180 but was it inserted into an already existing wall? There is a seam along the right wall which suggests a lengthening of the church at one time, but when? Just how much was rebuilt in the 1100s and how much was reused, or remained, from the preceding church? In the mid-1300s the church was

13. San Salvatore

remade "like new." Was this simply cosmetic work or were structural changes made? How much of the original church's foundation was used, how much of the doors, or walls?

We do know that the upper part of the facade, the row of hanging arches under the eaves and the stucco, date from the later 1800s.

The arches over the doors, with alternating bands of white and green marble (commonly categorized, rather unfairly to Lucca, as Pistoian) are typical of the 1100s. The doorways—with their wide white jambs and heavy architraves surmounted by arches in which the inside and outside curves do not share the same radius point—are duplicated throughout the city in churches of the 1100s and 1200s. San Salvatore lacks a proper bell tower, but the close-by tower which originally housed local nobility, was pressed into service. Today it serves as a nest for television antennae.

The Lintels

The most precious possessions of the church are the two decorated lintels. Despite being exposed to the elements for more than 800 years they are in remarkably good condition, a testament to the hardness of the stone the sculptors worked. (Compare the decayed state of the stone embellishments on the palazzi of the 1500s and 1600s.) More remarkable is that they reside in situ, and have never been rescued by a museum. They are part of a very small body of work, the narrative lintel, which is the earliest expression of Tuscan art. There are only nine existing examples of this art form in western Tuscany. San Salvatore has two of them. No admission charge.

Both lintels depict episodes from the life of Saint Nicholas. Nicholas has no other known relationship with the church, but he was one of the most popular saints of the 1100s.

Saint Nicholas

Saint Nicholas was the legendary bishop of Myra in Asia Minor, martyred under Diocletion in the 200s. He begins to appear in the west in the 800s and after 972 his cult spread into Germany when the Emperor married a Greek princess. His popularity exploded after 1087 when the Normans rescued his relics, re-interred them in Bari, and built a basilica which remains a popular pilgrimage site today. By about 1200 there were nearly 200 churches dedicated to him throughout Italy. (There are nearly 400 in England.)

His popularity among the Lucchesi is understandable: he is the patron of merchants and sailors. His rescue of a son from a foreign land must have made him frequently invoked by Lucchesi parents whose sons went abroad in trade. These invocations probably took place in San Salvatore. It is known that plays about St. Nicholas were performed in Lucca at least until the 1500s. In the middle ages the saint was equally popular with the Pisans; by 1192 its merchants had dedicated a church to him in Constantinople. The St. Nicholas story is best known from the *Golden Legend*, written about 1260. Its author, Jacobus de Voragine, was born near Genoa.

Side Door

The lintel over the side door is particularly valuable, because it is signed BIDUINO ME FECIT HOC (I, Biduino, made this). It can be dated to approximately 1180. (It is curious that the final word of this phrase did not fit on the tub and so is scrunched up in the background beside it; a surprising lack of planning for such an accomplished sculptor.) Its subject is **The Bath of Saint Nicholas**.

The incident is recounted in the *Golden Legend*: "While the infant was being bathed on the first day of his life, he stood straight up in the tub." In the sculpture the wide-eyed and oversized newborn saint stands up while being washed by two women. Biduino has placed his signature in the most  conspicuous place of the work, on the front of the tub, sharing equal billing, as it were, with the saint. In the background is inscribed, almost as an afterthought, "S. NICKOLAUS". The scene is symmetrically framed by columned buildings with domes and turrets. The figures in the upper turrets look toward and hail the saint; the one on the far left holds a cross, on the far right, a

13. SAN SALVATORE

book. Under the left dome a man apparently swings an incense burner. On the right are two old men leaning on staffs, and a rampant boar and lion face each other. The domed buildings are unusual and are probably meant to suggest the Oriental architecture of Saint Nicholas' birthplace in Asia Minor.

Front door

The elaborate lintel over the right front door is not signed but it almost certainly dates to the same period, about 1180, and is commonly assigned to the "circle of Biduino." It tells the *Story of the Son of Getron*, another episode from the *Golden Legend*.

Adeodatus ("god-given") was the son of Getron. While his parents were at church celebrating the feast of St. Nicholas, Adeodatus was captured by a pagan king, who enslaved him to serve as a cup-bearer in his palace. On St. Nicholas' day the following year Getron beseeched the Saint to rescue his son. Immediately Nicholas appeared at the king's table, clutched the boy up and transported him, still holding the king's cup, back to his parent's home.

The lintel narrates this story in three parts. On the left the pagan king sits, rather jauntily, at his table, attended by his queen and three retainers while Adeodatus to their right serves them drink. It is the moment when St. Nicholas appears and clutches the boy up by his hair. A tower in the rear provides a scene break. In the center scene St. Nicholas delivers Adeodatus, still holding his cup, to his mother. Three boys, ringing bells of thanksgiving, provide the next break. The final scene reiterates the first, this time

with the father seated at table accompanied by three guests. Adeodatus, returned to his proper station, now serves his parents and guests from the king's cup.

There is a lintel on the Cathedral of Barga which provides an interesting insight into the tight world of these medieval workmen. Its composition, the arrangement of figures and their poses, is identical to this lintel on San Salvatore. It shows a heavier hand, but is obviously a direct copy, presumably by a different artist. Perhaps the canons from Barga, on a visit to Lucca, hired an artist and said "make us one like that." It certainly shows the popularity of the Nicholas myth in the region during the 1100s, and of this episode in particular.

Interior

The interior is divided into three naves by rectangular stone columns of the 1100s. They support brick arches from which the former plaster covering has thankfully been stripped away, exposing the work of master bricklayers. The floor is littered with a dozen sarcophagi.

1. Circumcision, anon., 1600s, moved here from the oratory of the Name of Jesus (or *Oratorio dei Poveri*) in Via Santa Croce.

2. Plaque commemorating the restoration in 1990 by the *Arciconfraternita di Misericordia* on its 450th anniversary.

3. Crucifix, sculpted wood.

In San Salvatore you have the chance to examine and compare two crucifixes from the 1300s.

This one dates, most likely, to the end of that century. It was carved, except for the arms, from

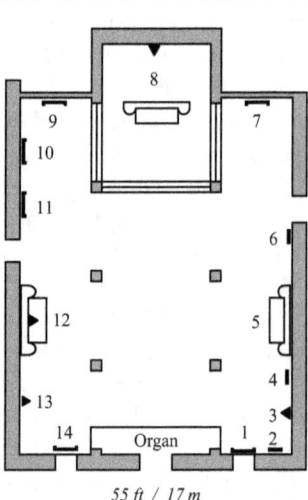

55 ft / 17 m

San Salvatore

13. SAN SALVATORE

a single block of walnut. The vertical axis of Christ's body aligns perfectly with the core of the tree from which it was carved. The sculptor must have used insufficiently aged wood, for a crack appeared straight down Christ's body from the neck through to the bottom of the *perizoma*. The head was spared because it was sculpted all on one side of the central pith. Similarly, each leg was cut from either side of the center of the tree. The restoration of the early 1990s has concealed this defect. The original artist did not hollow out the rear, as was often done to prevent splitting, but he was sensitive to the fracture lines, and oriented his sculpture to accommodate them as well as possible. The surface of the statue has suffered numerous interventions over the centuries and the original paint is unrecoverable. In the latest restoration work, for the exhibition of 1993, the top three coats of paint were removed by chemicals and scraper. The remaining coat was not the original, however—that apparently had been scraped off hundreds of years ago. The arms, it is generally agreed, are not original either. They are unnaturally horizontal, giving little suggestion of a body suspended by nails through the hands. The sorrowful face and emaciated body is what remains of the work that left the sculptor's hands 600 years ago.

4. Plaque in memory of the artist **Stefano Tofanelli** (1768-1812). Tofanelli, born near Lucca, was a major neoclassical artist and an eminent portraitist. When he was 16 he was sent to Rome with a stipend from Lucchese patrons. He spent much of his life in Rome but many of his works were destined for the environs of Lucca. He was particularly in demand for large works in the nearby villas of the nobility. He was appointed court painter by Elisa Baciocchi in 1805, and was elected a Senator of Lucca under Napoleon. His sepulcher is just to the right as you enter the main door.

5. This altar is a lovely example of Apuan marble working, attributed stylistically to the noted workshop of **Stagio Stagi** of Pietrasanta (1504-1563), which competed with the Civitali. It has been altered and adapted to its present purpose but it retains an exquisite frieze, well worth a notice. The altar was donated in memory of Giovanna and Biagio, the parents of an unknown patron. Their profiles are at either end of the altar top; sculpted cherubs hold inscriptions requesting their eternal salvation. The impressive high columns framing the altar are faux marble.

The altar was originally equipped for communion, indicated by the inscription above the curtains, Hoc Cibo Vivimus in Aeternum (with this food we live forever). It now houses an illuminated wood statue of the bound Christ, attributed to the sculptor **Giovanni Unti**, born in Lucca in 1786. This image of the grieving Christ belongs to the Misericordia, his humiliated and abandoned state the inspiration for their acts of mercy.

6. Plaque in memory of Giulio Menocchi, died 1626, age 50. He was a distinguished confidant, aide, and ambassador of several Popes. The plaque, placed by his brother, ends: "O Brother, with your death you have extinguished all my joy/ With your death our house has become a sepulcher."

7. *Ascension* by **Zacchia da Vezzano**, signed and dated, 1561. Restored 1975. This may be the last painting of Zacchia (ca.1500-1561) who was perhaps the leading Lucchese painter of the 1500s. His works have been widely dispersed; his self-portrait is in the Louvre. This is generally considered one of his lesser paintings, but it still shows, particularly in the faces of the disciples, the hand of a master. In the lower left corner he has written "those not skilled in the Christian religion—at least recognize the image of your Savior." Zacchia is called *Il Vecchio* (The Elder) to distinguish him from Lorenzo Zacchia "the younger" who was his student. The original site of the painting was in San Frediano.

8. High Altar; late 1500s. The main table, of white Apuan marble, is detached from the rear. The large columns fill the entire space of the sanctuary. At its top is a scroll bearing the symbol of the Hospital of the Misericordia: a large "M" on two silk sacks. The altar was originally in the Hospital of Misericordia, also called the hospital of San Luca, which was founded in the 1200s and demolished in the 1800s. It had been founded as a social service of the Court of Merchants, whose symbol was, appropriately, bags of silk.

Below the altar table is an illuminated figure of "Santa Faustina, Martire."

The *Crucifix* dates to the early 1300s. The entire body below the neck is one piece of wood, the head and arms being attached.

13. SAN SALVATORE

Unlike many wood pieces it was not hollowed out, and therefore is unusually heavy and has developed deep fissures in the rear. Before restoration, in 1993, it was presented in front of a baroque gold sunburst and was embellished with a heavy halo and crown of thorns. The statue had long ago been treated with a dark varnish which gave it a bronze appearance. This varnish was so durable it resisted paint remover, and had to be scraped off. Only the smallest fragments of original paint remain. The statue was stripped of its later additions, which included repaired fingers and toes, and was repainted fairly monochromatically with water colors. The cross had once belonged to the Knights of Jerusalem, and is therefore referred to as "the Templars' Cross."

At the left front corner of the presbytery is a contemporary, somewhat eerie, statue of Padre Pio, the 20th century saint who was canonized in 2002. Its inclusion in the church is a sign of San Salvatore's continuing popularity with supplicants.

9. *Madonna of Mercy with Saints* by **Alessandro Ardenti**, signed and dated 1565. At the top is the Holy Trinity. The likely identification of the saints: on the right, St. Anthony of Padua with a lily, guarding the Child; St. Augustine; St. Francis of Assisi; on the left, St. Joseph with staff; St. Jerome; a kneeling devotee. Ardenti (doc. 1539-1595) was from Faenza and settled in Turin but he was also quite active around Lucca and left paintings in a number of its churches.

Below, a lighted wooden case houses modern statues.

10. *Coronation of the Virgin* by **Gherardo delle Catene**, 1530s. The upper half of the painting depicts the Coronation, framed by cherubs, and angels portrayed as young maids. Below, bearing witness, are two bishops, two Old Testament figures (a king and a prophet?) and two obedient kneeling supplicants, who probably portray the patrons of the painting, of the family Gianetti; their crest is displayed in the center. Gherardo was from Modena, but was active around Lucca in the 1530s.

11. *Madonna with Sts. Zita, Joseph, Paolino, and Bambino Salvatore da Orta* by **Gaspare Mannucci**. Signed and dated 1638. Restored 1970. This painting attained more than artistic distinction when it was used in the canonization proceedings for Santa Zita in

1696. It was submitted as evidence that Zita was already revered locally as a Saint. This seems a superfluous testimony, considering how widely Zita's cult had spread in the preceding centuries. The reference to the painting had reasons more political than religious. In the lower left corner it bears the crest of the Arrighi family, who commissioned it. They were also prime movers in the effort to attain sainthood for Zita. Given the snail's pace at which such efforts generally proceed, we can be sure that by 1638 the family had already been active in associating their name with the saint and used this work of their own initiative as proof of her cult.

12. (Altar) Mock marble. This altar, dedicated to Our Lady of Fatima, with its illuminated statues of the Madonna surrounded by children, is one of the most frequented altars in town. Until 1916 this was the site of the crucifix now over the main altar.

13. Bust of Michele Bianchi, 1868. An accomplished portrait; the face of a Roman Senator.

14. *Assumption* by **Banduccio Trenta**. A modest painting and the only one signed by this artist. It is from the church of San Pietro Maggiore, which was demolished in the early 19th century for construction of Piazza Napoleone.

~

14. San Michele
The Church of Saint Michael

San Michele is often mistaken for the cathedral of Lucca. With its grandeur and extravagant façade, its location in the very center of town, as well as its propensity to appear on post cards, it is a reasonable misidentification.

The earliest reference to a church of San Michele *ad foro* or 'in the forum' is in 795. It was already a significant church, a place of pilgrimage, with a crypt holding saintly relics. You can still see the tops of the windows of this crypt on the outside of the apse; they were partly covered when the street level of the town was raised in the 1100s and 1200s.

Encroachment into the Roman forum must have begun quite early, the temptation to take advantage of the largest piece of vacant real estate in town proving irresistible. By 795 the church of San Michele was surrounded by "many houses" and a hospital. One of the purposes of these early hospitals was to serve pilgrims, and San Michele hosted many of them as travel began to revive following Charlemagne's conquest of the Lombards in 774.

Sometime before 1027 a monastery was built next to the church. In 1050, on the cusp of the medieval economic explosion, an Armenian pilgrim named Davino stopped in Lucca on his way to Santiago di Campostela, a worthy pilgrimage. He never made it. He died in Lucca in the hospital of San Michele and was buried in its adjoining cemetery. Miracles, a phenomenon more common in those times, began to be attributed to Davino. He was soon popularly proclaimed a saint and pilgrims followed.

In 1057 Anselmo became bishop of Lucca and began transforming Lucca's sacred architecture. He reconstructed the church of Sant'Alessandro and began construction of the Cathedral. When Anselmo became Pope Alexander II in 1061 he transferred Davino's relics into the crypt of the church of San Michele, giving his sainthood the papal imprimatur. With the necessary relics in place, Pope Alexander (who remained bishop of Lucca) began rebuilding the church in 1070—the same year he dedicated the Cathedral. He saw little progress in San Michele, however, since he died in 1073.

It is impossible to know how fast work progressed but the church was substantially complete less than a century later; the date 1163 can be found carved on an interior column. The lower portion of the bell tower, over the right transept, also dates from the early 1100s, as do the portals of the façade.

In the early 1200s the master mason Guidetto da Como and his workshop were employed to embellish the exterior. They were already busy in the city, working on upgrades to the Cathedral and Santa Maria Forisportam. This group provided one of the most significant bodies of work of medieval Tuscan architecture and sculpture.

In anticipation of raising the church roof, the elaborate façade gradually rose during the 1200s. It is something of a Tuscan tradition to build a church but not finish the exterior facing. In San Michele the process was reversed: build the façade and the roof will follow. But it never did, as you can see.

A good deal of finishing work somehow continued during the tumultuous 1300s, even during the Pisan domination, but the cost to Lucca of purchasing its freedom in 1369 depleted the local coffers and in 1370 work was suspended. With a new government,

14. SAN MICHELE

and peace with Florence in 1374, money was raised to complete the marble facing on the right side. In 1383 the renovations were abandoned. The roof never rose. The will was gone.

The need for repairs on a church, of course, never ends. Over the years San Michele was neglected until, by the time John Ruskin visited it, the magnificent front was crumbling away, with pieces of its inlay laying on the ground.

> *I sit in the open warm afternoon air, drawing the rich ornaments of the facade of St. Michele... I have been up all over it and on the roof to examine it in detail... The frost where the details are fine, has got underneath the inlaid pieces, and has in many places rent them off, tearing up the intermediate marble together with them, so as to uncoat the building an inch deep. Fragments of the carved porphyry are lying about everywhere. I have brought away three or four, and restored all I could to their places.*
>
> John Ruskin, May 6, 1845

A depressing sight, but then it was only six years earlier that the shops and stalls which had encrusted the great church had been demolished and the neglect of centuries began to be addressed. After Lucca joined a unified Italy attention to San Michele became a primary means of showing civic pride. Ruskin's façade was attended to, at times to the dismay of the purist. Columns were replaced and inlay re-laid, generally expertly and authentically. Decaying busts were also replaced, with contemporary personages occasionally substituted for their medieval predecessors. Notwithstanding such minor objections, San Michele remains a blessedly preserved example of the Lucchese contribution to medieval Tuscan architecture.

Exterior

Front. In the Middle Ages rivalry between neighboring towns was intense and churches were bragging pieces. San Michele and the Cathedral were the main pilgrimage sites in Lucca and the pilgrims were meant to be impressed. I'm sure they were. The façades of both churches almost shamelessly demand to be gawked at.

The lower level, with its high recessed arches, was built about 1100. It testifies to the flowering of Romanesque architecture in Tuscany, with a purely Lucchese presence. The enlivening of the traditional monolithic Romanesque was an expression of a suddenly self-confident society. Architects were still structurally constrained by the need for solidity and massiveness, and churches still retained their function as fortresses, true sanctuaries. But the spirit of the time demanded something more vibrant. Flat surfaces became rippled with pilasters and engaged columns. They were further broken by the recessed diamond shaped lozenges typical of the period; this was a precocious attempt to open up the solid walls of the Romanesque, an impulse finally realized by the Gothic when large windows became structurally feasible. The surface was further enlivened by alternating bands of green marble, a motif which was one of the typical and most resilient aspects of northern Tuscan medieval architecture.

The general effect of the lower level, however, is serene and simple. There are no elaborate archivolts; the doors are plain functional entrance ways. In the lower portion the sculptural impulse was given satisfaction in only a few places.

The **lintel** over the center door is a masterpiece of sculptural stonework and exemplifies a curious characteristic of the entire façade—there is nothing Christian about it. No Biblical scenes or stories. No didactic doorways. The facade of San Michele is a reflection and exaltation of the world outside the church. Those figures we call mythical—mermaids, gryphons, dragons—were not mythical at the time, only rare. (The unicorn does not figure in the local iconography.) This worldliness of the exterior emphasizes the transition undergone when entering the church, the interior being the realm of the sacred.

The central character of the lintel is a mermaid, one of the most popular medieval figures, appearing in similar form throughout Romanesque architecture. Today a mermaid seems unusual as the figure watching over the entrance to a church.
The intended symbolism is unknown but the mermaid is often

14. SAN MICHELE

interpreted as depicting the temptations of the flesh, at least of female flesh. Just above and to her right is the only religious symbolism of the lintel, a small figure of Archangel Michael slaying the dragon. He seems almost an afterthought, inserted into the main design and protruding beyond the border. To his right is a centaur, here with a female body, followed by two dragon-like figures, though the medieval world drew finer distinctions between types of dragons than we do: the first is a gryphon, a composite of lion and eagle, rulers of the earth and the sky; the one on the end is a wingless, more reptilian dragon, breathing fire. On the mermaid's left a lion attacks its prey, and framing the scene is the counterpart of the dragon on the right.

The capitals supporting the lintel are reminiscent of Lombard capitals which are found in old churches in the hills of Lucca. They may have been incorporated from the earlier building; many times when a church was rebuilt decorative fragments from the original were incorporated into the new building. The apse of San Michele has some further examples.

The celebration of the natural world pervades the colonnades of the galleries above. Bands of green and white marble inlay depicting wildlife and hunting scenes provide the foundation for the exuberant columns, no two alike, each trying to outdo the next in inventiveness and skill. Above each column is a bust, originally of local personalities. In the 1800s it was seen fit to substitute a few contemporary eminences, such as Napoleon III, Cavour, and Garibaldi. These modernizations, such as the sign "Eritrea" right in the center, can be a bit jarring but they meld well enough into the general effect and add another element of whimsy to a masterpiece which was never meant to be taken entirely seriously.

Reading the upper façade from the top down:

The Archangel Michael, 12 ft. high, towers precariously above, watching over the city. On his left wrist he wears a bracelet with faux gems. Catching a glint of one is as rare as finding a four leaf clover, and as auspicious. The angels on Michael's sides trumpet victory over sin and perdition.

1st row of inlay: hunters and falconers, lions, tigers, camels, wild boar, goats.

Columns: geometric inlay, medieval heads.

2nd row of inlay: animals.

Columns: at the ends are knotted columns, a conceit of the stone carver's art, and two elaborately carved columns with figures. The third from the left is a mermaid. The third from the right has a "Siamese twin" motif of figures reflecting and growing out of each other. In one column there is a remarkable juxtaposition of a female and equine head. Notice the rose window behind the columns, designed to let light into the projected interior, but it is still open to sky.

May 9th: "There is an exquisite star window at the end of the church of St. Michele, carved like lace. The French nailed up against it, destroying all the centre for ever, a great louis-quatorze escutcheon (which these wretches of Lucchese haven't spirit enough to pull down), with "Libertas" upon it, and they have mosaiced a tricolor into the middle of an inscription of the 15th century in the cathedral. I'm only afraid they haven't human soul enough ever to be damned."

John Ruskin, 1845.

The rose window has since been restored.

3rd row of inlay: hunting scenes and beastly conflict. Above the fourth column there is the rare beast the Amphisbaena, which has a head at either end and is coiled in the middle: it could move forward or backward with equal ease and by holding its heads together could form itself into a hoop and roll away from danger. It is surrounded by a number of gryphons and dragons. Interspersed are many geometric tondos, often with motifs which you will find reiterated in decorative brick around the city.

Columns: modern heads mixed indiscriminately with medieval ones and beasts. On the fifth from the right there is a figurine of mermaid and beasts.

14. SAN MICHELE

4th row of inlay: profusion of hunting scenes.

Columns: fifth from left, "Siamese twins" again, this time a merging of men and beasts. Right above this is an ostrich killing a snake and what appears to be Sagittarius. Especially notable are the fluted column (7th from left), the inlaid "negative image" (9th) and above this an elaborate angelic capital; and another with mermaid figures. The elaborately carved capital over the knotted column on the right portrays a siren or a harpy (a female head on a bird's body), an ancient depiction of temptation.

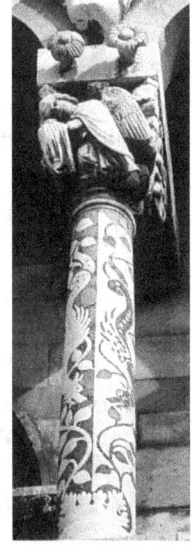

The lowest cornice, which separates the Romanesque façade beneath from the Gothic colonnades above, belongs to the earliest part of the church. It differs from the cornices separating the upper galleries, which are composed only of garlanded foliage, by incorporating the themes on the main lintel—hunting scenes with real and mythic animals. It is an extended meditation on medieval themes, with figures which would be more readily appreciated as masterpieces were they in a more observable location. Sirens and mermaids are again given prominence and there is an excellent hunter on horseback.

Not everyone thought such decoration as we find on San Michele to be appropriate to a church:

> *What is the point of this deformed beauty, this elegant deformity...The monstrous centaurs? The half-men?... The hunters sounding their horns? You can see a head with many bodies, or a body with many heads. Here we espy an animal with a serpent's tail, there a fish with animal's head. There we have a beast which is horse in front and a she-goat behind...In short there is such a wondrous diversity of figures, such ubiquitous variety, that there is more reading matter available in marble than in books, and one could spend the whole day marveling at one such representation than in meditating on the word of God.*

Saint Bernard (1090-1153)

The statue of **Mary and Child** on the front corner overlooking the piazza is a replica of the original by Matteo Civitali, which at long last, but too late, was removed to the interior of the church.

Step over to the **left side** (north) and you can see how work progressed over the centuries. Recessed above is the original clerestory. San Michele is an unfortunately dark church. It was originally better lit by its clerestory windows, but those on the south side were covered over by improvements in the 1300s. The windows on the less prominent north side would have met the same fate had projected work been accomplished but when funds ran out it was left unchanged. The upper brick row with windows was added later and mirrors the south side. These small high windows are barely adequate to their job. As you can see, the main wall also originally had high narrow windows.

On this side you can see how the grade around the building has risen over the centuries. Originally the church had a more elevated siting, with a much higher foundation and steps leading up to the doors, not plunked down squat is it is now. The cemetery of San Michele was along this side and on the wall are engraved funerary symbols and inscriptions, now cut off by the raised pavement. These mark sepulchers where the bones of the saintly, the eminent, and the philanthropic were deposited. The cemetery functioned until the 1500s.

The small sculpture on the corner of the left transept is a St. Michael of the 1100s.

It simply wouldn't do in Lucca to leave a church free standing, untethered to secular apartments. As it is, San Michele is one of only two churches you can walk around. (The other is San Giusto.) But even here a connecting elevated walkway was irresistible. The buildings on the north side of the church were the domain of the canons of San Michele and this walkway enabled them to move between their quarters and the church without having to cross the street.

As you walk over to the right side of the church you can see on the lower part of the front foundation, about three feet up, inscriptions similar to those on the north side. On one of them the word *sepultura* makes plain its import.

On the **right side** (south) the wall rises straight up through the second level. Here the clerestory was brought forward in the

14. SAN MICHELE

1330s as part of the planned enlargement and raising of the roof. The long colonnade on the mezzanine, tightly packed and without ornament, is much more classical than the earlier sections; it looks Roman or Greek, not Romanesque. The ornamentation has been simplified into alternating bands of green and white, already used in the earlier sections, but here accentuated and emboldened. Windows have been provided but never exploited: they open into dead space, not the interior of the church, since the renovations were never completed.

The medieval heads which crown the capitals are undoubtedly local portraits. Would that we knew anything about each one.

An easily missed but tantalizing feature of the lower wall is the medieval graffiti which is scattered along it. Some are scratched into the stone, others done with charcoal or reddish pigment. This graffiti was done between 1250 and the 1500s. If you look closely you can just make out the outlines. Many of the designs are of ships. The scrawling of ships on the sides of a church was a common practice, a sailor's supplication for safe voyage. The images, greatly faded, were done by people who knew their ships; they were probably sketching the one on which they were to depart. These images have recently been analyzed and correlated with known vessels of different periods. Most of them seem to date from the 1200s and 1300s.

Bell Tower. The grand blind arcade of the front and flanks of the church continues around the campanile. The tower dates from the 1100s and was completed in the 1200s, the date of the bells. The oldest bell was made in Pisa in 1215, another is dated 1258, and a third 1383 (to celebrate liberation from Pisa). Another bell, originally on the front of the church, dated 1273, is now in the Villa Guinigi Museum. Apparently the top of the bell tower was knocked down during the Pisan occupation, when any high point was a threat. The present crown is from 1772.

The **rear** and **apse** of the church contain carvings dating from the earliest stages of construction. The apse was often the first part of a church to be constructed since the altar and crypt area were needed so that services could begin before the entire building was finished. The lintel of the door to the left of the apse has a motif similar to the main front door—a lion killing a boar, a centaur, a dragon—although it is probably not by the same artist; the use of drill holes for emphasis is used much more here.

Along the base of the apse are visible the windows into the crypt with Lombardic designs, the crypt dating to the church of the 800s.

Interior

When entering the church you might reflect that you are doing what penitents, pilgrims, and tourists have been doing for more than 800 years. San Michele was conceived in 1070 and was substantially complete by 1163, the date carved into one of its pillars. The large panel crucifix suspended over the main altar is the artistic prize of the church; it dates to the 1100s and was part of the original decoration. In the medieval church the wall surfaces and columns were covered with frescoes, and a good deal more light entered within. The vaulted ceiling was added in the early 1500s, below the original wood roof. In the space between the two there are preserved frescoes from the 1300s.

Among the treasures in the medieval church, but now elsewhere are: a polyptych done by Angelo Puccinelli in 1393 and a panel painting for the relics of San Davino. These and much else were removed in the sweeping overhaul of all the churches in Christendom during the Catholic Reformation, initiated by the Council of Trent in 1545-1563. The side altars date from the 1600s.

1. Fresco (in niche) of **Nursing Madonna**, later 1300s, recently attributed to **Giuliano Di Simone**, one the major painters in Lucca at the time. It was repainted, restored, and elaborated several times over the centuries; it was last restored, dramatically, in 1990. It is a precious reminder of the frescoes which once covered the walls. Probably only the central portion of this fragment is by Giuliano; the surrounding parts were re-worked early in the next century. The iconography of the nursing Madonna was a prevalent motif in the Lucca-Pistoia area at the time. Giuliano di Simone's only signed and dated work has the same theme. The fresco had numerous tondos with portraits of prophets, but these are now almost entirely lost. A portrait of the donor, also nearly gone, was probably added *a secco*, as was the throne which is distinctly of a later period than the Madonna. The different periods are apparent, I think, even to an untrained eye.

14. San Michele

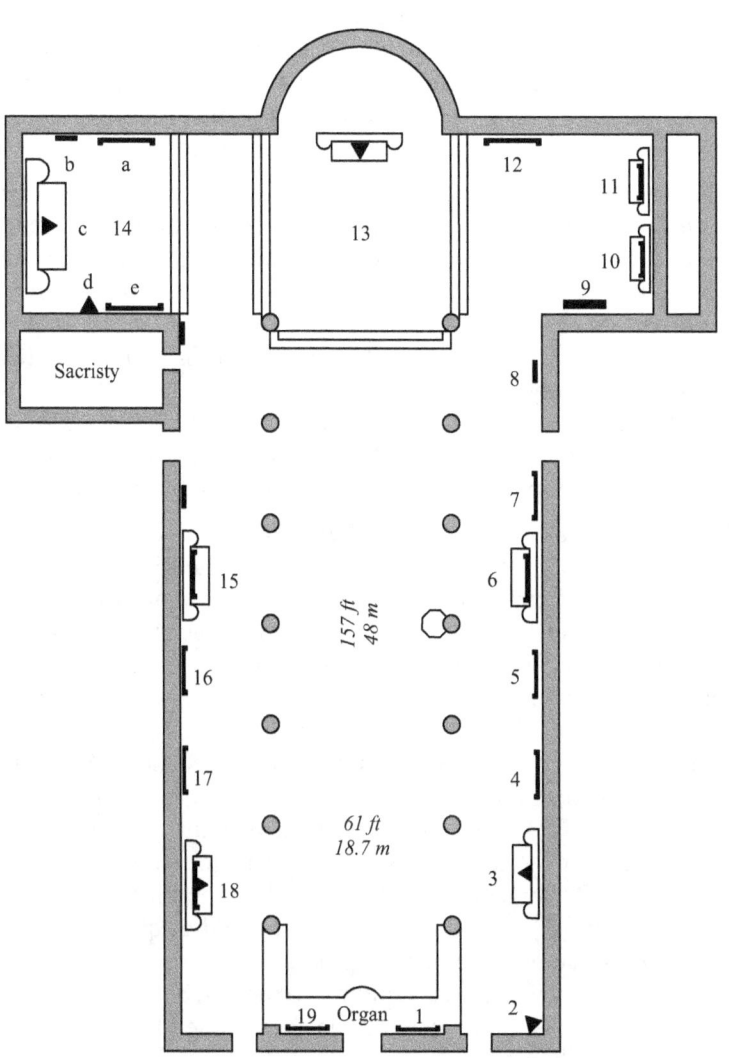

San Michele

2. Marble sculpture of *Madonna and Child* by Matteo Civitali (1436-1501). This sadly deteriorated sculpture resided outside for too many centuries. It was commissioned by Domenico Bertini (legislator, Palatine Count, and papal secretary) after the devastating plague of 1476-80. In its original position, overlooking the town square, the sculpture had an altar below it.

3. Altar of Santa Lucia. Above: a painted terracotta statue of *Santa Lucia*, 1500s, moved here when the small church of Santa Lucia (behind San Michele) was razed. St. Lucy holds the knife with which she cut out her eyes; they are displayed on the cup in her hand.

Below: glazed terracotta of *Madonna and Child* by **Luca della Robbia.** As lovely a Madonna as there is anywhere.

The altar was originally dedicated to the Crucifix and Saint Helen, as shown by the inscription at the top, and originally held the Filippino Lippi which is now at the head of the nave (#12).

4. *Martyrdom of St. Andrew* by Pietro Paolini. A dramatic painting by the most influential Lucchese artist of the 1600s. On the left is the X-shaped cross on which St. Andrew is about to crucified, in the year 60. He is shown here traditionally, as an old man with grey hair and beard. On the way to his crucifixion a great crowd gathered proclaiming his innocence but he begged them to not interfere. Seeing the cross he prayed "O good cross, take me away from the world of men and return me to my Master." Shedding his garments he gave them to his executioners. The figure standing over him is Aegeus, the proconsul of Patra in Greece who condemned him. Andrew was hung, not nailed, to the cross and being alive after two days the crowds called for his release. Aegeus relented but it was impossible to remove the Apostle. Aegeus was struck dead as he returned home.

Above the stained glass window, to the left, barely perceptible in the dimness, is a medieval animal head, one of several which inhabit the darkness.

5. *Madonna and Child with Sts. Stephen, Lorenzo, and John the Baptist* by Paolo Guidotti. Unusual and odd are terms frequently applied to Guidotti. There is something a little startling in his colors and compositions, which is appropriate for a man known for eccentricity and restlessness, who always seems to be scratching

14. SAN MICHELE

some unreachable artistic itch. The red robed figure is St. Stephen, the first martyr. The kneeling, barely clad, oddly proportioned and shod saint may be St. Lawrence, who was frequently painted with Stephen. In the face of John you might recognize the poor man being given water by Santa Zita, in Guidotti's painting in San Frediano.

6. Altar of Saint Michael. Marble statue of **St. Michael** set into a painting. Donated to the Republic in 1658 by the bishop of Manfredonia; originally located in the apse.

7. *St. Matthew*. Simple framed painting, anonymous, 1600s. At the top of the stained glass window above the painting is another medieval beast's head.

8. Plaque: in memory of Nicolao Gigli, patron of the church. Nicolao, the last of this distinguished and very wealthy clan, bequeathed his estate to the church. One of his ancestors, Silvestro, a deacon of the church, oversaw the transformation of the interior carried out in the 1500s, including the Gigli chapel in the north transept.

9. Monument to Silvestro Gigli, 1876, by **Vincenzo Consani** (Lucchese). This small monument makes some amends for the removal of the great monument by Baccio da Montelupo which was originally in the left transept. (See #14d.)

Silvestro died in 1521. He had a brilliant career but spent little time in Lucca. For years he served as Bishop of Worcester and was the King of England's ambassador to the Holy See, a position he held until his death.

10. (Altar) *Saint Filomena* (Philomena) by **Stefano Lembi**, 1867. In 1802 a Roman tomb was discovered which contained the bones of a young woman, a phial of blood (symbol of martyrdom), and an inscription identifying the remains as those of one Filomena. The relics promptly began performing miracles. Her cult spread quickly and was given a boost by the remarkable parish priest Jean-Baptiste Vianney. He had built a shrine to Filomena and attributed to her the miracles for which he was famous. By his death in 1859 he was receiving perhaps 20,000 pilgrims a year. One famous cure in 1835 led the Pope to authorize Filomena's local cults and in 1855 she was granted an official Mass and Office.

Scholars, however, were less impressed and picked away at the legend. A long rancorous debate ensued between the doubters and the credulous but in 1960 the Holy See rescinded its sanctification and suppressed the cult.

11. (Altar) Modern painted wood statue of *Joan of Arc* set into a painting of **St. Gaetano** (1480-1547), founder of the Theatine order, and **St. Philip Neri** (1515-1595), founder of the Oratorians. Neri's Congregation of the Oratory was so called because the first disciples met in a small oratory. They would call the faithful by ringing a small bell, such as the one you can see on the wall above the door on the opposite side of the church. Their use of music in their services gave us the musical form the Oratorio.

12. Sts. Rocco, Sebastian, Jerome, and Helen by **Filippino Lippi** (1457-1504), on wood. This very fine painting has been in the church since the early 1500s though it has moved around.

13. High Altar area. The altar, 1755, is by **Giovanni Vambré.** It holds the body of San Davino.

The *Crucifix*, tempera on panel, over the high altar is the greatest artistic treasure of the church. The earliest surviving painted cross in Tuscany, dated 1138, is in the nearby town of Sarzana. The San Michele Cross was done soon after, almost certainly no later than 1175. These crosses are the surviving font of Italian painting.

The crucifix shows Christ Triumphant (alive, eyes open), the standard depiction in the 1100s. Indeed a Papal Bull of 1054 forbade the image of Christ dead upon the cross. This would change in the following century with St. Francis and his vision of the Suffering Christ. The San Michele Cross was an expensive work, hosting jewels and gold. It was done for this church and was its centerpiece. It was restored in the 1950s.

Crypt. As the sign says, it cannot be visited, but if you are fortunate you may hear chanting emanating from below.

Apse, of plain stone. Stained glass windows: St. Lucy, St. Michael, and St. Davino.

14. Chapel of the Holy Sacrament.

a) *Marriage of the Virgin Mary*, oil on wood, by the Lucchese **Agostino Marti**. Signed and dated 1523. This was, until recently,

14. SAN MICHELE

his first known commission. Marti was one of the two leading painters in Lucca in the early 1500s (the other was his student and collaborator Zacchia da Vezzano). Few of his paintings remain in Lucca.

b) Plaque and bas-relief to Silvestro Giglio.

c) Altar of St. Silvester. A grand altar with a 1700s crucifix. On the upper sides are two sculptures representing Justice and Mercy. On the frontal is a polychrome inlay snake, from the 1800s.

d) Plaque and bas-relief of *Mary and Child*, marble, by **Raffaello da Montelupo**, 1500s. This is what remains of the funeral monument (1523) to Silvestro Gigli, a collaborative effort of Baccio da Montelupo, the architect of San Paolino, and his son Raffaello. The monument was dismantled and sold to a stone carver in the early 1800s; these fragments were later found in the church.

e) *St. Apollonia* by **Antonio Franchi**, 1600s. St. Apollonia died about 249, tortured by having her teeth pulled out with pincers. She is famous for having willingly leapt into the flames prepared for her, an act which caused a good deal of debate as to whether this was a permissible act of preemptive suicide.

f) Plaque, just outside the chapel, recording the restorations undertaken in 1837.

15. Altar of the Virgin Mary. Painting of *Mary and Child* in golden sunburst. The altar is dated 1637. This Madonna is known both as The Refuge of Sinners and "Ponte Rotto" because it is a copy of one in Ponte Rotto near Rome. At the top of the stained glass window just to the right of the altar there is a fine medieval lion head, difficult to see.

16. *St. Andrew Avellino*, anonymous, 1700s. Avellino (1521-1608) was a Theatine, the order founded by Gaetano (see #11). A Counter Reformation reformer, he was canonized in 1712, more for his character and proselytizing than for his miracles. He died of a stroke just as he began giving Mass, which became a popular theme for paintings of him, as here. His right eye looks straight into ours.

Above the stained glass window just left of the painting is a medieval eagle.

17. *St. Catherine*, 1695, by **Antonio Franchi** (1634-1709), called "The Lucchese" (though he spent most his life in Florence). A simple painting, typical of his later sacred work, done with great restraint by an artist once known for the "copious figures" in his paintings. It shows a St. Catherine very different from her pre-Reformation, tower-toting counterparts; here a palm and a lily are her only emblems of sainthood.

18. Altar of St. Anthony. Wood statue of *St. Anthony* set into an anonymous modern painting of the Holy Family. The macabre sepulcher set into the floor in front dates to the 1500s.

19. *St. Antonio Abate*, fresco, 1500s. By a masterful anonymous hand; thankfully preserved. Below is a recent baptismal font by **Francesco Petroni**, Lucchese, with the *Christening of Jesus*.

Works no longer in the church:

Madonna with Sts. Nicholas, Augustine, Michael, and Lucia, polyptych, 1393, by **Angelo Puccinelli**, done for the altar of St. Nicholas. It is today in the parish church of Varano, Lunigiana.

Ricognizione del corpo di San Davino, tempera on panel, by the hence so-called **Master of San Davino**. In the late 1500s the relics of the Saint were transferred to the main altar and this altar painting removed. It is now part of the Acton collection in Florence.

~

15. San Giusto

San Giusto is the only free-standing church in Lucca, unattached to another building, but even here the vacant walls were irresistible and now form the backdrop for bookseller's stalls. The church has three aisles, despite its small size, and is entered, uncommonly, from the east. If possible the churches of western Christendom faced west so that as you approached the altar you were walking towards Jerusalem.

The earliest mention of San Giusto is in 1040 but there was an earlier building on the site which dated to the 700s, during Lombard rule. At that time the area around San Giusto was the site of the Lombard court and palaces. From here Tuscany was ruled.

The present building is an exquisite example of Lucchese Romanesque architecture. The façade is superb. Reconstruction of the church was started in the late 1100s and continued into the 1300s. The heavy white door jambs and lintels date from the earliest phase of construction. The elaborate architrave over the center door dates from the early 1200s, a period of feverish building activity in Lucca, with a ready supply of workmen, masons, and sculptors. The sculptural work is generally attributed to the workshop of **Guidetto da Como**, the master who in 1204 left his signature on the façade of the Cathedral. A will dated 1323 left a substantial sum for the completion of the façade.

In the 1200s there was a raising of the church, marked by the alternate bands on the front and the change to brick on the sides. The original church was certainly not as high and probably lacked a bell tower. This is evident in the rear where the original slope of the roof can be seen on the campanile, which now rises in brick above the right aisle.

The façade recalls the churches of Santi Simone e Giuda and San Pietro Somaldi. The apse with its two rows of slit windows is similar to San Cristoforo.

The rebuilding of the church was closely tied to the rise of commerce at the time. San Giusto was the first home of the Merchants Association before it moved to San Cristoforo in the 1200s.

The piazza in front of San Giusto is the highest point in Lucca. From here the water sheds gently away in all directions at a remarkably constant grade. The drop from here to the walls is only five to ten feet, but painstaking city planning has assured that the water will disperse even without the use of sewers. It is likely that two thousand years ago, when Lucca was first built on a little island in the Serchio, the area of San Giusto was the highest refuge from the threatening waters.

Interior

The interior was completely refurbished in the mid 1600s in Baroque style. The art was supplied by the major artists working in Lucca at the time.

1. Over main door, fresco by **Giovanni Marracci** of the *Nativity*.

2. *Madonna with Sts. Francis and Apollonia* by **Girolamo Scaglia**.

3. *Pope Gregory the Great*, from the circle of **Paolo Biancucci**.

4. *Return from Egypt* perhaps by **Ferrucci**.

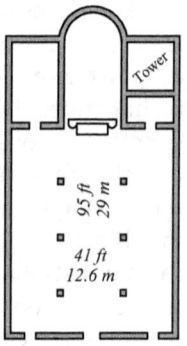

San Giusto

16. San Girolamo
St. Jerome

This church with a slate cupola, unusual for Lucca, has recently been restored and transformed into an auditorium. It had been closed for years and its possessions have been dispersed. It is built over the Roman wall, a portion of which is in the basement. By 1225, after the medieval wall was built, an oratorio dedicated to the Holy Trinity occupied this site, in the section of town called "the oaks."

In 1440, as recorded in the inscription over the main door, the oratorio was bought by Baldassare Manni, who would become bishop the following year. The church was built for the Gesuate brethren, whose patron was St. Jerome. A hospice was attached to the church and a convent was built in 1558, as recorded on a plaque along Via Garibaldi.

The **Gesuati**, properly called the Apostolic Clerics of St. Jerome, was a congregation of laymen founded about 1360 by Blessed Giovanni Colombini, a wealthy wool merchant from Siena who at age 50 (in 1354, in the aftermath of the great plague) experienced the Holy Spirit, gave away all his money, divorced his wife, and devoted himself to a life of mortification, poverty, and acts of mercy. His example proved so enticing to the young men of Siena that the authorities exiled him, which only provided Colombini with the opportunity to evangelize other towns.

When plague returned, the Sienese took it as retribution for their rejection of Colombini and he was called home. In 1367 the Pope gave official recognition to the order, and they adopted the uniform dress of a white tunic with square hood.

Their popular name, Gesuati, came from their practice of crying "Hail Jesus" and "Praised be Jesus" at the opening and close of their services, a practice reiterated on the inscription over the front door which ends with the invocation of Jesus Christ. The order was disbanded by the Pope in 1668, for straying too far from its founder's spirit.

In the 1700s the church was entirely renovated, but it was

soon closed by Napoleon. All that remains of the front loggia are the two corbels at either side of the exposed stone work. Fortunately, the glazed terracotta of *Madonna and Child with Sts. Peter and Jerome*, early 1500s, was allowed to remain. At one time the church hosted the Society of Barbers, an ancient benevolent brotherhood of surgeons who on holy days offered their services for free. They were, however, forbidden to cut hair.

Of the art work which was formerly in the church a good deal was undistinguished, but notable items were:

1. A Roman capital adapted for use as a holy water basin.

2. *St. Jerome* by the Lucchese **Paolo Biancucci**, which can now be seen in the Cathedral sacristy (the Ilaria room).

3. *Discovery of the True Cross* by Biancucci.

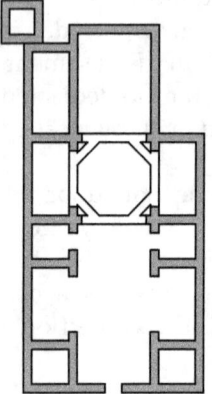

San Girolamo

~

17. San Frediano

"Such a church—so old—680 probably—Lombard—all glorious dark arches & columns—covered with holy frescoes…I don't know when I shall get away."

John Ruskin, May 1845

San Frediano is old, but not as old as Ruskin thought. There was a Lombard basilica on the same site in the 680s, dedicated to St. Frediano, but the present structure wasn't started until 1112. Still, we can forgive Ruskin for being off by a few centuries. San Frediano feels old. Despite both growth and decay, the church has stayed remarkably true to its original vision. It is hard to believe that many frescoes were left by Ruskin's time, but they did once cover the walls. A few remain today and we, with Ruskin, can restore the rest with a little imagination. It will take some time for us to get away.

San Frediano is everything a Romanesque church should be: solid, severe, simple. It seems a world apart from the other two great churches in Lucca, the Cathedral and San Michele. They look like something out of the Magic Kingdom, with endless invention and flights of fancy. San Frediano revels in its plainness. Except for that mosaic, incongruously perched, the façade is devoid of ornamentation, monochromatic, the flat surface broken only by shallow pilasters. Even the doors, often the only source of sculptural diversion in Romanesque churches, are plain, with only the central door slightly embellished by an understated frieze. I sometimes think that San Martino and San Michele were built for tourists, San Frediano for the Lucchesi.

It is the rarest of buildings, where everything was done right; function determined form and restraint ruled. That restraint has been remarkably maintained for almost 900 years. A church as central to the life of the city as San Frediano has attracted many benefactors over the years, eager to enhance their own glory and the glory of God. This usually means "improvements" and modernization. San Frediano has not been immune to this munificence: it has been raised and it has been widened. But the work was done with so little intrusion that the look and feel of the church, both inside and out, is almost unchanged from the way it looked and felt to the first medieval visitors.

There has been a church on this site for almost 1500 years. The first was built by Saint Frediano himself in the later 500s. He dedicated it to three saints: Vincent of Saragossa (martyred in 304 by being racked and roasted on a gridiron); Laurence (likewise roasted, in 258), and; Stephen (the very first martyr, stoned to death in the year 35). St. Frediano built his church outside the

17. SAN FREDIANO

Roman walls, next to the Jewish quarter. At the time he was the bishop, but he had been driven out of his cathedral in the center of town by the Lombards. He retreated here to re-establish a suitable presence. His church had the apse toward the east, the traditional orientation. The floor level was about 8 feet lower than the present.

By 685 the Lombards had converted from Arianism to orthodoxy and they began building churches with the enthusiasm of converts. One of the first they took in hand was St. Frediano's, which they rebuilt and rededicated to him, perhaps in expiation. It was an important undertaking and the work was carried out by the chief minister of King Cunipert. It became known as the Lombard Basilica. It was a grand building for the time, about 120 feet long, twice the length of the original church. It had the traditional basilica form, with three aisles, and it maintained the traditional orientation. The document of 685 mentions an adjacent monastery of San Frediano.

In the late 700s the bishop of Lucca had extensive work done, including the building of a crypt in which he placed the remains of St. Frediano. At this time crypts were becoming a common architectural feature for the veneration of relics, coinciding with beginnings of the pilgrimage movement.

Construction of the present building began in 1112, the same year as Lucca's first recorded earthquake, which may have precipitated the project. By this time Lucca was well on its way to becoming one of the richest cities in Europe. The local silk industry dominated the European market and would do so for the next two hundred years. The Bishop of Lucca, Rangerio, with newfound wealth, close ties to Rome, and an eye to his epitaph decided to institute a building project which would rival the Cathedral. The project was technically a reconstruction, but the transformation was dramatic.

The existing building was over four hundred years old and was undermined by the waters of the Serchio, which ran almost against the church's northern wall. The first order of business was to raise the foundation about eight feet. (The entire city was being raised piecemeal during the same period.) Then the church was turned 180 degrees on its axis. New town walls were being erected at the same time, which finally brought the church within the city proper, but they would have run too close to the front door if the church was not rotated. Since the present wall at this point incorporates the medieval one, you can appreciate how unsatisfactory it would have been to have the entrance where the apse is now.

Construction was sufficiently complete by 1147 for the new church to be consecrated by Pope Eugene III. At the same time he officially recognized the sanctity of its relics.

Exterior

Despite its later expansion the church you see today remains remarkably faithful to its original conception.

In the 1100s the structure was narrower and lower. The side walls were where the wide pilasters are on the façade, and the height of all three naves was lower. The side aisle roofs ran through the present circular windows. (The irregular stonework surrounding these windows indicates they are a later insertion.) The appearance of the church from the front would have been similar to Sant'Alessandro.

The **mosaic** was put into place in the later 1200s and is one of the masterpieces of that century. It is generally attributed to the workshop of the Berlinghieri family, on the basis of its Byzantine influences and because the

17. SAN FREDIANO

Berlinghieri were the dominant artistic influence in Lucca through the better part of the century. It has been suggested, however, that two different hands were at work on the upper and lower sections.

The use of a frontal mosaic is unique in Lucca and rare in Tuscany, though not so rare in Rome, and San Frediano has always had close ties to the holy city. The mosaic was a perfect solution to the problem of competitiveness which confronted San Frediano in the 1200s. Across town the Cathedral was already undergoing the transformation of its façade, in an ornate oriental fashion, and the caretakers of San Frediano, which had always functioned as a kind of alter-cathedral and rival, sensitive of its status, must have decided that some embellishment was in order. They decided not on a complete transformation, as with the Cathedral, but on maintaining the Romanesque base and adding color. The solution was actually quite obvious. Look at St. Alessandro to appreciate how San Frediano appeared at the time: the rectangular, plain surface fronting the central nave looks like nothing more than a picture frame, waiting to be filled. At San Frediano they did just that.

The work shows the *Ascension of Christ* in a mandorla held by two angels. Below are the twelve Apostles, looking up at the miraculous event. The writing makes clear the context: "Why do the Galileans look towards the sky? This, Galileans, is the son of God rising above."

An interesting footnote: we know that in 1301 Cimabue took over the mosaic in the Pisa Cathedral, his only certain work. He

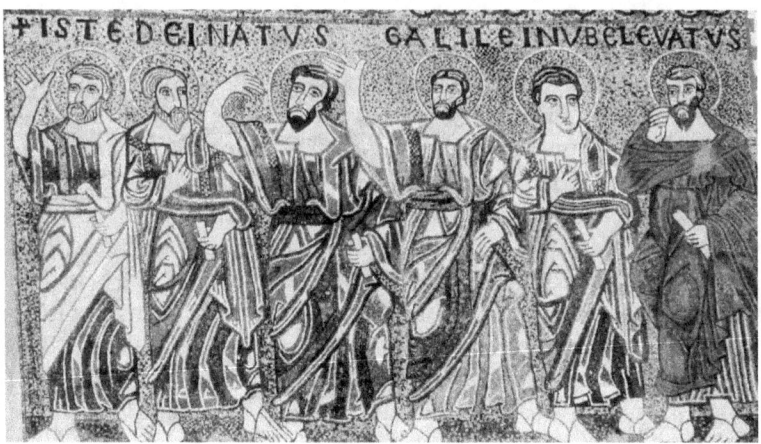

would have certainly been familiar with the San Frediano mosaic, which dates to the later 1200s.

The widening of the church was accomplished by incorporating into the church the chapels which had been built along its exterior walls. From the 1300s through the 1500s these chapels were constructed piecemeal, eventually requiring a general widening of the church, adding a 4th and 5th aisle. The project was undertaken with such care that despite the extensive nature of the alterations the original vision was preserved.

The massive bell tower betrays its original purpose as an impregnable refuge, a use which it has at times served.

Historical Events at San Frediano

June 13, 1314, was the darkest day in Lucca's history, the day the Pisans and Castruccio Castracani captured the city, beginning a half century of tyranny and repression. On the night of the 13th the Pisans invaded Lucchese territory, while within the city Castruccio prepared for a coup by turning the neighborhood of San Frediano into a Ghibelline stronghold, fortifying the massive bell tower of the church and the surrounding houses. As the rebels surged through the streets crying "Death to the traitors" and "Long live the People" the Guelfs began a counterattack and managed to retake the tower of San Frediano. They were on the verge of putting down the uprising when the Pisan troops arrived, set fire to the San Frediano postern and scaled the walls. The Guelfs retreated to outlying towns.

For two days the city was ruthlessly sacked, houses burned, possessions stolen. Since Lucca was at the time one of the wealthiest cities in Europe, the booty was immense. But the richest trove of all was unexpected—the papal treasure. Five years earlier Pope Cement V had moved the papal court to Avignon, the start of its 70 year long 'Babylonian Captivity." One of his cardinals was assigned the task of transporting the papal treasure to its new home. He did not set out, unfortunately, until 1312, by which time Emperor Henry VII, a bitter enemy of the Pope, had entered Italy, which made moving the treasure too risky, and the cardinal was forced to wait in Lucca. He died soon after, leaving most of the treasure in the sacristy of San Frediano, an amount estimated

17. SAN FREDIANO

at a million gold Florins. During the sack of the city the sacristy was looted by Castruccio, German mercenaries, and various citizens of Lucca. Several years later some of these citizens, now disenchanted with Castruccio and suffering excommunication because of him, sought to make peace with the Papacy and confessed their crime. The names included a number of the most prominent families in the neighborhood of San Frediano. It may well have been the presence of this treasure—which could hardly have been a secret—which made San Frediano the site chosen for the start of the uprising, and indeed may have persuaded wavering citizens to join the conspiracy.

Throughout most of its history the interests of San Frediano were closely tied to the papacy, but during the period of the Reformation it became a center of opposition and apostasy. In 1541 Peter Martyr—soon to be a famous reformer—was made prior of San Frediano by the Pope. He was probably sent to reform the morals of the canons, who had developed a scandalous reputation. In the years before his arrival the priesthood of Lucca had become notorious for sins involving pederasty, sodomy, and the molesting of nuns. The bishops in that period were frequently absent and oversight of the priesthood had fallen to the secular leaders of Lucca. Searching for less sordid sexual outlets, in 1540 the rulers issued a decree that "the prostitutes be not molested and may dwell safely in the city."

The iniquities of the brethren of San Frediano arose mainly from their supervision of the convent of San Giovanetto on Via Fillungo (former church #18). In April 1536 the town Elders requested the Papal authorities to prevent the frequent visits by the canons of San Frediano to the nuns in their charge. In May of that year offended relatives of the nuns broke into the monastery of San Frediano and tried to eject the canons by force. In December the nuns of San Giovanetto were found having affairs with two priests and the Prior of San Frediano fled the city. The priests were condemned to death and control of the nunnery was taken from San Frediano. It was this hotbed of sin that the reformer Peter Martyr was sent to clean up. As it turned out, however, the focus of his priorate would not be sex, but heresy.

Because of its close commercial relations with Germany Lucca was one of the first cities in Italy to catch the Protestant contagion.

In 1525 the Council General of Lucca decreed a ban on Lutheran writings, with appropriate fines and book burnings. But enforcement was feeble and the new thinking became fairly open and tolerated. Peter Martyr became its chief spokesman and he made Lucca the most heretical city in Italy. The actual bishop being absent, Martyr began to function in his stead. He assigned new canons to San Frediano and formed an ad hoc university which stressed instruction in Latin, Greek, and Hebrew for more accurate translations of the Biblical texts.

By the time Martyr arrived, Lutheran meetings in the church of Sant'Agostino were already beginning to draw attention outside of Lucca. Reports sent to the authorities in Rome claimed that in Lucca "Lutheran doctrines were...preached from her pulpits and published by her press...a considerable number of her citizens were in a state of ideological revolution." Another stated "The most corrupt place of all is Lucca, where it seems that the leading citizens are carried away by this madness." The informer went on to say that even his friend Master Gigli denied the Catholic doctrine of free will and was reported to have even performed Mass. Notices were put up in the streets which read "Give alms to Matteo Gigli who is missing his top storey and wants to sing his first Mass." Gigli was one of a number of prominent Lucchesi who were disciples of Martyr. He held meetings in his house and indeed administered the Lord's Supper.

Cardinal Bartolomeo Guidiccioni, an intimate of the Pope, had begun to assume some of the functions of the absentee bishop (and would become bishop in 1546). He heard the rumors from Lucca and wrote a letter to the Senators warning them that they must clean house before it was done for them. Before they could reply the Pope appointed six Cardinals, including Guidiccioni, as Inquisitors General and on July 21, 1542 he reconstituted the Roman Inquisition. It is fair to say that it was the situation in Lucca which was the immediate cause for the revival of the Inquisition.

Finally, in mid-July, the Senators began to act. One of them denounced the citizens who had succumbed to Lutheranism, demanded that the Senate confiscate their property and be rid of them, by exile or death. The Senate sent Nicolo Guidiccioni, nephew of the Cardinal, as envoy to the Pope. The Cardinal soon wrote home urging the expulsion of the main offenders. A new

17. SAN FREDIANO

decree was issued, banning heretical books and restoring "the cult of the bodies of such local saints as San Frediano."

The town fathers feared the loss of their independence; the merchant Balbani had reported from Brussels of overhearing a discussion between the Emperor, the Papal Nuncio, and Cosimo de'Medici's ambassador that if Lucca did not return to the fold it would be given to Florence, the worst conceivable fate for a Lucchese.

Martyr was summoned to Genoa to be examined. He chose, wisely, to flee to Strasburg, where he became a doctor of Theology and married a former nun. At the invitation of Thomas Cranmer he went to England and became a professor at Oxford. After Mary's accession to the throne of England he was arrested and compelled to leave the country. He finally settled in Zurich, where he taught Hebrew and corresponded with leading English Protestants.

In 1596 a fire in the church's archives destroyed most of its documents.

Interior

The low, squat appearance of the façade does not prepare you for the expansiveness of the interior. San Frediano is a big church. The antithesis of Gothic, it does not depend on ornamentation for effect but simply on unadorned space and light.

The central nave is separated from the side aisles by twelve massive columns with capitals. These are all spolia, reused pieces from Roman buildings. The plundering of classical buildings had been outlawed or tightly regulated throughout the Gothic and Lombard periods but with the construction boom of the Middle Ages the market in such objects began to flourish. The expense of procuring such pillars was daunting, however, and their use demonstrates the importance and wealth of San Frediano. Most contemporary churches used rectangular piers built of stone. In this case the ruins were probably bought from a dealer in Rome, where the prior of San Frediano had extensive connections.

On three of the pillars there are remains of the frescoes which once covered the interior of the church. If it was true that the interior was covered with wonderful frescoes when Ruskin visited in the 1840s, would that he had recorded more fully what he saw!

The 24 pillars are matched by 24 windows in the clerestory so San Frediano has an airiness, lightness, and openness which comes as a surprise after the close darkness of so many churches. In the winter, when the sun runs its low trajectory, the light through the windows courses slowly along the colonnade, at certain moments throwing every column into bright relief, an effect certainly designed.

The interior today is very plain, which adds to its grandeur. The sole remaining embellishment of the bare stone is the white band which runs along the walls and apse.

On the wall behind you as you enter the church is a magnificent Renaissance organ, rebuilt in 1667. Below the organ are two frescoes:

1. *The Visitation of Mary to Elizabeth*, (l-r) Sts. Peter, Joseph, Mary, Elizabeth, Zachariah, Paul. Commissioned in 1503. Bernard Berenson attributed this fresco to his "Maestro del Tondo Lathrop" who was later discovered to be **Michele Angelo di Pietro Membrini**, often considered the most accomplished Lucchese Renaissance artist. (His most famous work in Lucca is in San Pietro Somaldi.) Later attributions tended towards **Michele Ciampanti** or his son **Ansano,** but recent opinion is reverting back to Berenson's attribution, though possibly with the collaboration of one or both of the Ciampanti. All three were known to have worked together, and Ansano was commissioned in 1503 to decorate the organ above the painting.

2. *Mary and Child with Sts. John the Baptist, Agatha, Margaret of Antioch, and Sebastian*, 1508, fresco by **Amico Aspertini**. The Baptist points to a lamb on a book, the Agnus Dei or Lamb of God; Agatha is carrying on a book her breasts, cut off during her martyrdom (they are easily mistaken for the loaves of bread which are blessed on her feast day); at the feet of Margaret is the dragon that had tried unsuccessfully to swallow her; Sebastian is pierced by a single arrow. This is a good example of the work by the idiosyncratic Aspertini, who you will meet more fully in #19, the Chapel of St. Augustine.

17. SAN FREDIANO

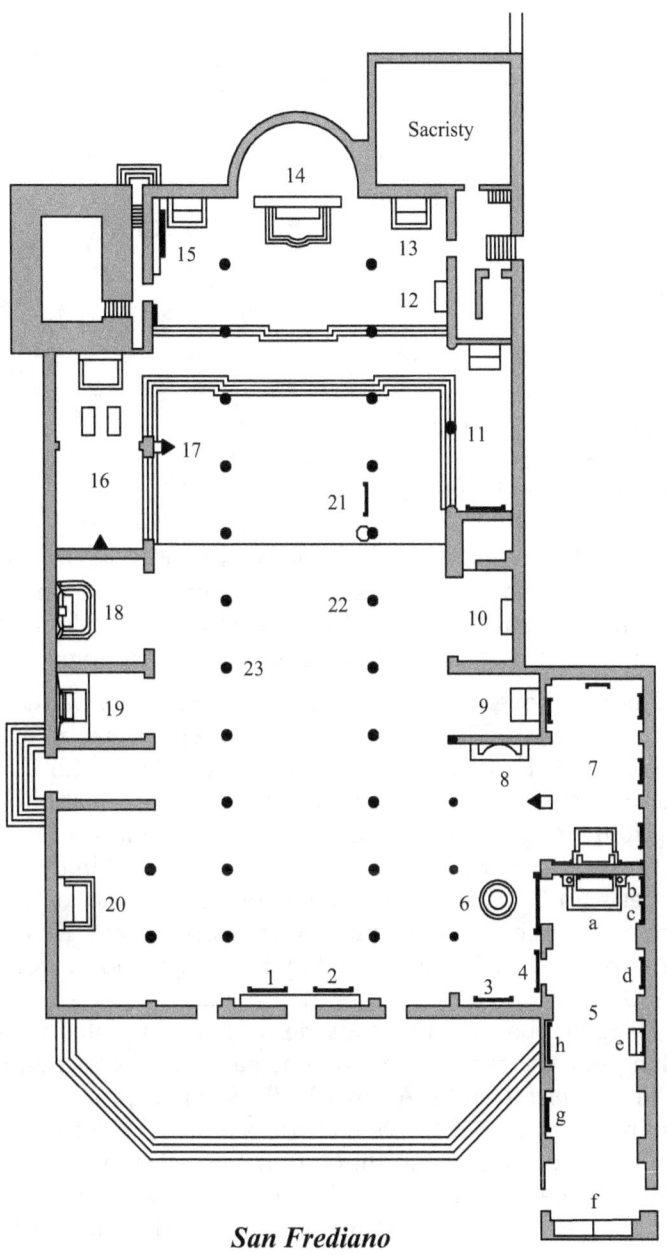

San Frediano

The two holy water stoups in front of the paintings are dated about 1505.

3. St. Peter in Cathedra; fresco, about 1372. To his sides are (l-r) Sts. Augustine, John the Baptist, Paul; above, the Passion Story. This fresco is a remnant of those which once covered the church. Its survival was a lucky accident: when the organ loft was built in the 1500s the painting was covered over and preserved. It was discovered and moved to this site in 1973. The artist is unknown, but hypotheses abound as to his identity and influences. It is one of the finest surviving Lucchese works of the period.

Fresco by Aspertini

Below is a small statue of John the Baptist, from the 1700s. It was atop the Font (#6) before the upper basin was restored in 1952.

4. Lunette (above door), **Madonna and Child with Santa Zita**, fresco, late 1200s. This is the first known representation of Zita, quite possibly by an artist who knew her; she died in 1278. She is wearing a typical servant's dress and is holding a loaf of bread. The cloth being held by the angels is Lucchese fabric of the day. On the right is St. Richard, the English saint buried in the Trenta Chapel (#16). The fresco was done under the influence of the Berlinghieri workshop, the dominant workshop in town. This fresco was also saved by being covered by the organ, and moved here in 1973.

Hanging above and on the sides of the iron grated window looking into the chapel is a monumental glazed terracotta relief of the *Annunciation* by **Andrea Della Robbia** (probably), with a bountiful border of leaves and fruits and a delightful row of cherubic faces below; the third from the left and two on the right are especially appealing. There are two standing cherubs with discreet fig leaves holding heraldic shields. This work was acquired in 1843.

17. SAN FREDIANO

5. Chapel of Santa Maria del Soccorso (Our Lady of Succor)
In 1509 Eufrosina Cenami received permission to construct this chapel in what was part of the cemetery of St. Catherine of Alexandria, and it is therefore also known as the Chapel of St. Catherine.

a) Main altar. Large fresco of *Madonna del Soccorso*, commissioned for this site when the chapel was built. It has been attributed to **Giuliano da Pisa**, his only known work.

b) *St. Barbara*, tempera on wood: later 1400s. It has been attributed to **Michele Ciampanti**.

c) *St. Catherine*, tempera on wood, attributed to **Giuliano di Simone**, ca. 1385. Restored in 1984. This is a fairly obscure corner for such a precious painting by the Lucchese master. Quite likely this is a panel from a triptych or polyptych for the altar of St. Catherine which was consecrated in 1220 and destroyed in 1810. This work was probably commissioned in 1385. Giuliano was resurrected only in recent decades; this attribution has been accepted since the '70s. The *Saint Deacon* fresco on the column in the main nave (5th left) is also attributed to Giuliano.

d) *Madonna and Child*, fresco, 1300s, recently restored, from the Cemetery of St. Catherine. It is also called Madonna del Pilastro or Madonna della Colonna, because it was detached from a column in the cemetery of St. Catherine in 1621.

e) Altar of Rest (*Riposo*). *Madonna del Riposo*, fresco, oval, 1300s, recently restored, from the Cemetery of St. Catherine.

f) Guidiccioni tombs, dated 1290, with some of the earliest known vernacular inscriptions. Some of the original paint of the family crests remains. The three columns are from the 1200s, with the symbols of the evangelists carved on the capitals. The crests on the left are of the Trenta family, from the 1700s. The columns and capitals were likely part of an ancient ambone (early pulpit).

g) *Madonna dei Busdraghi*, attrib. (by some) to **Perugino**. In 1531 Nicola Busdraghi paid for its restoration.

h) *Miracle of San Biagio* (St. Blaise) by **Giovan Domenico Ferrucci** (1619-1669). The miracle was the curing of a child who had a fish bone stuck in his throat. When Biagio was later imprisoned the child's mother brought him food and candles. He was torn apart with wool combs (curry combs), his symbol. Canterbury claimed his relics. This painting was originally in the

Cappella Cenami dedicated to San Biagio.

6. The *Font*

This large stone basin is one of Lucca's most famous possessions, a well-preserved sculptural masterpiece of the Middle Ages, dating to about 1150-1175. Its original function and location are debatable, but it seems most likely that it was a wash basin for the monks in the monastery of San Frediano or a cantharus placed outside the church for pilgrims. Water flowed from the upper basin through the twelve masks into the lower. Traditionally it is referred to as the Baptismal Font, but both its design and the subjects of its relief dictate against this being its original purpose.

The lower basin. Inspection of the floor beneath has shown that it has been in its present location for centuries. The bold relief sculptures depict biblical scenes which can be divided into two groups, by at least two separate artists, whose individual styles and themes are easily distinguishable.

I. On the west (towards the apse) the seven figures under acute arches separated by pillars are the work of Master Robert, who signed it on the rim above [ME FECIT ROBERTUS MAGIST(ER)...]. The identity of the figures is obscure but generally construed to represent the Good Shepard in the center, with three "prophets" on each side. Nothing else is known of Robert though he may be the same Roberto referred to in a document of 1177.

II. The next group to the right (counterclockwise) recounts scenes from Exodus. The first three figures, a woman and two men, one with an axe, probably represent the enslavement of the Jews in Egypt. In the next scene Miriam presents Moses' mother (disguised as a nurse) to Pharaoh's daughter who sits on her throne. The next figure, holding a dragon's tail, may be Aaron flinging his staff on the ground turning it into a serpent. Next, God, depicted as a face in an oval, appears to Moses in the burning bush. The crouching man to the right, holding out an arm covered

17. SAN FREDIANO

with boils or sores represents the plagues which God inflicted on the Egyptians. (One wonders if the missing face was broken off because it was so terrible.) Notice the use of trees and foliage to unify the scene, the use of drill holes to add texture, the finely executed scales and wings of the dragon, and the drapery which is obviously by the same hand as the preceding scene (for instance in the treatment of the knees).

Following this there is a clear seam. The scene to the right depicts the Egyptian army, dressed as medieval cavalry, with helmets and chain mail, drowning in the Red Sea. Following this is Jehovah presenting the tablets of the Law to Moses, and finally a single figure of Moses expounding the Law.

The *upper basin and cover* are by a different hand. This part of the fountain was removed during the 1700s to the gardens of Villa Mansi. Become a plaything, the cover was vandalized and the heads of all the figures broken off. In the 1890s it was acquired by the National Museum in Florence, but was returned to Lucca in 1952.

The theme is a typical Romanesque mixing of the Biblical with the mythic, sacred and profane. At the top of the support column is a ring of heads, still well preserved, of men and beasts. The water from the basin poured out through twelve grotesque masks. On the cover are depicted the twelve months, a popular medieval theme. Above these are the twelve disciples.

At the door to the chapel of Santa Zita is a glazed terracotta statue of **St. Bartolomeo**, placed here in 1842.

7. Chapel of Santa Zita.

Santa Zita was buried here in 1278, in what was then part of the cemetery of Saint Catherine. In 1410 the Fatinelli family, her masters, closed off the chapel from the rest of the cemetery and built the vaulted ceiling. The superb (and expensive—300 gold florins) ironwork which today separates the chapel from the baptistery is from this 1410 work.

In 1605 the family renovated the chapel, and donated a new marble altar. Their final restoration was done in 1849 by the last member of the family shortly before his death. The chapel was again restored in 1955 and 2007. The present glass case containing the body of the saint was made in 1956.

Santa Zita died 27 April 1278. April 24 to 27 every year the glass tomb is put into another of silvered wood and placed in the center nave.

Santa Zita

Zita was born about 1218 in the village of Monsagrati, 10 miles northwest of Lucca. At the age of 12 she was sent to the city to work as a servant in the house of the Fatinelli family, who were probably the feudal lords her village. Zita was the nickname given her by the other servants when she arrived. It meant spinster, a bit cruel but prophetic.

She was unprepossessing: about 4' 9", with a short right leg and curvature of the spine. By the time of her death at age 60 she had lost all her teeth and her feet were deformed, as were her knees from long hours of praying on the hard floor of San Frediano.

When young she was the butt of jokes and harsh treatment by her masters, but rose to become in charge of the household. Hence she is portrayed with a bunch of keys, and is the saint to invoke for lost keys.

She became famous for her frequent presence in San Frediano, and for her charity to the poor (often at the expense of her master). Within months of her death in 1278 the Bishop authorized her public veneration and in 1308 the Republic declared April 27 to be a public holiday. The festival is still celebrated. She was canonized in 1696.

Her cult spread quickly. In the *Inferno* Dante refers to Lucca as the town of Santa Zita. In England she had numerous shrines, and appears in Winchester Cathedral and Westminster.

Chapel Paintings:

On the altar has recently been placed the oil painting of St. Zita offering a drink to a pilgrim by **Paolo Guidotti**, dating from the painter's sojourn in Lucca, 1611-1617. The other paintings, later 1600s, by **Francesco Del Tintore,** student of Pietro Paolini, recount the most famous episodes of her life. Her miracles focus on the everyday hardships and concerns of the poor—bread and warmth. They include: Zita with an angel; Miracle of the beans (Zita gives beans to the poor, and yet the master's cupboard

17. SAN FREDIANO

does not diminish); Zita with the Fatinelli family; Miracle of the bread baked by angels (while Zita remains lost in prayer in San Frediano, angels perform her chores); an angel returns the coat to Zita's master (on a cold night her master had given Zita his best coat to wear to church, but she lent it to a freezing man, who absconded with it; the next morning it was returned by a mysterious stranger—Christ?); Miracle of the bread turned to flowers (Zita was spiriting bread out of the house in her apron to give to the poor; when confronted by her master who demanded to know what she was carrying, she opened her apron and it was filled only with flowers); Zita giving bread to a hungry man.

8. Exiting the chapel, on your right is an altar by **Matteo Civitali**, 1489. Never completed, it was moved to this site in the church in 1598 and converted to a baptismal font. The fresco, *Baptism of Christ*, is by **Lorenzo Castellotti**, 1700s.

9. Chapel of the Most Precious Blood, or Chapel of Saint Biagio. Patron family: Cenami. It has a number of treasures. An elaborate, high domed chapel, it was built in 1456 and modernized in 1602. It may have been designed at this time by Filippo Penitesi, who designed the Chapel of Santa Zita. Notice the excellent execution of the frieze arch as you enter. The niches in the chapel were destined for sculpture, but remain empty.

On the left wall is one of the great paintings of Lucca, *The Deposition* by **Paolo Guidotti**. At one time it was attributed, optimistically, to Caravaggio. It certainly exhibits his technique of dramatic lighting—tenebrism—which captivated Italian painters at the end of the 1500s. Until recently it was generally attributed to Pietro Paolini, a native son of Lucca. Since 1992 it has been reassigned to Guidotti, another native of Lucca, whose reputation has been on the rise.

On the right wall, a considerably less distinguished painting, *Nativity* by **Pietro Sorri,** 1608, restored 1977. Sorri (1556-1622) was a journeyman painter, well represented in Lucca.

The Altar: a marble relief, beautiful in parts, one of the most important works of **Giovanni Battista Baratta** (1670-1747). Into it is set a reliquary holding the blood of Christ. When Volto Santo first washed up on a nearby shore, found within it was the blood which is in the reliquary before you. It has had a peripatetic history.

First appropriated by the town of Sarzana, in 790 a certain Jacob absconded with it and gave it to his brother Giovanni, the Bishop of Lucca. At the time a relic was required to sanctify a new church, which he had built in a nearby town. 600 years later this church was demolished and its order, the Olivetan Benedictines, brought it to Silice, where it remained a further 300 years, until the Olivetans were suppressed by Napoleon. It then passed to his sister Elisa, ruler of Lucca, and she in turn donated it to San Frediano. Since 1837 it has been in this chapel.

Reliquary of Christ's Blood

Beneath the altar is the sarcophagus of Beato Corrado, Bishop of Lucca (935-964). When the body was uncovered in 1602 it was found to be in a state of perfect preservation, in its hand an olive branch whose leaves were still green.

The pavement was restored in 1600 with crests of the Cenami: lions rampant in gold. They were excised under the Jacobins.

10. Chapel of the Annunciation (formerly Chapel of St. Agnes). Patron family: Sandei. The chapel was begun by 1384, utilizing a room of the former monastery.

On the left wall is the painting *Saint Apollonia* by **Girolamo Scaglia**. It was traditionally ascribed to **Antonio Franchi** (called The Lucchese), but when it was restored in 1957 it was found to be signed by Scaglia, and dated 1646. (Franchi was 3 years old.) Scaglia (1620-1686), born and died in Lucca, has been unjustly ignored until recently. He has quite a few paintings in town.

On the right wall, *Saint Michael slaying the dragon* by **Camillo Ciai**, 1665.

17. San Frediano

On the altar, *Annunciation* by **Gaspare Mannucci**, (1575-1642). It has vibrant coloring, its play of grey, yellow, and red revealed by the 1994 restoration. The composition is divided diagonally, Mary in her bright red dress emerging from the darkness, the angel and the heavens behind in the yellow of sunlight, grays dividing them, the angel's clothes yellow and grey, as is the lily in his hand. The more I look at it the more I like it.

It was apparently in this room that the papal treasure was hidden, which was stolen by Castruccio.

11. Chapel of the Assumption and Crucifix. Patron family: Micheli/Magrini. A large double vaulted chapel, with bare stone walls but a lovely, restored ceiling. Built about 1500 by the Micheli family, restored 1856 by the Guinigi Magrini.

On the altar is the remains of a *Crucifixion* fresco from the 1200s, restored and moved here in 1997 from the Chapel of Santa Zita, and therefore known as *The Crucifixion of St. Zita*.

On the opposite wall is a wood ancona with raised figures of the *Assumption of Mary* by **Masseo Civitali**, master of intaglio and marquetry, nephew of the famous Matteo. An unusual and interesting work, cleaned in 2005 with stunning result.

12. *Tomb of Lazaro Papi*. Inscribed: "Colonel for the English in Bengal, then a praised writer of verse and history…His friends built this in 1835." Among his works are a translation of Milton and a history of the French Revolution.

13. Altar of Saint Fausta. *Martydom of St. Fausta* by the Sienese **Pietro Sorri** (1556-1622), restored 1997. The original altar to St. Fausta was dedicated in 1157. The present altar was placed here in 1566. The Fausta whose remains are venerated here was the wife of Saint Cassio (#15). The painting, however, shows the horrible death of the Saint Fausta who was martyred by having spikes driven into her body and being boiled alive.

14. High Altar and Crypt

A small section of the pavement to the right of the altar was moved here from the choir in the late 1600s. The body of San Frediano is open for viewing on the 18th November.

15. Altar of Saint Cassio. The original altar to St. Cassio was dedicated in 1140. The present altar was erected in 1566. **St. Cassio**

Exorcising a Demon as King Totila Watches by the Pisan **Aurelio Lomi**, 1595. This dramatic painting is a good example of Lormi, a late Mannerist well thought of by his contemporaries.

Cassio was the bishop of Narni from 536-558. Totila was the last Ostrogoth king who, having recovered most of Italy from the Byzantines (he captured Rome in 546 after a three month siege), was attacked first by Belisarius, then by Narses, who finally defeated him in 552. (The following year Narses laid siege to Lucca.)

In the year 878 Adalberto I, Duke of Tuscany, and his brother-in-law Lamberto, duke of Spoleto, invaded the Papal States and made off with the remains of Cassio and Fausta, which he deposited in San Frediano. They were consecrated in 1140 (for consecration of the new church), and in 1446 they were transferred to their respective altars. In 1679, after 800 years in Lucca, the bones of both Cassio and Fausta were returned to Narni, except for small pieces which were retained to maintain the sanctity of the altars. The festival of St. Cassio is celebrated in Lucca on Oct. 16.

To the left of the altar is *The Monolith of Saint Frediano*. This large limestone slab likely dates to the time of Saint Frediano. According to legend it was transported to Lucca from the nearby Pisan mountains by the miraculous aid of St. Vincenzo, on a cart pulled by two young oxen. It was almost certainly used as the altar in the church built by Saint Frediano in the 500s. Under the slab are sculptures, probably of the 700s, of the young bulls which pulled the cart.

To the left of the monolith is the *Sarcophagus Cover* of the tomb of San Frediano. The original inscription, with characters identifiable as from the 500s states that this is the tomb of Frediano: "HOC C.TUMULUM FRIGIANI..." When it was recovered during the construction of the 1100s, a new inscription was added on the side.

There have probably been three relocations of the remains of St. Frediano. Originally they were placed in the church he built which was dedicated to San Lorenzo; during excavations in 1950 there was discovered a sarcophagus with the dimensions which match this cover. He was probably moved again during the construction of the Lombard basilica about 690, and finally placed in the crypt below the altar of the present church in the 1100s.

17. San Frediano

16. Trenta chapel.

This chapel, built by one of the wealthiest families of the 1400s was restored in 2003 in an admirably minimalist fashion, the frescoed ceiling and walls retrieved as much as possible, the rest left plain.

The chapel is famous for the sculpted *Altarpiece* by **Jacopo Della Quercia**, one of his finest and best preserved works. It was made between 1416 and 1422. In the center are Mary and Child, flanked by (l-r) St. Ursula (she has also been identified as St. Lucy), St. Lawrence, St. Jerome and St. Richard, each in his own niche. Above them are busts of unidentified Evangelists or prophets. During the 1600s an attempt at modernization shaved about 6 inches off the rear.

On the predella below (l-r): St. Catherine of Alexandria; the martyrdom of St. Ursula and her companions; the martyrdom of St. Lawrence; Pietà; St. Jerome removing a thorn from a lion's paw; a person cured of possession by the relics of St. Richard; St. Ursula (or St. Christina). It is widely thought that the predella was not part of the original design and was probably added in 1422.

Below the altar is a small sarcophagus holding the relics of St. Richard. It was placed here in 1416.

St. Richard (often called 'King of the English') was from Wessex. While on a pilgrimage to the Holy Land he and his two sons stayed with the Trenta family in Lucca, where he took ill and died. The Trenta made him their protector and he was soon locally elevated to sainthood. His feast is still celebrated on February 7 in San Frediano.

His sons proceeded on their pilgrimage, Winnibald staying seven years in Rome, and Willibald proceeding to Palestine. An account of his travels, the *Hodoeporicon*, is the first travel book written by an Anglo-Saxon. In 730 he returned to Italy and restored

Monte Cassino to prosperity. He was then sent to Germany where he became bishop of Eichstatt, and where he and his brother founded a Benedictine monastery. They were joined by their sister Walburga, who became abbess. Walburga's feast day was May 1, and gave Walpurgis Night its name. Not only Richard, but all three of his children, are revered as saints.

On the floor in front of the altar are marble tomb slabs of Lorenzo Trenta and his wife Isabetta, probably also by Jacopo della Quercia; they are dated 1416. Considering that these sarcophagi were by the same hand that sculpted Ilaria del Carretto, how unfortunate it is that centuries of feet were permitted to tread on them and wear them away.

Placed recently in the chapel is a painted wood *Mary Annunciate*, attributed to **Matteo Civitali**, about 1480. Restored 1956.

17. Statue of *St. Peter* by **Vincenzo de Bartolomeo Civitali**, 1506, marble. The inscription states that it was the first work of Vincenzo. It was a gift to the Republic and was placed in the church in 1842.

18. Gentili Chapel. Also called Chapel of Sts. Stephen, Philip, and James and Chapel of the Virgin of Hope. Its construction was provided for in a Gentili will of 1398. This chapel was destroyed by fire in 1596. In 1796 during work in a nearby courtyard a fresco of the Immaculate Conception was discovered which the Bishop donated to the Gentili chapel with the title Immaculate Virgin of Hope. A new marble altar by **Giovanni Cecchi** was installed with figures of Saints James and Philip. On the side walls are two paintings by **Gaspare Martini**, 1824: *The Flight to Egypt* and the *Visit of Mary with Elizabeth*.

19. Chapel of St. Augustine (or of the Cross, referring to Volto Santo). The chapel was entirely reconstructed beginning in 1505 by the prior of San Frediano, Pasquino Cenami (of the immensely rich family). It is on the site traditionally believed to be the original location of Volto Santo in Lucca. The original chapel was built in the early 800s by the brother and successor to Bishop John I, who is credited with bringing Volto Santo to Lucca. To decorate the present chapel Cenami commissioned **Amico Aspertini**, whom we have already met at #2. The frescoes are frequently reproduced in books on Lucca because they depict two of the most famous

17. SAN FREDIANO

Lucchese figures: Volto Santo and Saint Frediano.

In 1845 Ruskin wrote "One thing I must do, & that is get... leave from the monks to take tracings of these frescoes of Aspertini's for they are chipping off and fading away, and I have no doubt will be scraped off or whitewashed over when I come back again." This was not allowed to happen, but his comments do cause one to reflect on what is restored and what is original. Ruskin despised restoration and would have been content to let them flake away, though not whitewashed.

On the left:
  1. Volto Santo is transported from Luni to Lucca.
  2. St. Ambrose baptizes St. Augustine.
  3. (lunette) Deposition.
On the right:
  1. St. Frediano changes the course of the Serchio.
  2. Nativity of Christ.
  3. (lunette) St. Augustine delivers his rules to his followers.

On the entrance arch are monochrome frescoes of four scenes from the life of Christ and the portraits of Saints Fausta, Cassio, Richard, and Zita.

20. Buonvisi Chapel. Dedicated to St. Anna. Built in 1511 by Benedetto Buonvisi. Renovated in the late 1700s to its present appearance.

On the altar: *St. Anna Adoring the Child Jesus* by **Stefano Tofanelli**. Placed here in 1812, replacing a painting by Francesco Francia (today in the National Gallery, London). Tofanelli also did the ceiling.

Right of altar: *Nativity of Mary* by **Francesco Antonio Cecchi**.
Left of altar: *Death of St. Anna* by **Bernardino Nocchi**, 1804.
Left wall: *Sepulchre of Buonviso Buonvisi*.

In the 1500s the Buonvisi family was by far the wealthiest in Lucca. This served as their family chapel. They also provided three cardinals to Rome who are represented by the three cardinal's hats under the arches. They were Buonviso (1561-1603), Girolamo (1607-1677), and Francesco (1626-1700). The latter two were also bishops of Lucca.

21. Fresco, north wall of main nave, ***Martyrdom of the Levite Saints Vincenzo, Stefano, and Lorenzo***, mid-1100s. By legend it marks the place where the previous church ended.

22. Fresco, 5th column left. ***Saint Deacon***, perhaps by **Giuliano di Simone**. Possibly of St. Stefano or Lorenzo, one of the three Levites to whom St. Frediano dedicated his church.

23. Fresco, 6th column right. ***Virgin Annunciate***.

~

Sant' Andrea

18. Sant'Andrea
St. Andrew

The first record of Sant'Andrea is in 1077 but it probably has its origins in the Lombard era. For centuries it bore the toponym *in pelleria*, that is, in the leatherworking district. There were a number of *pellerie* in town, dating at least to Lombard, and probably to Roman, times. San Tommaso still bears the designation, since its district was where the industry was centralized when the others were shut down in the 1300s. They had all been located along the several canals or sewer ditches which traversed the town. One of these canals ran down Via Sant'Andrea past the church. In the civic reforms of the early 1300s the canal was filled in and paved over, removing a blight on what was becoming a fashionable neighborhood.

The church itself was rebuilt in the late 1100s, during the period when it seemed the entire town was being torn down and built up again. The lower, original, portion is a fine example of Lucchese Romanesque: the ashlar of soothing slate-like, almost oily, gray stone; the main door with its heavy white jambs and lintel, high arch, and protecting lions; the similar side door with its arch of bichrome voussoirs; the high slit windows; the barely protruding apse, here graced by a small cupola and flanked by blind arches. The frieze over the front door, early 1200s, almost certainly came from the workshop of **Guidetto**, which at the same time was working on San Giusto, San Michele, and the Cathedral. Theirs also are the flanking lions which threaten but do not devour the men in their jaws.

The building survived unaltered until the 1680s when the roof was raised and the loggia on its upper front was replaced by purely functional stone work. The slit windows were filled in, replaced by larger rectangular ones above.

Sant'Andrea may have originally been a church of tanners, but as the area gentrified in the 1200s and 1300s it became the beneficiary of numerous bequests by wealthy local families (though not it seems, of the Guinigi, whose tower is just down the road). The interior of the medieval building was later transformed by the resurgent wealth after liberation from Pisa, and by the artistic tastes of the nascent Renaissance.

The sacking and burning of the town archives in 1314 destroyed most city records and the turbulence of the succeeding decades was not conducive to regular record keeping. After liberation in 1369, however, documentation becomes prolific and we can track the flow of the commissions and bequests which transformed the artistic landscape of the city. Sant'Andrea was blessed, though not atypically.

In 1373 a Bernardini left 10 florins for a painting to be placed over the door which faced his house across the street to the north.

In 1383 a Forteguerra who lived in the neighborhood had an altar built along the right aisle, and was given permission to construct his tomb next to it. He instructed his executors to spend "whatever amount they thought opportune." This was his primary bequest, but he also left significant amounts to a half dozen other churches and monasteries.

The same year, 1383, the merchant Bonagiunta expressed his desire to be buried in the tomb of his brothers in the church, where there would be placed a monument carrying their crest and the "trademark of his shop." For this he left the impressive sum of 3000 florins for ornamenting the church, with the stipulation that "for the three altars in the choir there should be built three chapels, frescoed and ornamented like those in the church of San Salvatore in Mustolio, with his crest." When he died in 1390 the bishop administered the will. It was probably this bequest which paid for the triptych by **Spinello Aretino**.

In 1390 another Bonagiunta left 200 lire for church improvements to include a chapel and an altar with "a beautiful painting." He also left money to the Cathedral, but if it was not needed there, it was to go to Sant'Andrea. For this munificence he was allowed to build a tomb displaying his family crest.

Sant'Andrea survived intact until well into the Counter Reformation period, but by the late 1600s it was badly in need of repair and restoration. In the 1680s the roof was raised, clearly evident on the exterior. The interior was given a vaulted, plastered roof, a new interior wall built over the original, and the art and altars were replaced according to the current aesthetic. This incarnation has survived fairly well, though some of the art has

18. Sant'Andrea

migrated. Today, though irregularly open, the church continues its sacred function, as it has for the last 800 years.

Interior

The commanding high altar is one of the few works in Lucca by its eminent but peripatetic native son, **Domenico Martinelli** (1650-1718). Most of his architectural work was done in Rome and central Europe. He left Lucca after a dispute with the directors of the Cathedral, and did not return home until 1715, three years before his death.

In the church:

St. Luigi (Aloysius) Gonzaga by **Francesco Antonio Cecchi** (born Lucca 1717).

St. Antonio Abate, wood statue from San Ponziano, attributed recently to **Baccio da Montelupo**.

Also belonging to the church is a painted terracotta relief of *Madonna and Child* by **Matteo Civitali**, though how and when it came here is unknown. It has only recently been rescued from relative obscurity, being cleaned and studied for the Civitali exhibit of 2004.

Formerly in the church:

An exquisite triptych, *Madonna and Child with Saints Paolino, John the Baptist, Jeremiah, and Andrew* by **Spinello Aretino**. It survived in the church until 1850. This was the period which, as one of the painting's cataloguers wrote,

> "signaled the beginning of a systematic impoverishment of the artistic patrimony on Italian soil, mirrored mainly by the enrichment of the great public and private collections of Europe."

The painting, still in its original frame, was about to be illicitly sold to a Hungarian baron when it was rescued by decree of the Tuscan government, which transferred it for safekeeping to Florence, where it still resides in the Galleria dell'Accademia. The prospects for its repatriation are dim, even though Lucca could now presumably be entrusted with it.

~

San Frediano font

19. San Cristoforo
St. Christopher

Neither its location at the entry to Via Fillungo, nor its distinguished architecture, nor its historical significance were ultimately enough to ensure San Cristoforo's role as an operating church. It functions now as a monument to those Lucchesi who have fallen in war—which does ensure its maintenance. This new role is appropriate, since San Cristoforo early acquired civic functions, undoubtedly because of its location in the center of the merchant area.

The earliest document regarding the church is dated 1053, which refers to it as next to the *Canto d'Arco*, the archway which joined two towers at the entrance to Via Fillungo. The archway was erected in 963, apparently for the visit of Emperor Otto I.

By 1150, the existing church was the site of the lay Court, in which it delivered its rulings and next to which it had offices. This court was called the Curia of San Cristoforo, even after it had moved from the church. It was replaced in occupancy by the pre-eminent business association in the city, the University of Merchants of Wool and Silk, which had been located in the nearby church of San Giusto until burgeoning business required a larger home.

When reconstruction of San Cristoforo began in the mid-1100s **Diotisalvi** was chosen as architect. He designed the Baptistery in Pisa and probably contributed to San Michele. In San Cristoforo he gave us one of the most coherently conceived and executed facades in Lucca, a masterpiece of Pisan Romanesque, dignified and classical. He used the favored device of high blind arcades, here adapting them to the entrance way. The two side doors with their own smaller archways introduce a secondary symmetry which breaks up that of the large arches. The side doors are classic Lucchese whereas the main door shows the advance of the Gothic, less common in Lucca. It has a masterful architrave with lush foliage, flanked by lions which are now almost worn away. Sculpted about the year 1200, the architrave is attributed to the workshop of **Guidetto**, which was busy in town at the time.

The fine use of two-tone marble gives chromatic character to the surface.

The upper part of the façade, which is about a century later, maintains the horizontal banding. It has an unusual, for Lucca, large rosette, and at the top are the small hanging arches we encounter so often on apses. The effect is somewhat Gothic and rather at odds with the lower level.

The close association of the church with the merchants' association was emphasized by cementing into the face of the building, just right of the main door, arranged as a cross, the steel bars (dated 1286) which were the standard lengths for folds of Lucchese silk: 86 cm & 45 cm (34", 18"). They have recently been removed.

The tribulations of church maintenance are made clear in documents from the 1300s in the archbishop's library. In 1345, three years after the Pisans took possession of Lucca, San Cristoforo was still without a roof. The original roof had been a temporary measure to serve until the upper level of the façade was finished. The façade was now complete, but the building fund was empty. In Tuscan churches the façade of the church was often left to last, and not infrequently never finished. Lucca had the opposite propensity, to build the embellishment first, trusting that the main structure would follow, but that likewise might never happen, as in San Michele.

Pisan dominance, despised as it was, conferred stability on Lucca after years of chaos. It was finally possible to attend to things like collapsing buildings. The Bishop, surveying the situation, "recommended to all the faithful of Lucca the church of San Cristoforo, which for a long time has been uncovered, and exposed to the dangers of ill weather." He offered an indulgence of 40 days to anyone who gave money or labor to getting the roof up, and he also guaranteed the annual proceeds from 6 lbs. of oil for rebuilding the sacristy. Being the home of the merchants, the motivation was not only ecclesiastical: San Cristoforo was a symbol of Lucca and its restoration was essential to the regeneration of the city. Three years later, 1348, the year of the great plague, a Castracani died and left 80 lire for the "reconstruction" of the church.

By 1373, four years after liberation, the integrity of the building

19. San Cristoforo

was ensured, and the interior could now be attended to. One merchant, though he wanted to be buried in the Cathedral, left a goodly sum, 500 florins, to build and maintain an altar (which included a priest to say mass).

But roofs are a curse. Once again, in February 1389 one Labruccio, "Master of roofs," contracted "to cover all the nave and the other needed parts, before the first of June." This must have been part of a major rededication because in April a commission was let out to Domenico Fazino for a painting of the Annunciation with Archangel Michael "similar to the one in San Donato outside Lucca", the only certain work of the master. And yet two years later the presbytery was still sufficiently "in danger" for the Bishop to finance its restoration.

The church is tightly constrained by surrounding buildings. Originally there was an alley on the right, which remained until the 1800s, when the space finally became irresistible. The buildings which are attached on the left of the church were originally the sacristy and storage space. The sacristy was converted in 1681 into the **Oratorio of Saint Charles Borromeo**, dedicated to the great reformer of the previous century.

The oddly shaped campanile in the rear is built on the foundations of an early tower.

Interior

The church is long and narrow, with a shallow apse and a wood truss ceiling. Rectangular pillars support broad, high arches. It has been stripped to its structural components.

On the first pillar on the right is a 1300s fresco of ***Madonna and Child*** and an epigraph by the children of Civitali recording the place where his sepulcher had once been.

Although the exterior of San Cristoforo has survived quite well for centuries the interior has been completely denuded. In its barrenness it provides an appropriately solemn memorial to the citizens of Lucca who have died in war. Their names are inscribed on the walls.

In front of the left hand pillar is the tomb of the painters Coli and Gherardi.

Nearby—

Opposite the entrance to the church is the lovely restored medieval house of the Taddicioni and next to it the same family's "tower of travails."

At the rear of the church, running up from Via Santa Croce, was an alleyway called Vicolo San Carlo. After at least a thousand years as a public way, in 1890 the commune relinquished all rights to the thoroughfare and granted quiet title to the eminent Busdraghi family, who then fenced it off for their personal use. It has recently been reopened to the public. In one of those acts of historical salvation and exploitation which Lucca values, a wonderfully preserved medieval groined passageway, rubbing against the apse and campanile, now leads into a chic *botiqueria*. At the entrance to the *vicolo* there were two towers, their remains still discernible, and the **Oratorio of the Poor** (former church #24) built in 1544, which was affiliated with San Cristoforo. Soon after its construction it became a center of the heretical Lutheran movement, a lapse from which it recovered after the expulsion of the Protestants. It was finally closed in 1920.

~

20. Santi Giovanni e Reparata
Sts. John and Reparata, and the Baptistery

The first written evidence regarding a church on the site of San Giovanni, as it is usually called, is dated 754. That church was dedicated to Santa Reparata, the same saint to whom the cathedral of Florence was dedicated. The present building was erected in the 1170s and 1180s, the date 1187 being engraved on the sill over the main entrance.

Since we can so closely date it San Giovanni serves as a snapshot of Lucchese church architecture in the late 1100s. It has been noted that it shows strong Lombard influences in its external decorations, its capitals, its use of hanging arches, its solid stone walls and clerestory. It provides a good place to pause and reflect on the influence of the Lombards—the Longobards—on Lucca. By 1170 the Longobards had long been displaced as the city's rulers. Four hundred years earlier, in 774, they had been conquered by Charlemagne. And yet, as you read through the documents which have survived regarding San Giovanni you are struck by the continuing dominance of Lombard—Germanic—names: Idelbrando, Lamberto, Glandolfo, Rolando, Manfredo. They dominate the records into the 1200s, which reminds us that when we speak of Lombard influence in Lucchese architecture we are rarely referring to the period of Lombard rule, but to their much longer lasting cultural influence.

Thanks to extensive excavations carried out during the 1970s and 1980s the entire basement of the church of San Giovanni and of the adjacent Baptistery is an archaeological site, permitting you a rare glimpse of what lies beneath the city, dating back to Roman times.

The Archaeological Site and Early History of the Church

When you descend the stairs at the rear of the church you see what appears be a basement full of rubble, which are the remains of about one thousand years of Lucca's history.

Not far from the foot of the stairs in the floor of the north transept (which leads to the baptistery) there are some fragments of mosaic floor which date to about the first century AD. They are at the ground level of the Roman city, which was about 8 feet below that of today. The quality of the mosaic indicates a significant building and the presence of water troughs suggest that it was probably used for baths.

After the Edict of Milan in 313 granted tolerance to Christians the Church began to thrive and to alter the urban landscape. In most cities the religious center developed close to the walls, away from the forum. In Lucca this was in the southeast quadrant, along the road which led to Rome. It was here that the bishop established his seat. Most visitors would pass by on their way to the forum and the business center of town. The bishop of Lucca soon became an important personage, one of the participants at the Council of Sardica in 343.

In 374 Ambrose became bishop of Milan and in the 380s he erected his Basilica. It was a defining moment in Christian architecture. Following Ambrose's example a wave of church construction swept through central and northern Italy. In the 390s an impressive church was built in Lucca, on the present site of San Giovanni. Befitting the seat of a powerful bishop the new cathedral was impressively large; its floor plan was almost identical to the current church. Along the north wall of the excavation you can see the sustaining pillars of the original wall. The remains of the original apse are also clear, with the foundation of the present apse built up against it. On the ground surrounding the walkways of the site there are remains of the mosaic floor of the church, which was about two feet above the Roman floor. The original church probably had only one nave, with no central columns. The rectangular posts which line the basement and which appear to be the foundations of columns were, apparently, not structural. It has been suggested that they served as the base for heavy iron lamps which illuminated the church.

Almost as soon as the church was finished Roman civilization began its slow and inexorable decline. In 401 the Visigoths invaded and in 410 they occupied Rome. The cathedral in Lucca declined as well and the character of the building changed. In the 500s it began to be used as a burial ground. About twenty tombs were discovered in the main body of the church, another twenty in the baptistery. The Romans had forbidden burial within the city walls

20. San Giovanni

but with the rise of Christianity this prohibition had ended and the desire to be buried in the holy ground of a church had spread.

The use of the church for burials coincides with a general deterioration of society. The 500s were a terrible period for Italy. From 535 to 555 the Gothic Wars devastated the country. In 553 Lucca was besieged and finally taken by the Byzantines. With the countryside ravaged by marauding armies people took refuge in the city, even for burials, and churches were the most secure place. The sad state of the church during this period is clear in the deterioration of the original baptistery, which not only fell into disuse for baptisms but was used intensively as a cemetery.

In 568 the Lombards invaded Italy and soon after had occupied Lucca. At the time St. Frediano was bishop of Lucca and this church was his seat. The Lombards were Arians and one of their first acts was to desecrate the Catholic churches. St. Frediano was driven from his church and forced to found a new one, outside the city walls.

The 600s are a time of obscurity, truly a dark age. There was certainly very little building going on in Lucca. Revival began at the end of the century, but it was not until the 700s that there was any true recovery. The first mention we have of the new church on this site, Santa Reparata, is in 754 when Bishop Valprando left a bequest to it before he went off to war with the Lombard king Astolfo. He left somewhat more to San Martino, intimating that by now San Martino had become the new cathedral. About this time another renovation was undertaken in Santa Reparata, work probably to make the church serviceable again after it had fallen into decay. You can see where the north wall was strengthened between the columns, using a typical Lombard masonry technique of river jacks aligned in a herringbone design, in rows of alternating diagonals.

A major reconstruction took place in the late 700s or early 800s. This was a period when church construction was flourishing in Lucca. It was also the beginning of the age of pilgrimage and Lucca was an important stop on the main road from France to Rome, the Via Francigena. Since visiting the relics of saints was a primary purpose of pilgrimage trade in relics became an important and profitable business. Relics were also necessary to sanctify an altar; a decree of 801 declared that all altars without relics must be destroyed.

The most important relics were those which sanctified the main altar of the church. To house these it became increasingly popular to build crypts which held the relics directly beneath the main altar. The first crypts were small but with the growth of pilgrimage they grew large enough to accommodate the influx of the faithful who wanted to touch the relics. In Santa Reparata the crypt was excavated a few feet below the main floor, and the floor of the apse area was raised, creating a chamber for pilgrims to walk through. You can easily see this area: two short flights of steps, down to the crypt and up to the altar, still exist on the south (right) side as does a small portion of the raised marble floor. The pilgrims would enter from one side, step into the short corridor in the center of the crypt to touch the reliquary, and then exit up the other set of stairs. A constant flow of pilgrims could thus be accommodated.

The crypt in the church of Santa Reparata was built to host the remains of St. Pantaleone, who was martyred in 304 and became a widely popular saint in the 700s and 800s. His reliquary was unearthed in 1714, the result of deliberate search. It was known, by a document of 984, that Pantaleone had become a patron saint of the church, which meant that his relics should be found below the main altar. They were—pieces of cranium, teeth, jaw, and fingers—in a box clearly inscribed with his name and identified as the "body of the martyr." The building of the crypt can be quite closely dated to between 780-820, probably earlier in the period. Giovanni I was bishop from 780-801 and he built the crypt in San Frediano. At almost the same time the new cathedral of San Martino also availed itself of a crypt and fresh relics.

In the years surrounding the turn of the millennium Santa Reparata underwent some significant changes. The front wall was pulled back and two towers were built on the front corners. The foundation of the northerly one was uncovered during the excavations; its massiveness commands our attention. A large ambone, an early altar, was installed so the priest could address the congregation from outside the sacred altar space. It is towards the right transept. A wall was also built to separate the area for services from the greater portion of the nave. On this wall, on the side opposite the altar, are a good deal of graffiti depicting, among

20. SAN GIOVANNI

other things, the story of Santa Reparata. A new set of steps was also put in on the north side, leading up to a higher level.

The precise dating of this extensive work is difficult and it may have been spread out over many decades. Putting the ambone in the area of the congregation was part of a movement to integrate the followers into the service. The erection of the wall which drastically shortened the nave, however, must have been related to the total reconstruction of the church. The nearby Cathedral of San Martino was completely rebuilt in the years 1060-1070 with a floor elevation about 9 feet above that of the nearby Santa Reparata. Indeed, beginning in this period the entire ground level of the city was being raised, so it was only a matter of time before Santa Reparata would have to elevated, but the work seems to have been put off for almost a century.

In the area beyond the wall with graffiti there are four large basins, which are the remains of furnaces for the making of brick and for smelting metal. The wall enabled services to be continued in the church while the work of construction went on. This brick furnace was one of the earliest in the area of medieval Lucca and marks the beginning of the transition to brick construction which would flourish over the next few centuries. It must have been built because there were no existing brick furnaces available within a reasonable distance. It is certainly significant that the graffiti is found on only one side of the wall, that facing the workman's area, while the side facing the area where services were still taking place was left unblemished.

As the walls for the new church rose in tandem with the ground level outside, the steps on the north wall would have permitted the congregants to walk down to the area of the old church where services were still being held.

The **baptistery** had a troubled and frequently disrupted history. At about the time the first church was being constructed in the 390s work on an ambitious baptistery began. It was to have three (or perhaps four) apses, arranged like a clover leaf, with a circular basin in the center. This building was either never completed or fell quickly into disuse. In the 500s it was used only as a burial ground. In the later 600s to early 700s it was reconstructed by the Lombards. Their baptistery rose on pillars, the remains of which have been exposed. The impressive square mosaic font was the centerpiece of the Lombard baptistery.

The present baptistery was built in conjunction with the new church in the late 1100s. The lovely brick cupola was erected in the 1300s. It took more than a century after the first brick kilns were built in the basement of San Giovanni for the Lucchese workmen to acquire the skill to build this testament to their art.

The Present Church

The present building was constructed between the years about 1160 and 1187. The dates can be fixed quite closely. In 1153 the Pope issued a bull placing the church under his protection and construction probably began soon after. Documents reveal that during the 1160s and '70s donations to the church increased dramatically. Most revealingly, during the archaeological excavations a stash of coins was found. It had been deliberately placed in the new foundation and almost certainly marked the commencement of construction. The coins can be dated to about 1160. 1187 is inscribed in the architrave of the entrance door, dating the completion of the project. It was an impressive achievement to carry out in twenty-five or thirty years.

By the time construction began on San Giovanni, the need was urgent. The entire city was being raised. The nearby San Martino, finished almost one hundred years earlier, was already at the new elevation, and most other buildings in the city were at least nearing completion. San Giovanni was still sitting in a hole. The city was a fervor of construction but funding for this church was probably hard to come by. Ever since the building of the cathedral the canons of San Giovanni had struggled to maintain their separate domain. Documents show an ongoing dispute with San Martino about respective rights and jurisdictions which began in the 900s and picked up in the 1160s. San Giovanni was, however, fortunate enough to have the protection of the papacy, as each successive Pope issued a bull reaffirming the rights and possessions of the church and its canons.

The challenge of maintaining such a grand church over the centuries was formidable. By 1344 it was urgently in need of a new roof. In 1388 there was a devastating fire. The roof of the baptistery was a constant challenge. In 1393 it was given a lead covering. In

20. San Giovanni

1449 it needed intervention, and in 1560 it threatened collapse and had to be shored up. In the early 1600s the lead was removed to lessen the weight, but in 1762 it was put back. Although from the exterior the cupola of the baptistery is unremarkable, the splendor of the interior has been revealed in the latest restoration. It is an elegant display of the bricklayer's art as it soars above us.

In the first decades of the 1600s there were extensive modifications to the church. A new façade was installed, which closed in the aisle doors but, fortunately, the medieval center doorway was retained. A new ceiling was installed, the one we see today.

In 1692 the chapel of Sant'Ignazio was added. In 1806 the church was closed by Napoleon's sister, Elisa, who intended to convert the building to the State Archives, but it was reopened in 1828 under the Bourbons and restorations undertaken.

Interior

The interior is fairly denuded but is lovely and grand in its sparseness.

On the rear wall to the right of the main altar is the ***Cenotaph of Matilda of Canossa*** by the Lucchese **Vincenzo Consani** (1818-1887).

This is an appropriate place to recollect the life of this remarkable woman, one of the most influential rulers of her time, often called the Great Countess. She was born in 1046, possibly in Lucca. After the murder of her father and the death of her siblings she was the sole inheritor of vast landholdings in Italy and Lorraine. Befitting her position her extensive education included military training and she became one of the great warrior queens, personally leading her army numerous times against the Emperor, generally with success. She became politically intimate friends with Pope Alexander II (formerly bishop of Lucca) and was even closer with his successor, Pope Gregory VII. She is most commonly remembered for her castle at Canossa, in the Apennines north of Lucca, where the Emperor waited for three days barefoot in the snow, seeking an audience with Pope Gregory. Matilda bequeathed all of her lands to the Church, which became a source of constant dispute between the papacy and the Emperor. She died in 1115 and in the 1600s her body was interred in Saint Peter's in Rome.

Main Altar. Below the altar is the reliquary box of St. Pantaleone which was discovered in 1714. The fresco of the apse ceiling is the *Annunciation* by the Lucchese **Paolo Guidotti** (1560-1629).

On the wall of the left transept there are frescoes from the late 1300s, attributed to **Giuliano di Simone**. On the left is *Madonna Enthroned with St. Nicola and Catherine* and on the right *Sts. Ginese, Sebastiano and Barbara*.

On the west wall of the baptistery: *Mary with Child* by **Ansano Ciampanti** (1474-1535).

On the south wall are the somewhat damaged remains of a fresco of the *Baptism of Christ*, late 1300s.

In 1692 the **Chapel of St. Ignazio** was attached to the church, one of the most interesting Baroque projects in Lucca. The cupola is frescoed with the *Glory of St. Ignzaio* by **Giovanni Marracci**. The right altar hosts *St. Francis de Sales* by Marracci. On the rear altar is *St. Ignazio with the Rule* by **G. Locatelli**, and on the left *St. Luigi Gonzaga*, anon.

~

21. The Cathedral of San Martino

San Martino was founded, according to plausible tradition, in the 580s by Saint Frediano when he was bishop of Lucca. The Lombards had occupied Lucca about 570 and one of their first acts was to drive Bishop Frediano out of town and raze his cathedral, which was almost certainly where San Giovanni is now. He built a new church outside the walls on the site of the present San Frediano and then, having in notably short order made accommodations with the new rulers, returned to town to establish a new seat of authority nearby to the original.

By 700 we leave legend behind and begin to have documentary evidence in the form of parchments. (In 778 Bishop Peredeo established the Cathedral Archives, bless his soul.) The 700s were growth years for Lucca and its cathedral. Surrounding buildings were torn down and new chapels were built. By 767 it had an atrium where parishioners and pilgrims could prepare themselves for entrance to the sanctum. In 780 Bishop Giovanni transferred the relics of St. Regolo from Populonia, on the east coast of Italy, to the cathedral. As a child Giovanni had been cured by the intercession of this saint; when he became bishop he was able to demonstrate his thanks. At the time, pirates were ravaging the area around Populonia, which provided the new bishop with an excuse to rescue the relics from danger. Bishop Giovanni also instituted the devotion to Volto Santo, the unique crucifix which would become Lucca's main pilgrimage attraction and the symbol of Lucca's communities abroad.

Although nothing remains of Frediano's church, early texts provide some information about it. The apse was decorated with a mosaic of Christ enthroned. To house the relics of St. Regolo, Giovanni built a crypt, modeled on that in St. Peter's in Rome, which enabled the pilgrims to come into contact with the relics. On the floor directly above the crypt, he placed the altar to St. Martin.

The 800s were a century of decline for the churches of Lucca. Few new ones were built and the old ones fell into decay, including the cathedral, which needed extensive repairs by 820. The same decline was not experienced by the ruling secular class. By the late 800s Adalberto I and II (father and son) had raised the Dukedom of Lucca to nearly royal status, and maintained a palace which aroused the envy of the Emperor. But the churches were neglected, part of a general religious decline reflected starkly in the degeneracy of the papacy. The 900s were no better and by 1000 it must have been a rare church which did not have empty coffers, leaking roofs, and flaking frescoes.

The situation changed quickly after the turn of the millennium. By the mid-1000s the Church and the Papacy were in the midst of a dramatic reformation which would reach its climax under Gregory VII (1073-1085). Before becoming pope Gregory had orchestrated the election to the papacy of his confidant and advisor Anselmo da Baggio, the Bishop of Lucca. Anselmo took the papal name Alexander II and served from 1061 to 1073.

In 1060 Bishop Anselmo undertook the reconstruction of the Cathedral. Ten years later the task was sufficiently complete for

21. Cathedral of San Martino

the church to be consecrated. It would not be quite correct to say that the building was finished in 1070—major structural work and changes would go on for the next four centuries—but it was able to hold holy services. Almost nothing of Anselmo's building remains apparent today. It was considerably shorter, extending only to the present transepts. Whether the original building had transepts is unknown but quite likely it did not. It had an apse; perhaps three. An anonymous reference of the 14th century says it had five aisles, but there is no other evidence for this. It seems probable that a wood truss roof was in place at the time of consecration, though some construction may well have still been going on. There was a crypt, with the main altar raised above it, and there were twelve altars. There was an atrium, or portico, though not the one we see today.

During the first decades following its establishment extensive building projects associated with the Cathedral were undertaken. A hospice was built for pilgrims, sponsored by Countess Beatrice and her daughter Matilda. It was equipped with a cloister, orchards, infirmary, granary, and kitchens. The religious institution had a large lay administration, which was required to live communally (at least in theory; enforcement of the rule was the focus of reforms throughout the Middle Ages). Land records of the later 1000s and the 1100s show that the Cathedral real estate spread south to Sant'Alessandro Minore (former church #29). This complex, which housed the canons and other functionaries, operated as a well-equipped monastery.

The large piazza which was cleared in front of the church served as the commercial center of the city, where the bankers and merchants carried on their trades. And, of course, there was the worker's area: barracks, kitchens, furnaces, store yards, carpentry shops, stone yards, and the shops of the people who served the workers. There are several records of the expropriation of lands and the destruction of buildings to enable the workmen to get on with their work. There were also extensive facilities for clergy and parishioners: a cemetery, a library, living quarters for the priests, their own cloister and kitchen.

In the 1170s documentation about the Cathedral becomes generous, coinciding with a resurgence of work. In 1177 the

Fraternity of Santa Croce was established to provide governance of the religious institution. (In Lucca, Santa Croce refers to Volto Santo.) Three years later the Works (*Opera*) of the Bell Tower was established; it was time to tackle the completion of this structure. In 1181 regulations were written for dividing up the income of the church among its various departments. The Cathedral was becoming a corporation. In 1190 the Works of the Façade (*Opera dell Frontespizio*) was formed, which helps us date this emblematic part of the church.

From 1190 we can also trace the Masters of the Works and fairly reliably follow the renovations. The first Master, **Guidetto**, is the most famous, and elusive. In 1204 he signed a column on the lowest loggia of the facade. Unfortunately, variations on his name—Guido, Guidone, etc.—pop up too frequently as the name of a Master throughout northern Tuscany during these decades. At times it seems a master had to be named Guido. An example in town is in Santa Maria Corteorlandini, where there is an epigraph dated 1188 by "Guidus Magister." Was this the same Guidetto or Guido who then went on to work on the Cathedral, or a relative or countryman of his? (Most masons famously came from Como, *comacino* becoming a general term for mason.) In any case, we can safely say that Guidetto's workshop dominated the art of stone working in Lucca in the later 1100s and early 1200s. They almost certainly worked on San Michele, Santa Maria Corteorlandini, and San Giusto and provided sculptural elements of other churches.

To Guidetto we can attribute the overall design of the façade: the asymmetrical archways leading into the portico, and the three loggias above with their extravagantly carved columns. By 1210 these elements of the façade must have been largely complete, since Guidetto moved on to Prato in 1209. He was followed by one **Pretese,** who served for almost 30 years, attending to the endless finishing work and relaying the floor of the church. His successor, **Lombardo** (we know he was a descendent of Guido, but which Guido?) served from 1238-1259, a period of intense activity. He oversaw not only the sculptural completion of the atrium but the lengthening of the church. His successor, who served until 1295, undertook completion of the bell-tower which was finally completed by 1277, the date of the oldest bell.

21. Cathedral of San Martino

The century covered by these four Masters of the Works of San Martino spanned Lucca's apogee in commerce, art, and pilgrimage. This status was to be challenged severely in the following decades as Lucca fell victim to the conflict between Guelphs and Ghibellines. In 1295 this struggle broke out into violence. The area around the Cathedral was Ghibelline and much of the fighting took place in this neighborhood. In 1300 the Guelphs cemented their victory by razing their enemies' houses to the ground, including the Antelminelli's (Castruccio's family), thus bequeathing to us Piazza Antelminelli.

The decade following the Guelph victory was a time of popular enthusiasm, civic participation by the lesser classes, and urban renewal. In 1308 the government issued extensive new statutes. They also made plans for completing the Cathedral, beginning by constructing a new apse. The work apparently got off to a good start but was severely disrupted barely six years later when Pisa defeated and sacked Lucca. Work would have resumed in 1314 when Castruccio Castracani made Lucca the capital of his blossoming empire. An inscription on the apse suggests that it had reached a height of about 17 feet by 1320.

Throughout this tumultuous period (1295-1320) the Master was one **Matteo**, who must have often wished for a more peaceful post. His successor, **Bonaventura Rolenzi**, assumed the position the same year Castruccio Castracani was made Captain for Life, 1320. The new Master set immediately to work, building new storage facilities and forging two new bells. But most of Castruccio's funds must have gone to other endeavors, such as building his fortress, the Augusta, and providing for his army. When he died in 1328 the situation became too chaotic for much to be accomplished on the Cathedral. The following year rioting broke out in town, and the Emperor stepped in. The Pope placed the city under interdict, for its multitude of sins, sacred and secular. The year after that Florence laid siege to the city. Yet by 1334 Master Bonaventura felt secure enough to go looking for workers in Pisa, Florence and even at the source, Como. To entice them to Lucca the government offered work for five years, free from all obligations of citizenship (except for the *gabelle*, the universal tax, and the obligation to work on the fortress of Montecarlo, Lucca's outpost against Florence).

When Lucca's excommunication was finally lifted in 1340 by Pope Benedict XII it was on the condition that the Lucchesi erect a chapel in San Martino dedicated to Saint Benedict. The burden of such an obligation at this particular time was great. In August of 1341 Lucca came under siege by the Pisans which lasted almost a year and ended with Lucca's capitulation and nearly thirty years of subjugation. Nonetheless, the workshop managed to finish the chapel in four years and it was consecrated in 1345.

Master Bonaventura not only labored during the most difficult of times, he was also in charge of more than the Cathedral. In 1342 he was responsible for re-roofing San Giovanni, and in 1344 he was in charge of the new façade of Santa Giulia. He also directed the installation of a new cemetery on the north side of the Cathedral. The demand for plots would escalate with the Great Plague of 1348, which also brought Master Bonaventura's life to an end.

Pisa ruled Lucca from 1342 until 1369, considered the darkest period in Lucca's history, mainly because the conqueror was Pisa, with whom the conflict had the nature of a feud. Yet the initial terms of submission were remarkably generous. Pisa would assume control of the foreign affairs and defense of the city (though the Lucchesi would pay for it), but internally the citizens would continue to govern themselves.

Denied a wider area for their ambitions, the Lucchesi were driven to internal squabbling and turf fights. The process of selecting the next Master became a matter of great civic attention. Since 1274 his selection had been the domain of the Fraternity of Santa Croce (formed in 1170), a group of socially eminent laymen who had wrested control from the canons. In 1348, however, the commune itself assumed dominion over the cathedral. Sixty citizens were assigned the task of deciding how the next Master of the Works would be chosen. Obviously reluctant to accept the responsibility, they voted 59-1 to grant the authority to the Anziani, the city-fathers, who in their turn voted to turn the decision over to Nicolao Sornachi. There were exacting requirements: the new Master had to be born in and a citizen of Lucca, of legitimate birth and childless. If at any point he did acquire a child he would be terminated. He could be married, however, and if he left a widow

21. Cathedral of San Martino

she would be provided for by the State. He was forbidden to sell the treasure of Volto Santo to raise funds. There were to be two sets of books, their format finely delineated. He was to have two co-administrators from the ruling families, a Guinigi and a Boccella. Despite all these arrangements not much happened; the demands of the Pisan overlord were too great, the coffers of the city too thin.

In 1370, for the first time in over fifty years, Lucca was an independent and self-governing republic. Finishing the cathedral assumed urgency. The first task was to build a chapel giving thanks for Lucca's liberty. The larger task was to renovate and enlarge the building according to plans envisioned 130 years before. This was the most ambitious and hazardous job of all, constructing the transepts—the great crossing.

The magnitude of the task quickly became apparent. In April of 1371 the Republic contracted for 25 cartloads of marble. This raised the question of whether the bridges across the Serchio could support such loads. They could not. The problem then became how repairs would be paid for. It took a year and a half of study and squabbling before a solution was reached: the Republic would pay to rebuild two of the bridges, and charge tolls. The third bridge would be the responsibility of the Cathedral Works, but they must provide passage for free.

The overriding issue was the structural integrity of the building itself. The opinion of the experts was that the entire structure would have to be shored up and that the two columns where the nave was to meet the transept would have to be torn down and rebuilt. The new columns would be massive octagons, 4½ feet in diameter, and expensive—600 florins. The experts thought that with these provisions the work could proceed up to the vaulting, although there were no guarantees; in case something went wrong all involved were granted immunity from lawsuits. Indeed, a few years later, in 1379, it was discovered that one of the pillars was in danger of collapse, threatening the entire building, and it would have to be rebuilt. The money appropriated for the project had all been spent, so more had to be found. Money was always the overriding obstacle. Confiscation of property was a good method for coming up with funds; after liberation those who had conspired against the State had their possessions appropriated. No one, however, had more ready money than a money-lender, and the quickest way to raise cash was to enforce the laws against usury and take the ill-gotten gains from the usurers. Up to 10,000 florins was authorized to be taken from this source.

Progress was piecemeal, altars and paintings being installed while major structural work was still going on. In 1381, the altar of Sant'Antonio was rebuilt and provided with a painting by **Paolo di Lazzarino**, who, judging from the frequency of his name in the records, was perhaps the most prominent painter in Lucca in the 14th century, but who has left no certain works. In 1383 the relics of St. Regolo and other saints were distributed among new altars, at a cost of 350 florins. Yet the following year work on the pillars was still going on. Not until they were finished could work on the new arches and vaulting begin, where the masons would labor long, with very heavy materials, at very great heights.

1400 saw Paolo Guinigi come to power and a new Master of the Works installed, but there wasn't much progress until 1411 when Guinigi appointed a new Master, **Nuccio di Giovanni,** and work finally moved towards completion. Funds were raised, buildings surrounding the cathedral were torn down and by about 1416 the south (right) transept was finally completed. Nuccio died in 1419 and it fell to his successor, **Ciucchino Avvocati,** to finally complete the north transept. He got the work done, but perhaps with insufficient care; the north transept has been a source of concern and repair almost since it was finished. A century after its birth it was decaying due to excessive humidity, and the problem plagues it today. As the 21st century began the north transept had been shored up and filled with scaffolding for years, as a new generation of masons and architects tried to fix its flaws. Once again, finding the money was the main problem.

By the 1430s work on the structure of San Martino was complete. Now the transformation of the interior could be undertaken—installing new pavement, painting the ceiling (more scaffolding!), commissioning new statues, monuments, frescoes, and altars. Not the work of a decade or two. In 1452 the contract for building the wood choir stalls was awarded to **Leonardo Marti**, in a detailed contract: the work had to be done within five years,

21. Cathedral of San Martino

with two rows, the second higher, with intaglio and marquetry. Today you can examine the result in the Villa Guinigi Museum.

The most dramatic transformation began in the 1470s under the direction **Domenico Bertini** and the workshop of **Matteo Civitali**. The present pavement, the exalted sculptures concentrated in the right transept, the present shrine of Volto Santo, and the exquisite pulpit were their work, Bertini as patron and a director of the Works of Santa Croce, Civitali as artistic master. Civitali died in 1501 and Bertini five years later. He had been granted permission to commission new paintings for the altars, but with his death this was put on hold. When new altars were built in the late 1500s the solution would espouse the principles of the Catholic Reformation, identical marble altars lining the sides, with identically sized paintings arrayed pedagogically: on the right side the stages of the life of Christ, on the left, of Mary. The altar paintings were all done in the 1590s, though two have been replaced. In the mid-1500s the Chapel of the Holy Sacrament was added, and the Chapel of Liberty rebuilt soon after. The major projects of the 1600s were the Chapel of the Sanctuary and, later in the century, the frescoing of the apse vault by the collaborators Coli and Gherardi.

The building could at last be considered finished and since that time the charge of the Office of Works has been to maintain the great structure. In the first decade of the 21st century the guardians returned to their chores with vigor, restoring the art and repairing the structure, allowing a new generation to appreciate its wonders.

Exterior

Close inspection of the ornamentation on the façade bears delightful surprises. The overall style is very similar to San Michele—the rounded cornices, the inlaid frieze, the inventive columns—though San Michele is even more relentlessly inventive and extravagant.

The Façade, looking at it from the top down, left to right:

Top loggia of six arches. The green and white inlay is entirely of hunting scenes. On each end are hunters; between them are lions, an antelope, a falconer on horseback, fighting animals, mythical beasts. The columns below have knotted pairs at the ends; between them are plain and decorated columns surmounted by elaborate capitals of beasts and heads.

Middle loggia. The inlay is of more hunting scenes with endless variation. There are a few stunning columns, including a sculptural extravaganza of interlocking fighting beasts, and a graceful spiral.

Bottom loggia. Here the inlay is primarily geometric and floral designs in roundels, with a few more hunting scenes. The columns are a wonder of inventiveness: mermaids, a graceful spiral, intertwined serpents, another supported by a squatting, heavy laden Hercules. On the right end there is long haired herald with a unique cap, holding a scroll which reads *"Mill CCIIII Condidit electi ta pulchras dextra Guidecti."* This is the signature of Master Guidetto, in 1204.

The cornice below, with hunting scenes and fighting beasts interspersed among the usual floral design, deserves to be at eye level. The corbels of the row supporting the St. Martin statue are themselves sculptural delights; notice the man and bear embracing under the statue. The statue is a reproduction; the original is now inside the church.

The Portico

The columns in the front were sculpted in the mid-1100s. Though worn and slightly defaced, they bear close attention.

The engaged column on the second pillar shows, on the bottom, Adam and Eve separated by the tree of good and evil. Above this is the Tree of Jesse, which recounts the lineage of Jesus; the names of several of his ancestors are written on scrolls. The tree rises up to Mary and above her is Christ in a mandorla. The tree of Jesse was a popular subject throughout western Europe at this time.

Tree of Jesse

21. CATHEDRAL OF SAN MARTINO

The earliest known representation is about 1080 in an illuminated book from Prague. A famous stained glass treatment in Chartres Cathedral is dated almost the same time as this column in Lucca. The smaller recessed columns to its sides are masterpieces of intricacy, enlivened by liberal use of drill holes.

The pillar to the right has columns lavish with floral designs and interesting vignettes: pairings of animals, a knight, a mermaid, centaur, gryphon, antelope. Considering the many centuries this work has been exposed to the elements it is remarkably readable, and the skill of its sculptors evident. The rear of the capital is very well preserved, skillful and charming, though the iconography is obscure.

The **Labyrinth** dates to the 1100s. The inscription reads "Here is the labyrinth built by Daedalus of Crete, from which no one who entered could escape, except Theseus who was helped by the thread of Ariadne." Labyrinths were common in medieval cathedrals, though few remain. Daedalus, famous for his ingenuity, served almost as the patron saint of medieval masons.

Inner Face, left to right:

In the first blind arcade is an epigraph, a transcription of the original of 1070:

> *"The resplendent work of this great temple was begun under Pope Alexander II, for his own use and that of the bishop. He built the surrounding buildings where the temporal powers made hospitals. He sanctified them and protected them under pain of eternal excommunication. The foundation was laid in 1060 and the temple was brought to completion and consecrated 10 years later."*

Left doorway. In the tympanum above, the **Deposition from the Cross.** On the lintel below, the **Annunciation, Nativity and Adoration of the Magi,** fairly decayed. These works are generally attributed to **Nicola Pisano**.

Arcade between the doorways. The upper panels are two

scenes from the life of St. Martin. The inscriptions below identify the scenes: **Martin raises a monk from the dead** and **Martin is proclaimed bishop by his monks**. In the panel below are six **Labours of the Months** (beginning from the left, December—July). Above the columns separating the months are the appropriate signs of the zodiac.

February

Below is another epigraph, dated 1111:

> "This is the oath sworn by all money changers and dealers in spices of this court, in the time of Bishop Rangiero, so that all men can exchange, sell, and buy with confidence. All changers and dealers will commit no theft, nor trick, nor falsification within the court of St. Martin nor in those houses in which men are given hospitality. Those who wish to dwell here as dealers in exchange or spices take this oath. Moreover, there also are officials who always guard this court and who see to it that any wrong that may have been done be amended. In the year of the Lord 1111. Let everyone coming peruse this inscription, and place trust in it, and fear nothing for himself."

Center door. In the tympanum, **Eternal Father in mandorla held by angels**. On the lintel, **Mary with the twelve apostles**.

In the next arcade, above, **Fire arises from the head of Martin as he gives mass** and **Martin casts out a demon**. Below, the following six labours of the months.

Right door. In the tympanum, **Martyrdom of St. Regolo** (beheaded); on the lintel, **St. Regolo teaches the true religion to the Arians**. In his hand he holds a scroll declaring the equality of Father, Son and Holy Ghost. The Arians to his right, portrayed as barbarians, hold a scroll declaring that the Son of God was divine in his origins. (The Arians denied the equality of  the Father and the Son; the Council of Nicaea was held in 325 to

21. Cathedral of San Martino

resolve the dispute.)

Continuing around the building, along the transepts and apse there are many sculptural delights. There are some quite remarkable visages separating the arches, but they are so high you would benefit from binoculars. Much of this exterior finishing was carried out in the 1300s, and employed some of the best artists available. Among the artists who have been suggested are Antonio Pardini, Domenico di Fatino, Jacopo della Quercia, his father Piero d'Angelo da Siena, and his friend and collaborator Francesco di Valdambrino.

Interior

Length: 276'. Width: 90'. Transept: 143'. Height: 90.5'

1. St. Martin. This equestrian statue of St. Martin giving his cloak to a pauper is one of the earliest examples of Tuscan sculpture. It dates almost certainly about 1200, from the workshop of Guidetto, although dates as late as 1300 have been suggested.

The following two large stone plaques date to the early 900s. They were rescued from the funerary monuments of the Count and Countess of Tuscany when the earlier Cathedral was torn down in 1060.

2. Plaque. (*Hoc igitur teguitur tumulo…*)

> "In this tomb is buried the Contessa Berta, kind and pious, of illustrious lineage. She was the wife of Adalberto, duke of Italy and the crown of her line. Descended from the King of France, Charles the pious was her ancestor. Of lovely countenance, but more lovely in her character. She was the daughter of Lotario, and her merits were even more splendid than his. She was fortunate in her life, with no adversary prevailing over her. With sage counsel she guided many governments, and the grace of God was always with her. People came from many parts for her wise and sweet conversation. For unfortunate exiles she was the kindest mother and she

CHURCHES

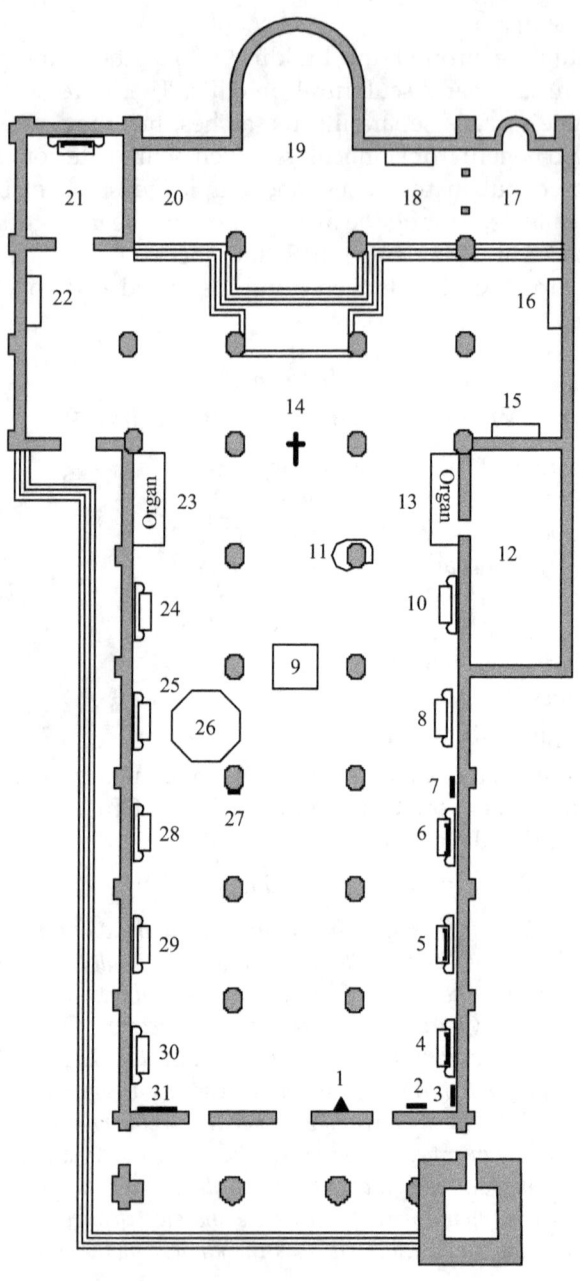

192

21. Cathedral of San Martino

always gave aid to pilgrims. A wise pillar of strength, she was virtuous and great, the light of her homeland. Alas, on the 8th of March she left this life, and lives in peace with the Lord. She was mourned in the East and in the West. All of Europe bemoans their loss; all France is in tears, as is Corsica, Sardinia, Greece, and Italy. Let all who read this pray for her eternal salvation, and so it shall be. Amen. In the year of our Lord 925.

3. Plaque. (*Hic populi leges...*) From the tomb of Adalberto II.

"Here lies the ruler of the people, buried under heavy stone. Here lies its leader and its peace, the succor of the country. Here lies the army and the defense. Their sorrow and their tears are here collected. Herein is sight for the blind, pity for the widows, feet for the lame, clothing for the naked, consolation for the poor; our Adalberto, pious and good Duke, terror of foreign peoples, bringing the greatest glory to his own soldiers. The ends of the earth [ultima Tule] know of his valor. Words cannot express his goodness. On the 17th of August he was here entombed, in the saddest of funerals. Whoever reads this, ask God for mercy on his soul, and help him with their prayers."

Berta and Adalberto were indeed illustrious personages, if not quite the pillars of virtue portrayed in their elegies. Adalberto's father, Adalberto I, was sufficiently powerful to raise an army of 4,000 and, with the Duke of Spoleto, to capture Rome, sack the city, and take the Pope prisoner, in 878. From 884 to 915 Adalberto II was Duke as well as Count of Lucca and Marquis of Tuscany, and was known as Adalberto the Rich. His sumptuous palace in Lucca aroused the envy of King Louis III who thought it more appropriate for the king himself than for one of his vassals. Berta is generally seen as the truly ambitious partner. She was the illegitimate daughter of Lothair, King of Lorraine. When her father tried to divorce his wife and marry Berta's mother it precipitated the conflict with the Pope which would eventually grow into the division of Guelphs and Ghibellines. Pope Nicholas I (the last Pope to be called Great) refused to legitimize the divorce, establishing the principle that only Christian marriage was valid. For the first time the Pope sat in judgment of a king and threatened him with excommunication. Berta's mother was excommunicated and summoned to Rome, but the death of Nicholas rendered the problem moot. Berta married the Count of Vienna, with whom she had two sons. When he died in 890 she married Adalberto, producing two more sons and two daughters. When this husband died in 915 the King of Italy arrested her and her son Guido, though they were later released and returned to rule Lucca, the mother being the force behind the throne. She died before seeing her son by her first marriage, Ugo di Provenza, become King of Italy.

4. (Altar) *Nativity of Christ*, 1594, by **Domenico Cresti,** called **Passignano** (after his birthplace). Cresti (1559-1638) was a student and then collaborator of Zuccari (who did the following painting). Together they completed the frescoes in the Duomo in Florence, begun by Vasari. They then went to work in the Vatican but were soon expelled from Rome amidst a scandal, and relocated in Venice in 1581, Cresti staying until 1588. He returned to Florence to do the decorations for the marriage of the Grand Duke, and during the 1590s became one of the city's most favored painters and a leading exponent of the Catholic Reformation. In the same decade he left several paintings in Lucca. After working for the Pope 1609–1614 he returned again to Florence where he ran one of the largest workshops in the city well into old age.

5. (Altar) *Adoration of the Magi*, 1598, by **Federico Zuccari**. Zuccari (1540-1609) was one of the most eminent painters of the period, and was instrumental in forming the Accademia di San Luca in Rome.

6. (Altar) *Last Supper*, 1594, by **Jacopo Robusti,** called **Tintoretto** (1519-1594). One of the best known paintings in Lucca. Commissioned when Tintoretto was over 70 years old, the painting was not delivered until 1594, the year of his death. His own involvement in the painting was certainly limited and it is probably mainly the work of his son, Domenico. The relatively low price paid for the commission seems to have taken this into account. Even so, the patrons of the Cathedral were dissatisfied and they considered selling it almost as soon as they received it. Notice the mother suckling a baby in the lower right.

21. Cathedral of San Martino

7. Plaque. (partly obscured by bench) *Hic iacet in vita felix...*

"Here lies the distinguished cleric Ranieri, leader and guide, first among the doctors (medici), strenuous, prudent and kind. Cleric or layman, man or woman, rich or poor, no one left without his help, given for free. His very presence often restored health. He was wealthy and munificent; fortunate in his life, more so in his death, where he will prosper even more. He died in the fourth month of 1134."

8. (Altar) *Crucifixion* by **Domenico Cresti**, 1598. Significantly restored.

9. *Judgment of Solomon,* inlaid marble pavement, by **Antonio di Ghino** of Siena, 1475-77. The design is generally attributed to Matteo Civitali, perhaps with Baldassare di Biagio. Civitali was certainly responsible for the quality of the finished work.

10. (Altar) *Resurrection* by **Michele Ridolfi**, 1825. Replaces a Resurrection by Paolo Guidotti, removed due its deterioration.

11. *Pulpit* by **Matteo Civitali**, 1494-1498. Civitali's last work, showing his complete mastery—look at the details of each band on the lower part. It was commissioned by Domencio Bertini (see #16).

12. *Sacristy*

This room was originally the Chapel of Sant'Apollinare and was attached to the exterior. It was later incorporated into the church as the sacristy. Its present appearance dates to the 1300s.

The centerpiece of the room is the *Sarcophagus of Ilaria del Carretto* by **Jacopo della Quercia**. It has been known to drive men mad with unrequitable love, John Ruskin foremost among them. No woman of flesh could seduce him after he had seen Ilaria (nor before, it must be said). As he recollected in old age:

> It is impossible to tell you the perfect sweetness of the lips & the closed eyes, nor the solemnity of the seal of death which is set upon the whole figure. The sculpture, as art, is in every way perfect—truth itself, but truth selected with inconceivable refinement of feeling. The cast of the drapery, for severe natural simplicity & perfect grace, I never saw equalled, nor the fall of the hands--you expect

every instant, or rather you seem to see every instant, the last sinking into death.

When Ruskin visited there was
no decoration nor work about it, not even enough for protection—you may stand beside it leaning on the pillow, and watching the twilight fade over the sweet, dead lips and arched eyes in their sealed close. With this I end my day and return home as the lamps begin to burn...

He never got over her, calling her "a supreme guide to me ever after."

Ilaria del Carretto was the second wife of Paolo Guinigi, who ruled Lucca as a fairly benevolent *signore* from 1400 to 1430. They were married in February 1403 in San Romano. She was 25 and he was 27. His first wife had died barely three years earlier, at the age of twelve. Ilaria gave birth to a son in 1404 but in December 1405 she died giving birth to a daughter. Della Quercia must have been given the commission for the tomb soon after; it was probably completed about 1407, shortly before the artist returned to his native Siena to sculpt the Fonte Gaia.

Also in the sacristy—

Madonna and Child with Sts. Peter, Clement, Sebastian, and Paul by **Domenico Ghirlandaio**, about 1475. The predella with scenes from the lives of the saints is generally attributed to **Bartolomeo di Giovanni** who worked with Ghirlandaio and painted other predellas for him. The lunette which has been placed above is perhaps by Vincenzo Frediani.

Saint Jerome by **Paolo Biancucci**, originally painted for the church of San Girolamo.

Crucifix by **Baccio da Montelupo**. Baccio was the architect of the church of San Paolino but he was best known for the numerous crucifixes which he did in Florence, and for his statue of St. John the Evangelist on the exterior of Orsanmichele.

St. Martin offering his cloak to a poor man by the Lucchese **Girolamo Scaglia**, about 1665. A very jaunty St. Martin in the guise of a 17th century cavalier.

Circumcision by **Jacopo Ligozzi** (1547-1627).

21. Cathedral of San Martino

13. *Organ* by **Domenico di Lorenzo**, 1481, reworked by the **Tronci** in 1792. The loft intaglio is by **Domenico di Zanobi**.

14. *Santa Giulia Cross* (See Santa Giulia, church #31.)

15. *Sarcophagus of Pietro di Noceto* by **Matteo Civitali**, 1472. The first documented work by Civitali. Noceto died in 1467 at age 70. He was an important figure at the Council of Basil (1432), secretary to Pope Niccolo V, and a good friend of Enea Silvio Piccolomini, the future Pope Pius II. For his services to Lucca he was given a house in the city in 1451 and the same year the Emperor made him a Count. Notice the lower frieze of fierce gryphons. Commissioned by his son Nicolao.

16. *Tomb of Domenico Bertini* by **Matteo Civitali**, 1478. The tomb was commissioned in 1476 by Bertini himself when he was about 60 years old; he was to live another 30 years. The form of the monument is an arcosolium, originally an arched niche in the catacombs; the style was revived in 1400s Florence. It is a work of remarkable restraint for such a wealthy and influential patron. The bust is a masterpiece, an unvarnished portrait of a man with sufficient accomplishments behind him, a firm and lean face but showing all its lines, especially around the eyes. You can see the determination in his face to "show me exactly as I am." You can also see the vitality which enabled him to live and work tirelessly another three decades. The luxurious Lucchese silk of his coat is perfectly captured in low relief. In 1524, for the construction of the chapel, the monument was disassembled and stored. Some parts were lost.

Bertini was Count Palatine, papal secretary to Sixtus IV, and many times held the highest offices of the Lucchese Republic. He was born 1410-1420, died 1506. In 1442 his father declared him an ungrateful son and disinherited him. In 1448 he was made an "original citizen" of Lucca, a great honor. He served as secretary and envoy to a succession of popes and in 1473 was governor of Orvieto. In 1477 he supported the application of Matteo and Bartolomeo Civitali for exemption from taxes to enable them to set up a printing press in Lucca. Its first product was an edition of Petrarch.

Bertini was elected an Elder many times and was intimately

involved in the affairs of the Republic, serving in diplomatic positions. As an *operaio* of Santa Croce he was very active as a patron of the Cathedral. He commissioned numerous works of Civitali: in 1474 the new altar of the Sacrament, in 1479 the sepulcher, in the '80s the balustrade of the choir and the acquasantiere, in 1484 the tempietto of Volto Santo, in the '90s the pulpit, and in 1497 the center door. For San Michele he commissioned the Madonna at the corner and for San Romano the sepulcher of San Romano. Bertini conceived of the new altars with unitary architecture and new paintings. He probably arranged for the painting by Ghirlandaio in the sacristy. In 1504 he was granted permission to arrange for new paintings on the altars, but died before this could be accomplished.

17. *Chapel of the Most Blessed Sacrament*. Its construction was authorized in 1524 and still in progress in 1539. To 1567 date the two elegant "facades" of two levels, which separate the chapel from the Cathedral proper. Vincenzo Civitali was made architect of the Cathedral expressly for this project. The iron grates were placed in front of the altar in 1579, the ones to the side in 1612. The monochromatic decoration of the vault with the sacred virtues (Faith, Hope, and Charity) with Moses is by **Stefano Tofanelli**.

Civitali's *Angels* were commissioned by Bertini in 1473 and completed by 1480. They are perhaps the most celebrated works of Matteo Civitali, for obvious reason. Notice the lovely lamb on front of the altar—similar to those on the holy water stoops.

The ***Ciborium*** in the form of a temple on columns is by Vincenzo Civitali, 1581; the base is from the 1300s.

18. *Altar of St. Regolo* by **Matteo Civitali**, 1484. Commissioned by Nicolao da Noceto. In the sarcophagus is the body of St. Regolo, which was moved to Lucca in 780 by Bishop Giovanni. (l-r), John the Baptist, San Regolo, St. Sebastian. Below each statue is a relief depicting the martydom of the saint.

19. Main altar and apse.

Main altar in stone and bronze is by **Giovanni Vambré**, 1763.

On the altar is a five part polyptych. Above it is the painted cross of Santa Giulia.

Stained glass is by **Pandolfo di Ugolino**, Pisan, 1485.

Vault of apse: *Trinity* by **Coli and Gherardi**, 1681.

21. CATHEDRAL OF SAN MARTINO

20. *Chapel of Liberty.*
In 1369 the Republic of Lucca erected an altar here in thanks for gaining its freedom from Pisa. The present altar is the work of **Giandomenica Bologna, called Giambologna** (1579). The bas-relief shows Lucca as it was in the 1500s. The sarcophagus in front of the altar is the tomb of bishop Nicodemo da Orbetello, dated 1434.

21. *Chapel of Sanctuary* by **Muzio Oddi** of Urbino (1569-1649). Built 1634-37 and completed in 1680 with a (now lost) painting by **Coli and Gherardi.** Interior redone in the late 1800s. On the altar: *Madonna and Child enthroned, with St. Stephen and John the Baptist,* signed and dated 1509 by **Fra Bartolomeo,** though Mariotto Albertinelli collaborated.

Berenson wrote that "to most people Fra Bartolomeo is a sort of synonym for pomposity...whereas the painter of that masterpiece of colour and light and shade, of graceful movement and charming feeling, the 'Madonna with the Baptist and St. Stephen' in the Cathedral at Lucca...is almost unknown."

22. *Guidiccioni monument,* commissioned by Bishop Alessandro II Guidiccioni in 1639 for himself and his predecessors Bartolomeo and Alessandro. Guidiccioni was responsible for the altars and the paintings on them. It is attributed to **Muzio Oddi.**

23. *Organ.* Loft intaglio by **Sante Landucci,** 1615.

24. (Altar) *Assumption of Maria* by **Stefano Tofanelli,** 1808. It replaces an *Assumption* by Pietro Sorri.

25. (Altar) *Visitation of Maria and Elizabeth* by **Jacopo Ligozzi,** 1596. Not well preserved.

26. *Volto Santo.* The Holy Face seems an odd name for a larger than life (8 ft.) crucifix but the visage is so unusual, soulful, and haunting that it is almost all you notice. Many believe that this is the true face of Christ and for centuries pilgrims came to Lucca, as they still do, to gaze upon their redeemer. Volto Santo became the symbol of Lucca, imprinted on its coins and copies erected wherever Lucchese merchant communities were established abroad.

According to legend the portrayal was begun by Nicodemus, who helped prepare the body of Christ for burial. The face was sculpted, however, by angels while Nicodemus slept. In the year 782 the crucifix arrived in a ship without crew or sails at the port of Luni, not far from Lucca. To determine the final abode of the relic it was placed in an ox cart without a driver. The oxen made their way to Lucca, where they stopped. The statue was first placed in San Frediano but was later moved to the Cathedral when it was completed in 1070. Within a reliquary chamber in the statue was found a vial of Christ's blood, which is still housed in San Frediano. The story is represented in a fresco by Amico Aspertini in that church.

According to history the facts are less certain. Based on comparative stylistic grounds, the statue appears to date from the 1100s-1200s. This has led to the hypothesis that the present work is a substitute for an earlier one which had deteriorated, though there is no real evidence for this. There are examples, in paintings dating to the 700s or earlier, of the crucifixion in which Christ is wearing a long tunic called a colobium so a date of 785 for the original work is not implausible. Similar works are found throughout Europe from the 1000s to the 1200s but whether they derive from the Lucchese work, or all derive from a common ancestor remains to be determined.

The lovely *tempietto* which houses Volto Santo was made by **Matteo Civitali** in 1484.

27. ***Manaia di Volto Santo***. On a column near the *tempietto* there is a crude axe head, above a plaque. This is the *manaia*, or executioner's axe, of Volto Santo. The inscription commemorates an event of 1334. Giovanni di Lorenzo di Arras had been condemned to death for a homicide, though he was innocent. He placed his fate in the hands of Volto Santo and was led to the execution block. When the axe came down the blade simply bent, with no harm to Giovanni. This happened three times and was considered a sign of the man's innocence. It was one of the more notable miracles attributed to the sacred image.

28. (Altar) ***Annunciation*** by **Giovanni Battista Paggi**, 1597.

29. (Altar) ***Presentation of Maria at the Temple*** by **Alessandro Allori**, called **Bronzino**, 1598. Considered a masterwork of his later life.

21. Cathedral of San Martino

30. (Altar) *Nativity of Mary* by **Giovanni Battista Paggi**, after 1597. Painted during Paggi's long sojourn in Tuscany, where he fled after killing a man in his native Genoa. There are three known sketches for the painting, one in the Louvre.

31. *Stories of Volto Santo*; *Trinity*; *Holy Conversations*; and *Lunettes of Prophets* by **Vincenzo Frediani**, frescoes, after 1470. He also did designs for stained glass in the apse.

~

San Leonardo

22. San Leonardo
St. Leonard

San Leonardo was built at the end of the 1100s, at the same time as the new medieval wall was being built. The old name of the church was San Leonardo *in capite borgo*, "at the top of the suburb." The *borgo*, which flourished around the north end of Via Fillungo, lay outside the Roman wall but for centuries had been an integral part of city life. The new wall encompassed much of this area, but still left a good many citizens outside. To accommodate them a new church was built, a stone's throw outside the new gate.

Living outside the walls meant a drastic decrease in security, and, therefore, of property values. This was a working class neighborhood of smiths and weavers, and at the end of the road (now called Via Michele Rossi) there were a mill and bakeries. San Leonardo was the only significant church serving this area in the Middle Ages (as it still is) and its parishioners were devoted, if not rich. Bequests to the church were heartfelt but modest: in 1383 a donation of cloth to embellish the crucifix and the statue of the Virgin; in 1429, in a more prosperous era, a local smith gave the goodly sum of "up to" 13 gold florins to buy a suitable set of vestments for the priest to perform Mass at the crucifix of the church. Unfortunately, neither this crucifix, nor any other part of the medieval church interior, remains, though the southerly wall still exists and is visible on the exterior.

In its early centuries the church suffered the trials of the unprotected. From the 1320s through the 1340s, the decades of Lucca's greatest tribulations, the church was closed, as one invader after another encamped outside the city gate and even in the church itself, which provided a solid fortification within bow shot of the city's northern gate, a threat so serious that for years the gate was kept closed. In 1349, in the midst of the Great Plague, the church was reconsecrated. The Pisans, who had taken Lucca in 1342, had imposed enough stability for this to be accomplished.

In 1376, a few years after Lucca regained its liberty, the *borgo* was beginning to rebound, bequests began to increase, and a thorough renovation was begun. Later work, in the 1570s, followed the dictates of the Catholic Reformation, with the result that the church lost its medieval treasures. This work coincided with the building of the Renaissance walls, which finally brought San Leonardo within the city proper.

The church was renovated again in the 1720s but under Napoleon it closed once more. In 1863 it came back to life, was enlarged and reconsecrated, and began a prolonged revival. The old *borgo* was becoming one of the more thriving parts of town, with an enlarged gate and even a steam trolley. Having some rare open space available within the walls, there were even a few new palazzi built. After the First World War the church's status was raised to a Priory with a Monsignor. A luxurious new chapel was opened and the façade of the church was redone in the uninspired classicism we see today. Only the exposed stonework on the right side remains to suggest the church's medieval origins.

Exterior

The façade, which dates only from 1920, transformed the building into the plainest church in Lucca. An engraving of one of its earlier incarnations shows a much more charming and inviting entrance, with a columned portico, which was later enclosed to enlarge the church.

The right side fortunately has been left unplastered, revealing the original wall and the renovations it has undergone. The central side door has been filled in and the remains of earlier arched windows can be seen here and there. Towards the front on this side, in the now plastered area of the former portico, is a curious relief of Saint Leonard. Although it is dated 1561 there is nothing of the Renaissance about it, appearing determinedly medieval. The saint holds the shackles which he is famous for releasing.

Saint Leonard

Supposedly a French nobleman of the 500s, St. Leonard's cult arose about the year 1000 and he became one of the most popular saints of the Middle Ages. He was the protector of women in childbirth and therefore had a wide and fervent following. Most famously, he was the patron saint of the imprisoned and enslaved,

22. SAN LEONARDO

with the miraculous power to free their chains. During the First Crusade, in 1099, the fate of prisoners of war became a European preoccupation and Leonard's cult got a boost in 1103 when the prince of Antioch was released from a Muslim prison after praying to the saint. By 1200 hundreds of churches dedicated to him had been built throughout Europe.

Interior

1. *San Vincenzo de Paoli* by **L. Luporini**, 1947. (Also reported as by **Isabella Sesti**, done in the 1930s.) An appropriate saint for the church of St. Leonard, St. Vincent de Paul (1581-1660) had himself been a prisoner, captured by pirates and enslaved in Tunisia. He spent much of his career administering to prisoners, especially those condemned to the French king's galleys. He also founded the first effective orphanage, and he is here depicted with one of his foundlings.

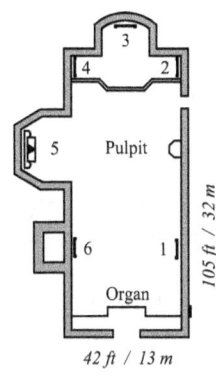
San Leonardo

2. *Madonna della Misericordia* by **Paolo Biancucci** (1596-1650). This painting came from the nearby Oratorio del Gonfalone (former church #17) built by the Confraternity of Mercy, which had been founded in San Leonardo. With her cloak the Madonna of Mercy shelters her devotees, among them, in their hooded robes, members of her brotherhood; in front, a freed slave kneels, his chains beside him.

3. High altar. *Mary in Glory with Sts. Leonard and Mark* by **Giovanni Marracci** (1637-1704). St. Leonard with shackles at his feet, and St. Mark with a lion, were the patrons of a hospice already in existence when the church was built next to it in 1188.

Marracci was a local painter who has been called, not unfairly, unexciting. Nonetheless, he found steady employment in town and has left a good number of works in its churches. He was a student of Biancucci, and therefore in the lineage of Paolini, but his dominant influence was probably Pietro di Cortona, with whom he studied in Rome.

The crucifix was done in 1920 by **Angelo Santini**.

4. *Madonna dei Miracoli* by **Gaspare Mannucci** (1575-1642). Painted for the opening of the Oratorio of the Gonfalone in 1616, this curious work recounts a miracle which happened nearby in 1588. A soldier assigned to guard the Porta dei Borghi, losing at a game of dice, threw one of the die at a nearby fresco of Virgin and Child, and in doing so found his arm immediately broken. In the painting the soldier, his right arm limp, stands in front of a painting which mirrors the fresco still found in the nearby gate. The Madonna casts a chastising look in his direction; the Christ Child looks at her while lurching away, as if frightened by the hurled die. Although born and buried in Florence, Mannucci spent much of his time in Lucca, and is well represented around town.

5. Chapel of our Lord (*Nostra Signore***).** Opened in 1917, this chapel is the focal point of daily worship in the church, with a continual flow of the faithful. Designed by **Giuseppe Lunardi**, it is a unique example of the Liberty style in Lucca's churches. The statue of the Virgin and Child was designed by **Augusto Passaglia** (1837-1918), a noted Lucchese sculptor, who also designed the left and center doors for the Duomo in Florence.

6. *St. Ann*, the mother of Mary, instructing her illustrious offspring. Early 20th century.

~

23. Combonian Fathers

This small church is also called Santissima Trinità e Sant'Anna. It was built in 1662 as a convent by a local order of Capuchins. It is today administered by the Comboni Missionaries, more commonly known in English as the Verona Fathers. The order was founded in 1867 by Blessed Antonio Daniele Comboni (1831-1881), the first Roman Catholic Bishop of Central Africa. In 1854 he was ordained a priest for the African mission and joined its Nile expedition 3 years later. In 1861 he was sent to Aden to bring ransomed slaves to Verona for education. The experience inspired him to develop a "Plan for the Regeneration of Africa." He died in Khartoum. He was Beatified in 1996.

Incorporated into a wall of the church is a stone with the date 1136, which may have come from the church of San Jacopo alla Tomba, which had been nearby (former church #33). It is also thought that the crucifix on the main altar came from the same church.

~

24. Benedettine del SS. Sacro
Benedictine Church of the Most Sacred

*T*his small chapel can be filled for services but it is rarely open for casual visits. It is attached to the monastery of St. Benedict and St. Scholastica.

~

25. San Pietro Somaldi

San Pietro Somaldi is one of Lucca's most venerable churches. In 754 the original church on the site was granted to one Auriperto, who is identified as a painter, and is therefore the first Lucchese artist whose name we know. (We have to wait 400 years for the next.) In 763 Auriperto's brother, Erimperto, had the family's ownership confirmed by Desiderio, the last of the Lombard kings (and the former Duke of Lucca). Erimperto in turn granted the church to Bishop Peredeo, reserving for his family, however, its use and its income. This was a fairly common practice, donating the family church to the bishop, thereby avoiding taxes, but maintaining the priesthood as a sinecure for the family. It was an effective way to provide for sons.

At that time the church was outside the walls although the town had already spilled beyond them. Of the forty-three churches recorded in Lucca in the 700s, seventeen were outside the walls.

San Pietro Somaldi was entirely rebuilt in the latter part of the 1100s. It is unlikely that the original church was as large as the present one; more likely it was about half as long, though any remains of the Lombard church await excavation. An interior inscription dates a major phase of construction, an extension towards the apse, to the 1190s. The lower part of the façade was complete by the mid-1200s; the date on the main door lintel is generally read as 1248. In the 1300s the roof of the nave was raised and the upper part of the façade was finished. The apse was also raised at this time and the upper part of the tower was rebuilt in brick.

For centuries the area around San Pietro Somaldi was one of several leather working districts in the city. These activities were shut down in the early 1300s, by which time the church was within the city walls. The canals which served the industry were diverted, and the neighborhood gradually became gentrified. Being an area with available workspace, it first became an artists' district and by the later 1300s it was the center of their workshops in the city; at least twenty artists are recorded as living in the neighborhood at the time. As the population expanded and recovered its wealth during the 1400s, available building space for the nouveau riche became scarce in the center of the city, and the area around San Pietro Somaldi became a choice area for new mansions, which still surround the church.

Exterior

The church is a beautifully preserved example of medieval Lucchese architecture, having suffered few structural revisions since the 1300s. The façade has blessedly maintained its integrity. The lower part, below the loggia, is a snapshot of architectural style of the early 1200s, with solid white door jambs surmounted by heavy architraves. The central door is surmounted by a relief of **Christ Consigning the Keys to St. Peter** which has been attributed to **Guido Bigarelli da Como**. The date inscribed has been variously read, often as 1203, but generally accepted to be MCCIIL,

25. SAN PIETRO SOMALDI

or 1248.

The lower stone part of the bell tower was most likely erected in the 1100s. It originally had an arched passageway at ground level which served as a public thoroughfare. The upper brick section was rebuilt in the 1300s, though restoration work was undertaken over the following centuries. A clock, not the present one, was installed in the latter 1870s.

Interior

1. (Altar) *Assumption of the Holy Virgin* by **Zacchia il Vecchio**, 1532, dated and initialed on the scroll on the left. The twelve apostles are examining the empty tomb of Mary as she is lifted up above the clouds by cherubs. There is a most curiously posed cherub below.

2. Protected by glass, this fresco fragment of the head of Christ was moved here from another location in the church. It appears to be of the same period, the 1300s, and perhaps by the same hand, as the fresco at #6. The working of the haloes is very similar.

3. This balcony could not, obviously, be used with the present ceiling. As with many churches in town the groin ceilings were added later, below the existing ceiling. There are heraldic crests on the front, a lion rampant on left, crossed swords on right.

4. (Altar) *Annunciation* by **Gaspare Mannucci** (1575-1642), signed, not dated. Though Mannucci was born and buried in Florence he was active in Lucca and has left a large number of paintings in its churches.

5. (Altar) *Blessing of St. Bona* by **Antonio Franchi**. Signed and dated 1663. Franchi (1638-1709) was called *the Lucchese*, though he spent most of his working life in Florence, rising to become the official portraitist of the Grand Duchess. His scholarly interests included philosophy and scientific inventions. He also wrote a work on the theory of painting. St. Bona

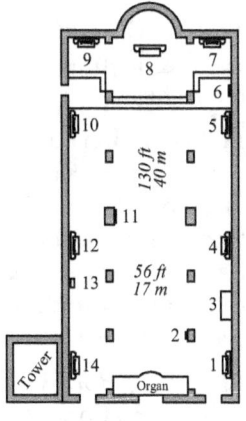

San Pietro Somaldi

was born in Pisa about 1150 and died there in 1207. She was famous for her pilgrimages; in 1962 Pope John 23rd declared her the companion of pilgrims.

6. *Holy Virgin and Child with two Saints*, lunette fresco, 1300s. This remnant of early church decoration was preserved by being hidden behind the organ for many years. St. Paul is on the left with a sword, St. Peter on the right with keys. It has recently been attributed to **Deodato Orlandi**.

7. (Altar) *St. Emidio* by **Stefano Tofanelli**, early 1800s. The saint appears to be ascending from Lucca, a view added later. There is a lovely marble tabernacle on the altar below. Tofanelli (1752-1812) was the most successful Lucchese painter of his time, though from age 16 to 50 he lived primarily in Rome. He returned to Lucca in 1801 where he was granted the positions of Senator and First Painter to Princess Elisa Bonaparte, working at her Villa Reale in Marlia and in the Palazzo Pubblico. He had earlier achieved fame for his work in the Villa Mansi in Segrominio. He is buried in San Salvatore.

8. High altar. Bare apse walls, formerly frescoed.

9. (Altar) *Holy Family with St. Anne* by **Nicolao Landucci** (1801-1868), dated 1848. The inscription at the top of the altar identifies the theme: "In honor of Anna, mother of the Blessed Virgin Mary." This may be Landucci's best painting.

10. (Altar) *Saint Peter* by **Tiberio Franchi**, 1600s. A copy of the striking painting by Guido Reni. Peter with arms outstretched beseeches heaven while a cock crows behind him.

11. Inscription on pillar. In 1190 (or 1191, or 1199) two bakers, who were rectors of the Confraternity of San Nicolao, gave 100 carts of prepared stone for the construction of the church, particularly for three of the arches. This inscription records their donation. At its end [*"Bonoditus depi(n)xit hoc."*] it specifies who was to paint them, one **Bonodito**, who thereby has become the third most ancient Lucchese artist whose name we know.

12. (Altar) *Holy Virgin and Child*, called Madonna of Mercy, by **Sebastiano Conca** (1680-1764). The most active altar in the church.

13. *Baptismal Font*, 1953. Bronze relief of shepherd and lambs.

25. San Pietro Somaldi

14. (Altar) *Sts. Antony of Egypt, Bartholomew, Francis, Vincenzo Ferrer (or Dominic), and Andrew*, tempera, dated 1497, by **Michelangelo di Pietbrini** (1484-1524). Membrini was for long known as Bernard Berenson's "Maestro del Tondo Lathrop." He probably painted this for the Lucchese merchant Antonio di Andrea di Bartolomeo who chose to have three of his namesake saints portrayed. St. Bartholomew, martyred by being flayed alive, holds the instrument of his death. The patron saint of tanners and skinners he is an appropriate saint for this church of the tanning district. St. Francis, with stigmata, is to his right and St. Antony of Egypt is in the center. St. Vincent Ferrer (or St. Dominic) is in the white habit and black cloak of the Order. He is the only one with shoes. St. Andrew holds a Roman cross, as was common in ancient pictures. He is more generally shown holding an X-shaped or Saint Andrew's cross.

Saint Anthony the Abbot supposedly lived from 251 to 356, and is therefore appropriately shown as an old man. At age 20 he abandoned the world to live in the desert as a hermit. He attracted followers and is honored as the founder of monasticism, so he is justifiably in the center of Membrini's painting. In 1095, just in time for the First Crusade, the Hospital Brothers of St. Anthony, aka the Antonites, was formed, and spread throughout Europe. Their symbol, the Tau (T) is reflected in the shape of Anthony's cane. One of the rights widely granted to the Antonites was to let their pigs roam freely in town, with small bells around their necks. In the painting one of these privileged creatures pokes out from St. Anthony's robes. In English the word tantony persists as the smallest pig of the litter or the smallest bell of the peal.

Organ. A small gem, by **Domenico Cacioli** (1687) with additions of 1864 and 1900 by **Filippo Tronci**. Tronci was a world famous master, making organs in India, Egypt, Buenos Aires, and Barcelona. When Puccini was young he played this instrument many times. He later carved his name on it as a tribute to Tronci and as a memento of his youthful employment.

In storage: *St. Buona* by **Giovanni Marracci**.

~

26. Santi Simone e Giuda
Sts. Simon and Jude

A little classic of medieval Lucchese architecture. The first record of the church is in 839, when it was built right up against the Roman wall, remains of which have been found in the basement of the adjoining building. New town walls were built in the 1200s, allowing an expansion of the church, which took the form of an entire reconstruction. There is a commemorative plaque on the front, dated 1258, somewhat obscure, referring to an opening in the city walls at that time. The church was completed soon after 1269 when a bequest was made to finish the façade.

It was a small church, but significant, and would become more so as the Guinigi family rose to preeminence and used it as a chapel for their family and supporters. In the mid-1300s the church received many bequests, from simple to extravagant. In 1347, during the Pisan occupation, the Bishop consecrated three new altars for the church with a wealth of relics. For the Altar of the Mother of Mary he deposited locks of Ann's hair and garments, parts of the shrouds of Christ and of Saint Eusebio, as well as the rock on which Archangel Gabriel delivered the "Ave Maria." For the altar of Saints Philip and James the Less there were relics of each Apostle and also of Saints Grisante and Daria (a peculiar collection which fixed the provenance of the painting by Spinello Aretino mentioned below). For the altar of Saints Sebastian and Fabian there were relics not only of those two saints, but of the 11,000 Virgins who were murdered in Cologne by Attila's Huns, and for good measure, the cloak of St. John the Evangelist.

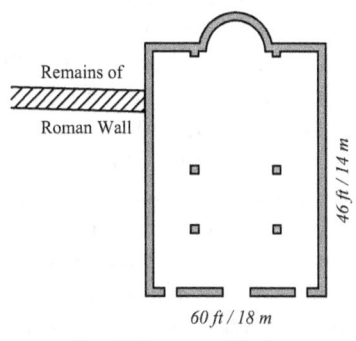

Santi Simone e Giuda

Saints Simon and Jude, two of the twelve apostles, were usually invoked together during the Middle Ages. Many churches were dedicated to them jointly and they share the same feast day. In *The Golden Legend*, which was considered authoritative in the Middle Ages, they are brothers of James the Less (whose relics are in the church) and were martyred together in Persia by pagan Magi. Jude, author of the New Testament epistle, has in modern times become the saint of lost causes: having the same name as Judas Iscariot, he is invoked only when the other saints have failed.

In May of 1348 Francesco Guinigi died and made generous bequests to the city, including 500 florins to pay for 3,000 masses for souls in purgatory. The Great Death was about to sweep into town, producing ample need for the bequest. He also sent, on his behalf, one pilgrim to Rome and one to St. James in western Spain, and he guaranteed fifteen florins to any Lucchese who made a similar pilgrimage. Guinigi thus reaped spiritual benefits for himself and his fellow citizens, and political ones for his family. In such ways are dynasties made. To the church of Simone e Giuda he left sufficient funds for a painting of the Blessed Virgin with Saints. A few years later, in 1354, the church had acquired enough possessions to require a new sacristy.

In the year of Lucca's liberation from Pisa, 1369, a citizen of the neighborhood died, and asked to be buried in the church in front an altar, for which a painting should be commissioned. It was to be a major work, and six years passed before the commission was granted to **Paolouccio di Lazzarino**, considered the most prominent Lucchese painter of the 1300s. It was to be large, to be done with fine gold and true colors, under the direction of Francesco Guinigi. The pay was 65 florins but Guinigi was so satisfied with the extravagant work that he added a bonus. The tabernacle frame was done by another master, **Nicoletto di Cionella**. The work is lost.

When Paolo Guinigi became Signore of Lucca in 1400 the church became the most elite chapel in town, and the beneficiary of particular munificence. But fortunes fade and works of art disappear. In the 1600s the church underwent interior renovations, received a new vaulted ceiling and a modernization of its artworks. Today it is just a vacant little church.

26. Santi Simone e Giuda

Among the works which the church once housed are:

1. A delicate painted wood statue of *St. Ansano* (ca. 1410-1420) which used to be attributed to the sculptor Valdambrino, but has now been elevated to his more eminent friend and collaborator, **Jacopo della Quercia**. Della Quercia was favored by Paolo Guinigi, who chose him to create the tomb of his young wife, Ilaria. Valdambrino also sculpted a St. Ansano, which can be seen in San Paolino. Della Quercia's work, stripped of its paint, is today in the Villa Guinigi Museum, a masterwork of carving, but a shade of its former artistic self.

2. A lovely triptych of an *Enthroned Madonna flanked by Sts. Philip, Grisante, Daria and James the Less* by **Spinello Aretino**, ca. 1380. This work follows by only a few years the work of Lazzarino, ample evidence that in the years after freedom from Pisa the church was becoming a favorite of the future Lord of Lucca. Aretino's work is now dispersed; the sides are in Parma and the center in Mexico City, though they were reunited in Lucca for an exhibition in 1998.

3. A painting of *Sts. Simon and Jude* by **Domenico Brugieri** (1678-1744), a native of Lucca who had a successful career not only in his birthplace but also in Rome.

4. A 1500s fresco of *Sts. Peter and Paul*, moved here from the Oratorio della Fratta when it was closed.

~

27. Oratorio degli Angeli Custodi
Oratory of the Guardian Angels

Just a few steps from the apse of SS. Simone e Giuda is the Oratorio of the Guardian Angels. From the street there is nothing to identify it or to suggest the ornate chapel which lies within. It was built in 1638, designed by the military architect **Vincenzo Paoli**, who at the time was working on the new walls, which were almost finished. The oratorio is a lovely, well preserved product of the Counter Reformation, which in the 1600s was transforming all the churches in Catholic Christendom. It is now the domain of the Archbishopric of Lucca, which also occupies the palazzo on the left. It is open irregularly, but visits can be arranged.

That each soul has its own protecting angel was a folk belief until the early 1100s, when Honorius of Autun clearly formulated the doctrine. In the 300s St. Ambrose had thought the righteous were denied such guardianship, to more glorify their struggle. St. Jerome thought that sin drove them away. Finally Honorius established to general satisfaction that at the moment the soul enters the body its own guardian angel enters with it. In the 1200s Thomas Aquinas thought that only lower angels served this purpose, while Duns Scotus believed that any angel might. Originally encompassed in the cult of Archangel Michael, the reverence for the Guardian Angels spread from Portugal in the 1500s and by the 1600s was popular in Italy. In 1670 the Pope gave the Guardian Angels an official feast day.

The interior of the oratorio is elaborately decorated, with eight side altars, each with a painting on the theme of angels. Until recently these were all attributed to the local artist Matteo Boselli, which led to an unduly elevated status for this mundane artist. The canvases actually present a broad panoply of the artists working in Lucca at the time, of varying talent. (Some of these attributions are still debated.)

Interior

1. *Story of Hagar* or *Hagar Saved in the Desert by Angels* by **Girolamo Scaglia**.

2. *Angels Transporting Volto Santo* by **Matteo Boselli**. (There appears to be a view of Lucca in background.)

3. *Jacob's Ladder* or *Jacob's Dream* by **Girolamo Scaglia**.

4. *Allegory of the Faith* by **Antonio Franchi**.

5. *Christ Served by Angels* by **Antonio Franchi**.

6. *Archangel Michael* by **Pier Filippo Mannucci**, 1661.

7. *Holy Family* by **Filippo Dinelli**, 1691.

8. *San Girolamo helped by angels*, anon.

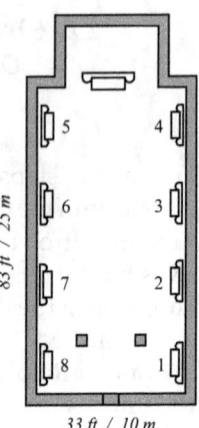

Angeli Custodi

The frescoes in the presbytery are attributed to **Giovan Domenico Lombardi**.

~

28. San Nicolao
St. Nicholas

San Nicolao was founded in 1332, during Lucca's darkest period. Castruccio Castracani had died four years earlier, bringing Lucca's territorial ambitions to a swift end. Upon his death the Holy Roman Emperor quickly came to town and quickly left, leaving behind a vicar to rule his new protectorate.

1329 was a terrible year. In March the Poggio family, recently returned from exile for treason, were battling in the streets with the Castracani. In the ensuing fighting a fire broke out in the Poggio neighborhood (where the Puccini museum is today) and it quickly spread through the center of town, around San Michele and the City Hall, where it destroyed most of the civic records. (The sack in 1314 by the Pisans had already destroyed many ancient documents.) The Emperor returned briefly to quell the riots but as soon as he departed the German troops he left behind rebelled and took control of the city. They offered to sell the town to Florence, but the deal fell through, so they began to plunder the countryside. In the town of Camaiore they massacred 400 of its citizens.

In June the soldiers offered Lucca to the Pisans, but this deal also fell apart. They finally found five Genoese noblemen to take it off their hands for 60,000 florins. Then, just after Christmas, Castruccio's sons attempted another coup. They managed to overrun the town but failed to take the citadel of the Augusta. Its troops were able to drive them out, back into exile.

1330 started out better but ended up worse. Breaking under the taxes needed to pay the local mercenaries, the skilled craftsmen began to flee town, primarily to Pisa. By July there were only six goldsmith shops in the city; a year earlier there had been nineteen. The flight of silk workers was so severe that in September a fine was levied on any who left, and amnesty granted for those who returned. Then members of the Quartigiano family plotted to betray Lucca to Florence; their plot was discovered and its leaders were beheaded. In October Florence made its move. It invaded Lucchese territory and laid siege to the city. Repaying the insult by Castruccio a decade earlier, they ran three victory races around the city: one by the cavalry, one by the infantry, and one by the camp prostitutes. Two hundred of the German knights in Lucca promptly went over to the Florentines. Everyone left in town manned the walls, except the bakers. By the end of the year Lucca was short of food, short of men, and out of money. After four and a half months, King John of Bohemia lifted the Guelph siege and in March 1331 he entered Lucca as Lord. Order was established, but Lucca was still suffering under a Papal interdict, expelled from the Church and denied its rites—no baptisms, marriages, or burials were to be blessed.

In 1333 the only bright spot for Lucca was that Florence suffered the worst floods in its history. The Castracani staged another coup and again the Empire had to liberate the city. Again it was expensive. The defense of the city at this time consisted of 260 knights and 900 footmen, all mercenaries. King John did allow the Guelph exiles to return and try to reclaim their property. All males who wished to remain in the city had to swear allegiance to the Emperor. We still, fortunately, have this list of names. Among them were the Busdraghi, who in the midst of all the troubles, were about to see their fortunes increase.

Fairly obscure until this time, the Busdraghi were somehow to thrive during the years of trial and become one of the leading merchant houses in Lucca, with offices in London and other cities. They owned land just inside the eastern wall, which was still fairly open space, and in 1332 the three brothers who headed the family donated the land and built the church of San Nicolao.

In two documents of 1334 they declared their intentions for restoring this section of town. In the first they recount how formerly there had been a hospice which had been established for "eleven abandoned and destitute virgins, with cloister and monastery." Being near the walls these "had been destroyed during the war and there was now no monastery, no hospice, no church." The dispersed virgins had been taken in by the Busdraghi family, and now that order was restored they intended to build a new Augustinian monastery, hospice and church, to be called Santa Maria della Croce. At the same time they made bequests for the expansion of San Nicolao by building a hospice "to receive the poor, the infirm, and virtuous clerics."

28. San Nicolao

These bequests, made on April 2, 1334, envisioned improving conditions under the protection of King John, but they were overly optimistic. On April 30 the Imperial Vicar announced that an attack by Florence was imminent. He went to Montecarlo to see to the defenses, leaving the town fathers to come up with the funds. Forced loans were extracted from the leading merchants, among them, no doubt, the Busdraghi who, perhaps anticipating such an event, had divested themselves of some of their land and money beforehand.

Although born in times of trouble the church managed to survive and even thrive, fitfully, along with the fortunes of the Busdraghi. Over the next decade the family became one of the political and commercial leaders of Lucca. By 1338 they were doing well enough to loan the King of England almost 2,000 pounds sterling, but they had trouble collecting the debt and their fortunes went into a long slow decline. Their church also faded from view, though we know that in 1390 there was a fire in the convent because the next year the Bishop raised money for its reconstruction.

In the 1500s the Busdraghi recovered their fortunes and prestige. Their church was rebuilt in the early 1600s and entered a period of prosperity. In the early 1700s the interior was refurbished and became the repository of works by some of the leading artists in Lucca. San Nicolao continued its mission of caring for and educating young ladies until the Napoleonic suppression in 1811. The church and school later reopened but by the 1880s they were taken over by the civic authorities. The former convent and cloister are still utilized as a school. The church itself is defunct and denuded. All that remains inside is the grand main altar, by Domenico Martinelli, and the vibrant frescoes by Lombardi.

Domenico Martinelli, born in Lucca in 1650, was an architect, engineer and painter. Ordained a priest at age 23, he soon had a dispute with Cathedral authorities and he left town for a secular career in Rome. He won first prize in architecture at the Accademia di San Luca and was elected to its membership when he was 33. His fame was made outside of Italy, in Vienna, Warsaw, Prague, Prussia, and Holland, building palazzi and villas. At age 49 he returned briefly to Rome to accept Honors from the *Accademia*, but a few years later had sufficiently offended its directors to get himself expelled, though they later relented.

In 1715, aged 65 and ill, he returned to Lucca. He was buried in San Paolino three years later.

Formerly in the church, now in the Villa Guinigi Museum:

By **Giovan Domenico Lombardi** (1682-1751)

1. *Appearance of the Virgin to San Nicolao*, painted for the main altar.
2. *Adoration of the Magi.*

By **Domenico Brugieri** (1678-1744)

1. *Presentation of Maria in the Temple.*
2. *Trinity with Saints Jerome and Augustine.*

~

29. Sant'Anastasio
St. Anastasius

Sant'Anastasio is first mentioned in 844, but it was certainly founded earlier, during the great wave of Lombard church construction in the 700s. (Beginning around 820 there was a drastic falling off of church foundations and gifts.) We hear of Sant'Anastasio again in 1053 when it bore the toponym *in lischia*, the area of the beech trees, which gives some sense of the population density within the Roman walls in the early Middle Ages. By the time the present building was erected the beech trees had certainly fallen victim to the developer's axe.

The building which you see before you can, with fair certainty, be dated between 1150 and 1210. It is a rarity among Lucca's medieval churches: the product of a single architectural conception, executed by a single generation of workmen, and (as such things go) nearly perfectly preserved. You can almost see the original blueprints when you look at it. More than any other church it is the work of one head and one hand. It is a site to bemoan the loss of the architect's name, for it surely had an architect. Some *one* designed this building.

Sant'Anastasio was conceived and built at the height of

Lucca's medieval prosperity. The old nobility were losing their land, largely to the Church, and relocating in the cities, where the Church had aligned itself with the populace, the *popolo*. A new civic structure was arising, more democratic, with greater diffusion of power. There was a rapidly developing economy based on trade, creating a vibrant merchant class. Lucca was a successful city, and behaved accordingly.

The 1100s and 1200s would be driven by this assertiveness, expand on it, and develop its political implications. The new walls, a massive civic undertaking which doubled the size of the city, were being constructed at the same time as Sant'Anastasio was being built. Within the walls the city was being transformed into a brick showcase, embellished by the decorative brick which had its first showing in Sant'Anastasio.

The church stands at the cusp of Lombard and Medieval architecture in Lucca. Showing a mastery of both worlds, it takes the elements of Romanesque Lucchese design and combines them into a composite which is startling in both its originality and its obviousness. Most churches are the result of consecutive aesthetic periods. We are used to seeing the façade, sides, and apse treated as separate elements, the result of centuries of remodeling. In Sant'Anastasio the relentless extension of a single motif around the entire building catches us by surprise.

Prior to Sant'Anastasio the churches of Lucca were usually built of stone. Now brick was to become the dominant medium. Brickwork tended to fall into two categories: purely functional walling, and; decorative details, such as friezed arches on doors and windows, or rows of pendant bows below eaves. The brickwork of Sant'Anastasio, however, presents us with a very different example of the mason's art, where the actual bricklaying, accentuated by the bands of white limestone, is the ornamentation. These are not walls which were ever meant for, or would permit, plastering over, or facing with finer material. It is the excellence of the workmanship which preserved it from later revisions.

Exterior

Despite its artistic unity, construction of Sant'Anastastio proceeded in stages. Along the exposed, north, side three nearly

29. Sant'Anastasio

vertical seams can be detected, giving us four stages. Construction presumably started with the apse. It was usual to start at the apse, since the altar and crypt were the key components of a church. Once they were in place, the church could be consecrated, so it was natural that they would be built and roofed first.

The detailing on the apse provides a fairly secure stylistic guide to its date. The interwoven hanging arches below the eaves had something of a vogue in the 1160s. The arches over the two right rear windows are examples of the earliest use of decorative brick in Lucca, about 1150. The arrowhead motif over the window to the right, and the diamond rows on the apse window itself, mimic but expand on motifs which could already be achieved with unworked brick, as was done just below the rear eaves, with a row of bricks set on edge.

The section just forward of the apse (about one-third of the wall) is almost entirely original and preserves the only complete original window. The seam between the apse and this section probably represents only a new construction phase, not an extended hiatus in work. But with the next section, which includes the side door and a decapitated window, we sense a mixture of periods. The arch over the door jumps out at us as of its time, the 1150s, with a diamond frieze outlining an assertively non-concentric arch. Yet it sits atop a doorway which recalls the Lombard churches of centuries earlier—heavy jambs and off-center lintel. The combination of these diverse elements provides an asymmetry common in other churches in town but surprising in the deliberateness of Sant'Anastasio. One wonders if the doorway itself is a relic of an earlier structure. With the foremost section we feel another break in time. There seems to have been a reworking of the wall in preparation for the façade. We expect a third window, which may have been removed.

On the façade the blank white wall of the lower portion is the only part which seems out of synch with the overall conception. It suggests an inspiration from Sant'Alessandro or San Frediano. The ceramic dishes below the eaves are datable to about 1210 and provide a good terminus date for construction. They seem to derive from an Islamic influence.

A faded inscription to the right of the front door was probably placed there while work was in progress.

> *"Contained in this small place is the priest Enrico, venerable for his life, wisdom, piety, and skills. Erudite, he established a school for cantors. An excellent and honorable minister of this church, he died the last day of September. Now he assists the Lord in redeeming the souls of this world. In 1167, O Choir, you were saddened."*

Interior

Nothing remains of the medieval furnishings. In 1584 the interior was restored with a barrel vault, and new altars were adorned with paintings by the best artists working in Lucca at the time.

Of the works reported to have been in the church:

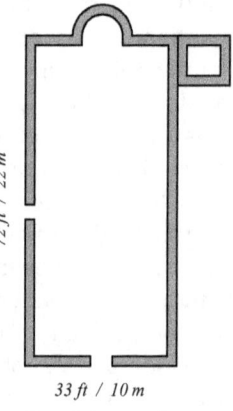

33 ft / 10 m
Sant' Anastasio

Crucifixion with Sts. Giuliano and Lorenzo by **Lorenzo Zacchia**, 1587.

Madonna and Child with four Saints (including Vincenzo and Anastasio) by **Luca di Costantino**. On the predella, ***Annunciation, Crucifixion, Resurrection***, dated 1460. At one time on the high altar.

Madonna and Child with Sts. John the Baptist and Leonardo by **A. Ardenti**, 1568.

Circumcision by **Jacopo Ligozzi**, signed and dated 1594. One of his major works. (Today in the Cathedral sacristy.)

Madonna with Sts. Rocco and Sebastian by **Matteo Boselli**.

In 2007 Sant'Anastasio was transferred to the Romanian Orthodox Church. It was repaired and refurbished so it can once again be visited. It now has a magnificent carved wood choir screen and new paintings.

~

30. Suffragio
Intercession for the Dead

The great plague of 1348 was only the first of many comings of the Black Death. In 1630 another terrible outbreak swept through Lucca. Unable to cope with the number of bodies, the citizens converted a courtyard in the center of town into a mass grave. As soon as the city began to recover it started planning a large church on the site as a memorial to the dead. The architect chosen was **Francesco Buonamici**, who had already made his fame working for the Jesuits in Malta. In 1646 the Confraternity of Suffragio, who prayed for the dead, moved into the new church from nearby Sant'Anastasio. Construction was completed in 1675 with the placement of the majestic high altar. After being closed for many years and falling into decay, Suffragio was renovated and reopened in 2004 as an auditorium for the music school which is housed in the adjoining palazzo.

The church was once embellished by works of the major artists working in Lucca, all in the style of the mature Catholic Reformation:

Giovanni Balducci, *The Doubting of St. Thomas*, 1605. The only painting not commissioned expressly for this church.

Matteo Boselli, *Crucifixion with Sts. Peter and Biagio*, 1630s.

Paolo Biancucci, *Madonna with Angels and Souls of Purgatory*.

Pietro Paolini, *Madonna and Child with Sts. Antonio da Padova and Carlo Borromeo*.

Filippo Gherardi, *Madonna with Souls in Purgatory*. This had been on the main altar.

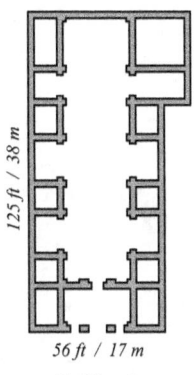

Suffragio

~

31. Santa Giulia
St. Julia

The origin of the church of Santa Giulia is lost in the mists of the Lombard period. There is a story that Desiderius (Duke of Tuscany and the last Lombard king) brought the relics of St. Giulia to Lucca. Desiderius assumed the kingship in 757 and was conquered by Charlemagne in 774. But the church may have preceded him and was only reconsecrated under his patronage. Excavations around the area of the apse have uncovered Lombard tombs and gold jewelry which have been dated to the first half of the 600s, which suggests that the original chapel may date to that time. (The finely wrought ornaments can be seen in the Villa Guinigi Museum.) The site may well have been sacred ground even earlier since a Roman fragment from the first century B.C. was found at the base of the *campanile*. It was not uncommon for a pagan temple to be converted to a Christian church.

We do know that just before the year 900 Santa Giulia was donated to the Bishop by the Allucingoli family; as were many of Lucca's churches, it was the fief of a noble Lombard family. With the fading of Lombard dominance many of these personal chapels were donated to the Bishop, often with the provision that the priest (who was one of the family) would be provided for. The Allucingoli family had a distinguished past and an eminent future. They would produce the only pope born in Lucca, Lucius III (1181-1185).

The next certain date regarding the church is 1295 when the Bishop offered 40 days indulgence to anyone who contributed to its rebuilding, calling it "ancient but now ruined and in total need of repair." The construction sequence is not easily resolved. As always, the questions are: what was added and what was only repaired? The original Lombard church was probably shorter. In 1857 a wall was uncovered in the basement, which the excavator thought marked the original façade. There is also a conspicuous seam in the exterior right wall, which strongly suggests the building of an addition onto the front. The apse and campanile are complicated, indicating staggered construction and adaptation to existing structures. Its brick work suggests the 1100s more than the late 1200s. An interesting comparison is with nearby Sant'Anastasio, the rear of which was certainly built between 1150 and 1200 and which seems to develop motifs already present in Santa Giulia, such as Sant'Anastasio's more elaborate hanging arches along the top of the apse.

The renovations initiated in 1295 would continue fitfully through Lucca's most tumultuous period. Most of the structural work was probably finished by the death of Castruccio in 1328 but then suspended during the chaos of the following years. Yet some work went on: in 1337 the bishop approved the erection of a small chapel inside the church. The Pisans took control the city in 1342, bringing tyranny but also stability and a resurgence of construction. We have the contract drawn up in 1344 for the last stage of construction, the façade. The document is quite detailed, specifying the type and color of stone to be used. The model was to be the Baptistery of San Giovanni and the similarities, especially to the north transept door of San Giovanni, are striking. The contract specified that other details were to be inspired by, and not inferior to (a tall order!) those found on Santa Maria della Rosa. The work was given to **Coluccio Collo**, "master marble mason of the city of Lucca, who lives in the neighborhood of San Pietro Somaldi," which was an artists' quarter. He promised to complete the work in eighteen months. It is quite possible that the upper part was expanded later, along with a slight raising of the roof, and that the *bifore* window, overlarge for the space, was added at this time.

The last major reconstruction was in the 1850s when the two large *bifore* windows on the right side were added. Smaller conical windows were filled in; the outline of one these is clear, and parts of two others are discernible in the seams and coloring of the

31. Santa Giulia

brick. The new windows were nicely done but are stylistically out of synch with the rest of the church.

Interior

The construction of the façade was accompanied by a general refurbishing of the interior. In 1346 **Paolo di Lazzarino** was paid for a painting on the high altar, the first record we have of an independent major work by this artist, who was the preeminent, or at least best recorded, Lucchese painter of the mid-1300s. This work is lost, as are all his others.

By far the most important piece in the medieval church was the tempera on panel *Crucifix*, dated 1200-1220, which now hangs over the high altar in the Cathedral, but which was painted for Santa Giulia. The Bishop's 1295 plea for donations refers to it as one of the reasons for saving the church, and attached a recounting of its famous miracle.

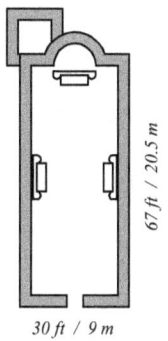

Santa Giulia

In the year 1230 a gambler, losing at dice and cursing his luck, picked up a stone and threw it at the holy image of the crucified Christ in Santa Giulia. He hit it on the eye, and the crucifix immediately began to bleed from the spot, the blood flowing down a marble column into a font of holy water. "That drop of blood is still today on the column, impressed into the marble, and it is impossible to wash it off. More than that, that same drop of blood which at first seemed so small, because of its divine power grew so that the bottom of the column in a short time was completely covered in blood."

Befitting such an apparition, the crucifix soon began performing additional miracles.

From an art history point of view the most important fact about the cross is that it is not from the Berlinghieri workshop. The Berlinghieri, because of available records, dominate our view of the 1200s Lucchese art world. The Santa Giulia Crucifix is one of our most valuable additions to this small body of works and indicates the presence of other workshops in town at the time.

The interior of the church has been renovated a number of

times. There were originally four side altars, which were reduced to two in the later 1500s. On the left altar was a painting of the Nativity, on the right, of St. Nicholas. The artists are unknown. In 1647 a Bernardini funded a new high altar as the site for the famous crucifix.

The church no longer holds services, but is occasionally open for civic functions.

~

32. San Benedetto in Gottella

A little gem of a Lucchese church, San Benedetto had existed for an unknown period of time when we first hear of it in 900. Given its small size and central location it was probably a Lombard family chapel before being donated to the Bishop, as was Santa Giulia in the same year of 900. The church was rebuilt, along with so many others, between roughly 1150 and 1200.

In 1200 it did not open onto a large piazza as it does today, but was confined to a narrow street. Just outside the front door were the tower and houses of the family of Castruccio Castracani, the Antelminelli. When Castruccio was Lord of Lucca in the early 1300s he took an interest in the little church and contributed to renovations, though what they were we don't know. The church was certainly finished by that time and it shows few signs of later interventions.

By the 1200s the church bore the toponym *in Gottella*, denoting it was the area where water basins were made, an insight into the separation of labor in the middle ages. (It has also been suggested that it derives from a family name, Gottella.)

Over the years the church has been the site of several of the confraternities which proliferated in town. In the 1600s it was the home of the Society of Grocers, an ancient association in existence since at least the early 1300s. Today the plaque on the front identifies it as the home of the *Confraternita*

30 ft / 9 m
San Benedetto

44 ft / 13 m

de' Legnaioli di Lucca—the woodworkers association, which was founded in 1608.

Exterior

The building seems to be a unitary piece, built over a limited time, but questions remain.

The façade shares a common basic motif with San Giusto and San Pietro Somaldi, a first order of gray stone surmounted by tightly spaced white and gray bands. In San Benedetto the single door is relatively broad with a well executed arch of white and green and a fresco of uncertain age. The arch is almost a semicircle, very subtly non-concentric.

The upper part of the facade has obviously suffered interventions. The two original windows were filled in, and a simple rectangular one was inserted just above the doorway.

The side is not so clear cut. The two large, plain windows are relatively recent and utilitarian, perhaps put in when the two on

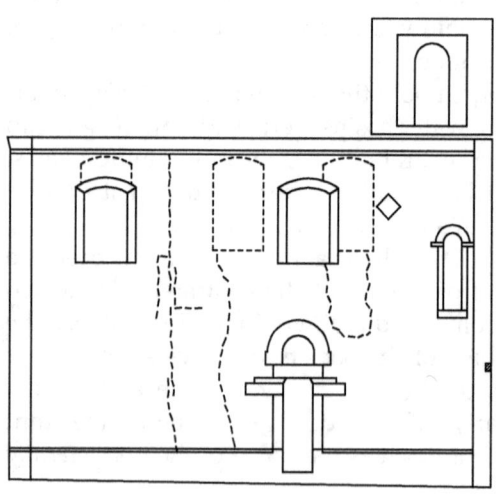
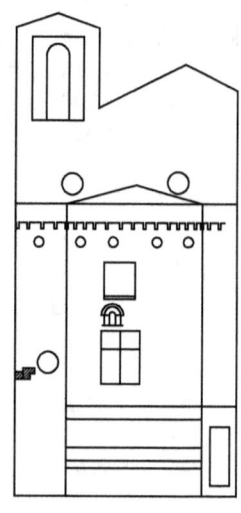

32. San Benedetto

the façade were closed. There were three large earlier windows, evidenced by seams. The only original window is curiously close to the rear. It doesn't seem to have any companions, though at two places it appears that they were at least started.

The side door is walled up. It was executed with careful symmetry of jambs, lintel, and arch, which was often not the case in earlier churches, where the pieces at hand were often made to serve. The considerable step up to the sill indicates the street level has not changed much at this point since the 1200s. The significant vertical seam towards the front suggests a hiatus in construction, but it may simply be a crack, since it spreads up from a seam in the foundation stones.

The original system for letting in light is curious. Besides the one side window of which we can be sure, there is a lozenge shaped opening near it; it is tempting to think this was repeated along the side before being obliterated by later windows. A similar system was employed in the apse side.

The apse end has three *oculi*, circular openings, as small windows, two above and one to the side. But the apse itself is the most curious feature, just a shallow off-center bump. The consensus is that it is not as early as the front part of the church, yet it is hard to believe it was not originally planned— the foundation is too consistent. The adjoining building which intrudes onto this face was obviously already in existence when the apse was built. It seems likely that when the total renovation of the late 1100s was undertaken the church was lengthened and the workers had to accommodate to existing conditions. The  decorative brick work also seems early, relying not on molded or carved decorations but on ordinary bricks arranged in a decorative fashion, as in the upper band where they are angled and recessed. Along the curve of the apse a herringbone laying of the bricks echoes the Lombard technique of "fish bone" stone work. A limit on the dating is provided by the row of shallow disks running below the crown, a technique fairly well known in the Pisa-Lucca area between about 1200—1250. A similar device is found in the upper façade of Sant'Anastasio.

The rectangular windows in the apse are late intrusions; of the original window only the upper part remains, of the same style as the one on the side. Next to the lower oculi the masons inserted, as they often did, fragments of early Lombard decoration, presumably remnants from the Lombard church. The small bell tower is a later addition.

Interior

Over the years the interior has been renovated and rearranged many times with changes in fashion and ownership. Of the medieval works the only one known is a painting of San Sebastian done by the Pistoian **Cecco di Francesco** in 1423. In the 1600s San Benedetto was the home of the Society of Saint Onofrio. One of the altars was rededicated to him and provided with a painting of the saint, now lost. The main altar retains the painting done in the 1590s by **Benedetto Brandimarte** of *Madonna and Child with Sts. Benedetto and Margherita*. It had been commissioned by the Society of Grocers, when they used the church as their headquarters.

In the pavement there is a sepulcher from the 1300s, of a young girl of the Antelminelli family.

~

33. Santa Maria dei Servi
St. Mary of the Servite Order

Shortly before the year 1233, seven wealthy Florentine merchants abandoned the worldly life and started a religious fraternity dedicated to serving the Blessed Virgin Mary. Their order grew quickly. In 1256 they were sanctioned by the Pope. In 1267 St. Philip Benizi became their leader and the Servites quickly spread through Germany and France and sent missionaries to India "to convert the Tartars." In 1304 the Pope issued a Bull in their favor, giving a further stimulus to their growth.

By 1254 the Servites already had enough members in Lucca to require their own church. They bought the rights to the private church of the Avvocati family, dedicated to St. Michael (*San Michele degli Avvocati*) which is first recorded in 1060, but probably dated to the 900s.

The first half of the 1300s was a period of constant tribulation for Lucca but after the Black Death in 1348 the city began to revive, though it was still under Pisan domination. In 1349 the Servites acquired adjacent land and the private chapel of the Corvaresi family, San Lorenzo, and began construction of a new, much larger church.

Such a large church required substantial fund raising and over the next decades some of the town's wealthiest families left bequests to it, the final burst coming in the 1380s when they began to specify that the money was to be used to complete the building (rather than to erect private altars). Many of these bequests required that the family have rights to burial in the church. These requests proliferated in the 1390s and early 1400s, and the church became the final resting place of some of the most important families in town.

Exterior

The exterior has not changed much from the way it looked in 1400: a great expanse of brick, plain except for the graceful and exquisitely detailed windows. It looks like the church of a mendicant order, a great hall more for preaching than for ritual. But from the beginning Santa Maria dei Servi was also a church of the wealthy families. They had subsidized it and were buried there. With the side of the church opening onto an unusually large piazza, they could not forebear embellishment on this side. It is an arresting show.

The effect is somewhat diminished by later renovations. The original proportions were better before the roof was raised, twice. The original roof eaves were supported by a row of corbels, now gone but their location can be seen.

The building of the church progressed in stages, from the apse forward, as funding was available. You can make out the seams which show the four stages of construction. You can also see a progression in the decorative brickwork on the window arches. The first stage included the left window, which is the simplest, devoid of any decorative brick. When work resumed the vision had expanded, a reflection of the economic and civic expansion Lucca was undergoing. The Guinigi family was solidifying its dominance and was building palazzi lush with decorative brick. By the time the next two windows were built they would incorporate masterworks of the local brick artisans, adding an exuberant filigree to the original model. The working of these two central windows is identical; they were cast literally from the same

33. Santa Maria Dei Servi

mold. The last window to be done substitutes a graceful garland for the geometric flowers of the middle two and subtly restructures the interior portion, creating a more open and better proportioned space. This window may, however, (once again reading the seams) be a later restoration, necessitated when it was damaged during the opening of the disappointing square window we have today. The patch around the rear window also makes one suspect unknown destruction and restoration.

The existing side door must be a later remodeling. The arch of the original can be seen above it. Just left of the door there is a pointed arch, perhaps the remains of an altar. Altars were often attached to the outside of a church, but only a few remain intact (on San Francesco and San Romano).

It is impossible to date the painting between the rear windows, since it has almost disappeared, the inevitable fate of outdoor frescoes.

The front of the church is very plain, a stark white arched doorway and a simple round window. Near the top you can see the original roof line. Above the doorway the location of a former roof or awning is etched in the brick. In the tympanum a fresco of the Annunciation is fading away.

To the right of the door is a small white plaque recording an unusual entombment (BALENAE PYSTRES TYMNI DELPHI...):

Front Door

> "Whales, sea mammals, tuna, dolphins, killer whales, and other monsters of the Ocean and the Mediterranean and all they have, or the Nile and the wonders it has, or the Ganges, may this beast make men give credence to you. The bones attest to the vastness of its mouth and the ribs to the rest of the body. The Tyrrhenian Sea threw it on the shores of Lucca in the year 1495. Nicolao Tegrimi put it here."

Interior

The entire interior was originally frescoed, of which a little remains along the lower right hand wall. The baroque ceiling, in sculpted wood, has 27 panels of various form and sizes, and includes the coat of arms of the Servites and the Comune of Lucca. It was built in 1627 by the Pisan **Pietro Giambelli** who did the intaglio for the choir loft over the front entrance.

In the later 1400s and early 1500s the Civitali workshop was active in the church. In the early 1600s the interior was radically remodeled, altars and paintings changed, the walls raised and a new roof put on. Work continued into the 1700s.

The church was the home of now lost treasures, but it retains others. Of the lost paintings, one was a grand altarpiece by the preeminent painter of the 1300s, Paolo di Lazzarino. It is known to us by legal proceedings concerning it, which describe it as "a large panel, gessoed, divided into five main parts, with the upper part also divided, value of 50 fiorini." In testimony before a grand jury the clerics of the church charged that Lazzarino entered the church and, while a friend created a distraction, he made off with the painting. The reason is not specified, but presumably he was not content with his payment. Both of the men were convicted, sentenced to two months in the Bishop's jail, a fine, and return of the painting. On appeal they were granted a hearing by the Roman curia, and then skipped town to Pisa. Eventually they were granted pardons by the Bishop and Paolo went on to execute other prestigious paintings for the town fathers. Not one remains.

In a niche to right of the main door is a statue of *St. Sebastian*, painted wood, 1400s. It has been interfered with extensively over the years, but is quite possibly by Matteo Civitali. It is similar to other St. Sebastians by Matteo, including one at the Met in New York.

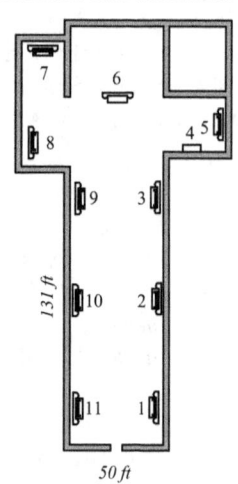

Santa Maria dei Servi

1. (Altar) *Madonna and Child with Sts. Philip Neri and Philip Benizi* by **Giovan Battista Vanni**, 1658. Neri (1515-1595) was the founder of the Oratorians.

2. (Altar)

3. (Altar) *Nativity of Mary* by **Matteo Rosselli**, 1636.

33. Santa Maria Dei Servi

4. *Monument to Giano Grillo*, 1480, attributed to **Raffaello da Montelupo** (whose father designed the church of San Paolino). Grillo was from Genoa; the work was commissioned by his son.

5. Transept altar. Painted *Crucifx*, mid-1400s, perhaps by Borghese di Pietro.

On the rear wall of the transept there is a marble aedicula, attributed to **Matteo Civitali**.

6. Main Altar. A lovely and unusual altar, covered by a filigreed wooden canopy supported by four polished columns.
Behind the altar is a painting of *St. Antonio with Trinity and St. Francesco Saverio* by **Franchi**.

To the left there is a tomb, damaged, with the figure of a woman, dated 1426.

7. *Chapel of the Sacrament*. This chapel was opened in 1713, a wonderful expression of the period. The altar, dated 1516, is by **Nicolao Civitali** and was moved from another part of the church. In the niche is a superb, though reworked, wood statue of *Mary Annunciate*, by **Matteo Civitali**.

Four paintings on the wall are by **Domenico Brugieri**, before 1721.

8. Transept altar. *Sts. Giorgio e Pellegrino Laziosi* by **Antonio Franchi**. Pellegrino Laziosi (1265-1345) was a Servite friar. Originally politically active as a supporter of the Ghibellines (anti-papist party) he once physically attacked Philip Benizi, who literally turned the other cheek, causing Pellegrino to repent and join the Servites. He was famous even in life for his miracles, and more so after his death.

The octagonal *acquasantiera*, imbedded into the wall near the door, is a work of 1300s.

9. (Altar) *Nativity* by **Pietro Paolini.**

10. (Altar) *Madonna dei Dolori* by **Matteo Rosselli.**

11. (Altar) *Presentation of Mary at the Temple* by **M. Rosselli.**

~

San Lorenzo

34. Oratorio di San Lorenzo
The Oratory of St. Lawrence

In April 1349, the church of Santa Maria dei Servi acquired a small adjoining chapel, San Lorenzo. The bubonic plague was taking its first year's toll and abandoned buildings were sold at bargain prices. Churches could no longer maintain the services to which they were committed by perpetual sacred contract. San Lorenzo, which had originally been the private church of the Corvaresi family, was in need of rescuing. The Servites assumed guardianship and were given permission to enlarge it, so long as they maintained the religious obligations. They were also warned not to encroach on public streets with any new construction.

Conjoined with Santa Maria dei Servi, San Lorenzo became an oratorio serving the monastery which had grown up between the two. The cloister of the monastery remains and can be visited. The façade of San Lorenzo, reflecting the main church, is an unadorned brick expanse, but windows have been opened and closed over the centuries.

San Lorenzo joined in the success of the Servites and about 1480 was significantly embellished. **Matteo Civitali**, who had a close relationship with the Order, was commissioned to sculpt a *Pietà*, one of his masterpieces, now in the Villa Guinigi Museum. *Pietà* was an appropriate theme for an order dedicated to Our Lady of Sorrows.

In the Napoleonic period the ancient church and convent of Santa Giustina was suppressed and demolished. Its displaced members found a new home in San Lorenzo, and brought with them, among other things, the painting of *San Silao* by **Paolo Guidotti** which still hangs over the main altar. St. Silao, an Irish or Scottish pilgrim who died in Lucca over 900 years ago, does not go unremembered in Lucca, though his relics and the cell where he died are lost.

The Oratorio is still well tended, and is occasionally open for visits. Do go in if the door is open. Its caretakers have a long tradition of taking care of strangers.

~

San Giuseppe

35. Oratorio di San Giuseppe
Oratory of Saint Joseph

This oratorio is all that remains of a substantial Gesuate convent founded in 1518. It has recently been restored and incorporated into the Cathedral Museum. (On the Gesuates see the church of San Girolamo.) The convent was closed under Napoleon, and used as a storehouse in the 1800s.

The glazed terracotta relief over the front entrance of *Mary and Child with Sts. Joseph and Jerome* is the work of a local artist of the later 1500s.

The interior was ornately redone in the 1600s with inlaid painted and gilded wood, of which some excellent examples remain, including the large choir loft on the front wall and the smaller one on the left.

1. Altar. *St. Catherine of Alexandria* by **Girolamo Scaglia**, mid-1600s.

2. *Flight to Egypt*, fresco, local artist, later 1500s.

3. Main Altar. *Sts. Joseph, Paul, and Jerome* by **Lorenzo Zacchia**, ca. 1560-1570, tempera on wood. This painting had for a long time been attributed to Filippino Lippi. The impressive altar is part of the mid-1600s renovations. Above the altar are partially covered remains of a late 1500s fresco of the *Coronation of the Virgin*.

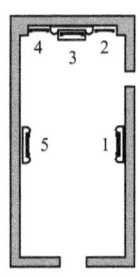

San Giuseppe

4. *Angel Appears to Joseph*, later 1500s, fresco, by a local artist.

5. Altar. *Immaculate Conception with Sts. Carlo Borromeo and Ignatius Loyola* by **Matteo Boselli**, mid-1600s.

~

36. Santa Maria della Rosa
St. Mary of the Roses

This exquisite little church was built to house the fresco which is on the high altar. Since the permit for construction was granted in 1309 the fresco must date from before that time and it is, therefore, one of the earliest examples of Lucchese painting.

The 1309 document states that the image was at that time in a chapel dedicated to St. Paul, which was built up against the east wall of the archbishop's residence. This wall was, in fact, the Roman city wall. It is today the only section which remains extant above ground.

The construction of the church proceeded in stages. The earliest portion is the rear where a statue of Madonna and Child is found on the exterior corner. Below the statue is an inscription bearing the names of the original benefactors, dated 1309. This first section was quite small, comprising only the first broad arch holding two *bifore* windows and a door. This doorway was opened, or perhaps reopened, in the 20th century. Photographs from 1900 show a solid wall with a large oculus.

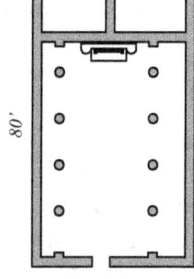

Santa Maria della Rosa

The original space must have been inadequate to house the number of devotees because in 1333 another grant was made permitting its enlargement. The same date is found inscribed over the central side door. In 1358 another grant of land was made for buildings associated with the church, and in 1378 an additional grant was made.

Most of the construction work was subsidized by the Society of Merchants which explains the sumptuousness of the stone carving. What is remarkable is the period in which it was done. 1309 is not a surprising date for the founding. The previous year the merchants and the *popolo* had taken power from the old nobility and instituted a broad range of civic reform. The next few years were perhaps the most optimistic in Lucca's history, at least for the merchant classes. A scant five years later, however, in

1314, this world collapsed as first Pisa ravaged the city and then Castruccio Castracani began his dictatorship. Castruccio brought stability and a certain prosperity, though with a heavy military burden, but immediately after his death in 1328 chaos reigned. By 1333 there was again some hope. The Emperor had arrived to establish order, and building projects around town were revived (for example, the church of San Nicolao). But things immediately fell apart. The next few years were the hardest in Lucca's history, and it is difficult to imagine that work progressed very quickly on the little church. Yet it did progress, a show of determination to create something beautiful in the midst of disorder.

In their 1906 book *The Story of Lucca* Janet Ross and Nelly Erichsen refer to Santa Maria della Rosa as "a queer little shanty of a church." What a beautiful shanty! Though it is difficult to do so without getting hit by a car, it is well worth your while spending time in the street deciphering the endlessly inventive carvings. Amidst the profusion of garlands and filigree, be sure to notice the many faces which dot the friezes—jesters, kings, prophets, ordinary townsfolk, and, undoubtedly, patrons.

The left wall of the church is the original Roman city wall, dating to at least the first century BC. The interior was upgraded in the 1400s and the 1600s. Under Napoleon it was briefly converted to a magazine, but it was soon reopened. In the early 2000s the exterior received a badly needed cleaning and the interior was pristined, restoring what fresco fragments remain.

This was the church in which Santa Gemma Galgani made her daily devotions. She preferred to sit at the rear of the church where her seat is noted with a small plaque.

~

37. Santa Maria Forisportam
St. Mary outside the gate

"Absolutely for the first time I now saw what medieval builders were, and what they meant. I took the simplest of all facades for analysis, that of Santa Maria Foris-Portam, and thereon literally began the study of architecture."

John Ruskin, recalling his visit at age 26, in 1845.

Townsfolk generally refer to this church as Santa Maria Bianca, the white St. Mary.

There was a church dedicated to St. Mary on the site as early as 768. At that time it was just beyond the eastern gate of the Roman wall, so it was called *forisportam*—"outside the gate." The gate was located where Via Santa Croce enters the piazza in front of the church. This street was the main Roman road across town, and the column in the piazza was the terminus for races which were run along it.

The grandeur of the church reveals how much the town had expanded beyond its walls by the beginning of the medieval period. By the same time there was a major church outside each of the four gates: the others were San Frediano, San Donato, and San Pier Maggiore.

Construction of the present building began about 1150. Although fortifications had been built beyond it, the completion of the medieval wall was still decades away.

The towering brick over the central nave, the result of a late raising of the roof, is visually jarring and an offense to the architectural integrity, but it did achieve its purpose of aggrandizing the interior. Ignoring this accretion, we are left with a splendid example of Lucchese-Pisan Romanesque, dignified but with the first impulses of playfulness.

The exterior is clearly modeled on the Cathedral of Pisa, though the façade of Santa Maria Bianca is more sober than that in Pisa, the false upper loggias in Lucca giving it a flattened aspect. As in Pisa the lower front consists of seven high blind arches, three holding the doorways, and the primary embellishments are the recessed lozenges within the arches. Atop this level, the loggias in Lucca look as if the first row on the Pisa cathedral were removed and the second and third rows simply dropped down. In Lucca the loggias are themselves blind, or false, rather than the true loggias in Pisa. The blind arcades continue along the sides and the grand apse, giving the building a unified architectural vision.

Santa Maria Bianca did not fare well over its first centuries. In the 1400s it was almost abandoned, and by 1512 it was in such decay that services were in jeopardy. A stipend was finally obtained from the State, and in 1516 Giovanni Guinigi donated the extravagant amount of 1000 gold ducats. The work, unfortunately, went well beyond repairs. The grand crypt, which had traversed the entire transept, was filled in and the floor above it was lowered, giving the church a uniform level. The old ambone (early pulpit) was destroyed, as was the choir area.

37. Santa Maria Forisportam

The windows along the nave were closed. Most offensively, the medieval frescoes were covered with plaster and stucco imitations of marble finery were installed. This work had been overseen by the respected architect Michele Arnolfini but later evaluations called it a "bastardization," "disgrace," "disaster." By the 1830s restorations were deemed appropriate, but little could reasonably be done except to remove the plaster and expose the original stone. The medieval decorations were gone forever.

The facade of the church has some of the best examples of Lucchese architectural sculpture of the 1100s and 1200s. The jambs of each door have classically inspired capitals, supporting massive, densely carved architraves. The one over the left door appears to be inspired by Roman sarcophagi, with a lion and a gryphon to the sides of a rosette. In the arch a Byzantine inspired Madonna and Child has been replaced by a copy; the original (now in the Villa Guinigi Museum) probably dated from the 1100s, though earlier dates have been suggested. In the  space over the main door is a low relief of the *Coronation of Mary*, and over the right hand door is a 1200s sculpture of a bishop. The animal sculptures, two atop each corner, and four above the loggias, are difficult to appreciate in their current location. They were probably moved here from the interior when it was dismantled in the 1500s and they may have been part of the original ambone. On the pilaster on the left are two typical Lombard woven bands, which probably came from the earlier church.

On the rear of the church you can see the upper parts of the windows which once opened into the expansive crypt.

Interior

The columns are of granite and marble, not local. There is such a wealth of ruins reused that we can deduce that the ancient church was an ornate Roman structure.

1. Paleochristian *sarcophagus*, about the 300s. On the left is the Good Shepherd, in the center Daniel and the lion, on the right the Vigilant Shepherd. This was donated by the Bernardini family, who had an extensive archaeological collection.

Above it, in a little alcove is a fresco. The border is foliage, and the center is a book with the verse of Mark 3:16: "Whoever believes in me and is baptized has everlasting life."

2. Above the door, a fresco lunette of **Nursing Madonna** from the 1300s, recently restored. It has been attributed to the Sienese

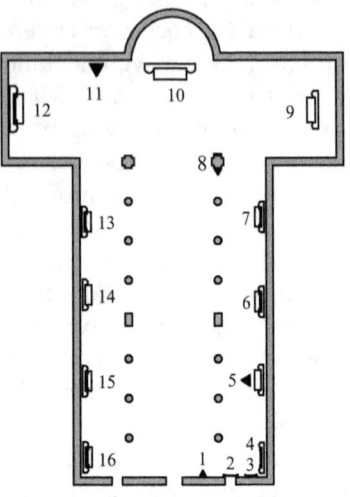

Santa Maria Forisportam

Martino di Bartolomeo, but this is the subject of a lively debate. **Giovanni di Pietro da Napoli** has also been suggested.

3. Undistinguished modern painting above a wood "mini altar" which identifies it as *"Beato Angelo Orsucci Domenicano, Lucchese martire nel Giappone."* Angelo Orsucci, scion of a noble Lucca family, was born in 1573 and died a Dominican martyr in Japan in 1622, for which he was beatified. He was born on Via Guinigi, where he is commemorated by a plaque.

4. (Altar) **Coronation of Mary** by **Girolamo Scaglia**, 1659. The altar table has been removed, revealing a fresco from the earlier decoration of the church. It was preserved by the placement of the altar. These fresco remains are from the early 1400s but have several layers. The more recent are Mary and Child on the left, and on the right a kneeling knight with his head being held for execution. The knight's tunic bears the same design as the crests along the border. Where the top fresco has broken off is an earlier one, a simple geometric design in red. Further back in time are the faint remains of painting where frescoes have flaked off. A bit of the original tile floor has also been exposed.

37. Santa Maria Forisportam

Fresco, early 1400s

5. (Altar) Small terra-cotta of *Mary and Child*. In front, a statue of Santa Gemma Galgani (1878-1903), life size.

6. (Altar) *Crucifixion and Trinity with Sts. Francis and Jerome* by **Alessandro Ardenti**, later 1500s, restored 1996. There is a Di Poggio family tomb in front.

7. (Altar) *St. Lucy* by **Giovan Francesco Barbieri**. The saint holds a cup with her eyes on it, though her own eyes look fine. Barbieri, a first rate Bolognese painter who suffered in the shadow of his countryman and contemporary Guido Reni, left two paintings in Lucca (that we know of), both in this church.

8. Wood *Crucifix* on column, 3' high. Notice the exquisite small frieze above on the column. High on the rear side of the same column are the bare remains of a fresco. Below it is an interesting plaque, which gives tables for calculating the time in other places according to the meridian of Lucca, determined by Enrico Pucci in 1875, with corrections for every day of the year.

9. Altar (right transept). A grand altar with an undistinguished painting but a truly exquisite *ciborium* by **Giovanni Vambré**.

10. Main Altar, 1595, by **Vincenzo Civitali**. The upper part was completed in the 1700s with two angels on the sides. It is a wonderful large white altar which derives grandeur from the monochrome material. Notice the diamond lozenges which reiterate those on the church façade. The excellent large *Madonna* statue (1761) also benefits from the monochrome effect.

11. *Monument to Antonio Mazzarosa* by **Vincenzo Consani**, 1870.

12. Altar of the Sacrament (left transept). *Assumption with Sts. Francis and Alessandro* by **Giovan Francesco Barbieri**, called *Il Guercino*, (1591-1666). To the left of the altar is a sepulchre plaque dated 1291. Two Mazzarosa family tombs in front.

13. (Altar) *Sts. Michael Archangel, Liborio, and Augustine* by **Giovanni Marracci**. Restored 1997. A very young, almost feminine St. Michael with quite a feathered hat, holds the scales of justice and a shield; no dragon. Marracci was born in nearby Camaiore and studied with Pietro Paolino in Lucca.

14. (Altar) *Crucifix*.

15. (Altar) *Mary, Child, Saint, and Nun*, framed in a sunburst.

16. (Altar) *Sts. Carlo, Rocco, and Giovanni Evanglelista*, 1600s.

Notice the elaborately carved wooden balcony for the organ, with quite ferocious faces, tongues out.

Formerly in the church:

The Cumaean Sybil by **Alessandro Ardenti**, now in the Villa Guinigi Museum.

Madonna with Sts. Lorenzo and Gervasio by **Gaspare Mannucci**, now also in the Guinigi museum.

In the Sacristy: central part of a polyptych, *Death and Assumption of the Virgin* by **Angelo Puccinelli**, 1386.

~

38. Santissima Trinità
The Most Holy Trinity

The second youngest church in Lucca (Suffragio is a half century later). The Company of the Most Holy Trinity was formed in 1562 to give aid to pilgrims and the sick. In 1589 they acquired land from the nearby Monastery of San Micheletto, and from the Franciotti family, to build a church and hospital. The construction of the church was promoted by the influential Bishop Alessandro I Guidiccioni and the work went quickly. The date over the doorway is 1591. (Guidiccioni was bishop for 51 years, and a member of his illustrious family held the office for over 90 consecutive years.) Located directly opposite the entrance to Villa Buonvisi, the façade of the church was designed to provide a pleasing view from the villa, which had been built a few years earlier as the grandest residence in Lucca. The church complex encompassed the entire block. It still serves as a school.

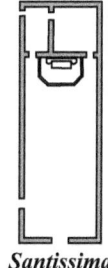

Santissima Trinita

The roof collapsed in 1918, but it has been made good and the church today is a quiet place of worship, watched over by the sisters, whom you will often find at devotions.

There was originally only the central altar. The altars on the sides were installed in the 1800s.

The right altar hosts a marble sculpture by **Matteo Civitali**, moved here from San Ponziano. Its subject is the *Madonna del Latte* (Nursing Madonna) but it is popularly known as *Madonna della Tosse*, or Madonna of the Cough, because it was famous for its ability to cure this affliction. Dated 1482-1485, it is one Civitali's most famous works. It is similar to one done in painted and gilded terracotta more than a decade earlier and which until recently had been attributed to Verrochio. It has been suggested that both may have been

inspired by a work by Jan Van Eyck, about 1435-1440, which is known as the Madonna of Lucca, from its earliest known location. (It is now in Frankfurt.)

The main altar, installed in 1595, hosts a painting of *The Trinity, Madonna, and Sts. John the Baptist, Paolino, Sebastian, Antonio, and Catherine*. It is one of the last works of **Pietro Paolini**, from the 1670s, but much of it must have been done by his workshop and it is far from one of his masterpieces.

The left altar has *St. Francis di Sales* by **Pietro Nocchi** (1783-1854). Nocchi's father, an engraver and painter, was born in Lucca but he went to Rome with Stefano Tofanelli in 1769 and remained there. Pietro, born in Rome, returned to Lucca in 1806 and succeeded Tofanelli as teacher of painting in the Accademia. He did many portraits, including of Elisa, as well as church paintings.

Also in the church are an *Immaculate Conception* by **Giovanni Marracci** (1637-1704) and a *Volto Santo* by **Pier Filippo Mannucci** (1601-1669).

Behind the high altar, and opening into the church, is the choir of the monastery. Its vault was frescoed at the end of the 1500s by **Pietro Sorri** though this was painted over by **Domenico Brugieri** about 1720, at the same time he painted six canvases for the church.

In the sacristy there is a *Holy Trinity with Sts. Carlo Borromeo and Leonardo* by **Giovan Domenico Ferrucci**, who was closely connected with the order.

~

39. San Micheletto
St. Michael Archangel

San Micheletto was a large monastic complex, and it is still today a large open space in the constrained world of Lucca. You are welcome to wander around the grounds.

When the monastery was built in the early 700s it was well outside the Roman walls, and it would remain outside the medieval walls. You can still see the medieval gate a block away. Fortunately, the site has recently been adopted by the *Cassa di Risparmio di Lucca* (Lucca Savings Bank) which has restored it and transformed it into a cultural center. It is the home of the Ragghianti foundation, a seminal influence in the revival of Lucchese studies, with an excellent library.

In 721 a wealthy Lombard nobleman named Pertualdo, inspired by his pilgrimage to Rome, returned home to Lucca and established the monastery of St. Michael Archangel.

The monastery flourished and expanded, having sufficient

endowments (it was located, after all, in the capital of Tuscany) and the space to do so. In 757 the Duke of Lucca, Desiderius, would become king. Desiderius and his kingdom would fall to Charlemagne in 774, but most of the Lombard nobles would maintain their influence. In 778 Peredeo, Bishop of Lucca and son of the founder of San Micheletto, made his last will and testament, leaving the monastery, still his personal property, to the Cathedral (that is, to the next Bishop). The great wave of Lombard philanthropy, however, was at an end. Donations to the Church would continue, but they seem to have been disposals of burdensome property (let the bishop pay for the upkeep) more than displays of munificence.

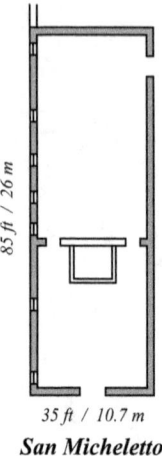

San Micheletto

Peredeo, bishop from 755 to 779, was taken prisoner by Charlemagne along with many other bishops. They were not so much hostages as impressed advisors on Italian affairs. Peredeo was permitted to retain his bishopric, which he well deserved, having been extraordinarily active in building and repairing the churches, monasteries, and hospitals of Lucca.

In the 830s descendants of the founders of San Micheletto relinquished their rights to nearby San Bartolomeo (later San Ponziano) and assigned them to San Micheletto. One of these benefactors was Peter, bishop of Lucca from 819-834. He was of Lombard lineage and close to the Pope. By his time bishops were filling the void in the temporal order caused by the demise of the Lombards and the remoteness of the French overlords. The inevitable result was the enrichment of the bishop.

Peter founded or sponsored a good number of other religious and benevolent establishments, asserting the preeminence which Lucca still claimed in Tuscany. The latter part of his reign was shaped first by the invasion of the Saracens in 828, and then by marauding pirates a year later. The Duke of Tuscany, Bonifacio, defeated both of the enemies and Lucca profited accordingly. Salvation from imminent disaster led, as always, to a new round of thanksgiving offerings, to the benefit of San Micheletto.

The Lombard sway slowly faded. The Papacy became

39. SAN MICHELETTO

increasingly corrupt and the Emperor more remote. The result was that local political and religious reform became possible, and thrived. Reformist monastic orders such as the Cluniacs were ascendant. These willing hands were more than content to take on the burden of property management from Rome. By 1141 San Micheletto was in the hands of the Benedictines and the enthusiasm of a new generation of monks revived the venerable institution.

The document of 1141 calls the church *San Benedetto in Silice*, declaring its shift in allegiance to St. Benedicts's rule, but it was soon to return to the patronage of its original saint.

An inscription, originally on the exterior but later moved inside, reads: "The honest doctor, Angelo, a righteous man, a priest of Christ, lies in this tomb. I made this church of yours, Michael, so help me enter your celestial resting-place. I went to Christ in November 1195." So, sometime between 1141 and 1195 the church was rebuilt and rededicated to its original saint, Archangel Michael, giving us the building we see today.

Centuries pass. In 1433 the "church, a house adjoining, orchard, and other belongings" were given to the Mother Superior of the Sisters of the Third Order (Franciscan) at the price of four pounds of wax each year for 4 years.

In 1455 the monastery had the good luck to acquire as benefactor the widow Catherine Sbarra, from one of the oldest and wealthiest families in Lucca. She entered at age 50 and lived there until she was 80. When she came, there were only four sisters but the monastery's fortunes soon improved dramatically. It attracted new members, including nobility, and was recognized by the Pope. In 1477 the sisters were accepted as members of the Order of Poor Clares.

In 1608 the proprietorship of the monastery changed again, this time given to the Capuchins, who ruled it until 1812. These industrious monks gave it its modern form and by 1664 there were five dormitories, two infirmaries, kitchens, granaries, and orchards.

In 1796 the monastery was blessed by the miracle of Sister Maria Luisa Biagini, who upon receiving a vision of the Virgin Mary was instantaneously cured of a fatal illness. Work immediately began on transforming her cell into a chapel.

But the monastery was soon to be embroiled in the Napoleonic incursions. A document of 1799 records that "the infantry and cavalry constantly coming and going, and expecting a large column of troops" the quartermaster requested beds from the monks. He suggested they cope by using sacking, sleeping on the ground, or two to a bed.

Yet the monastery survived and in 1804 restoration work began. Then in 1806 came the great suppression of religious orders. Members of some orders were forcibly united with others and San Micheletto, being so large, was expected to host displaced monks. Each monastery, however, was its own little world and the unification seldom went smoothly. In San Micheletto the resident monks refused to share their cells, relegating the newcomers to the infirmary. Soon after, under Princess Elisa, the monastery was transformed into a school for girls.

The greatest threat to its continued existence was Elisa's urban renewal efforts. She opened a new gate through the walls, ending the isolation and serenity of the area. One of her plans envisioned a road from the new Piazza Napoleone to the new Porta Elisa, which would have gone straight through San Michelletto. In the end a more modest road was built, from the medieval gate to the new one, which preserved the monastery.

By a decree of 1811 the ruling Baciocchi family took possession of the belongings of all religious orders. The next year the religious buildings were stripped—organs for their metal, fine woodwork and choral seats to be used as firewood. San Micheletto was to be turned into stables for the royal residence at Villa Buonvisi, though the fall of Napoleon saved it from this fate.

The monks returned in 1818 but tribulations continued. In 1827 all monasteries became public property, and in 1865 there was a new round of suppression. Finally in 1896, in accordance with the law that when there were fewer than six inhabitants the institution would become extinct, San Micheletto became public property. During the First World War the monastery served as a military hospital and afterwards became a technical school. In 1972

39. San Micheletto

Cassa Di Risparmio became the proprietor, planning on turning it into elderly housing. Then in 1979 the scholar Ragghianti made a donation to establish a Center for the Study of Art, contributing his library and archives. In the 1980s extensive renovations began and the complex was gradually transformed into a cultural center, hosting among other things the intimate world class concerts of the Lucca music society.

Third Orders

In the earliest days of Christianity the use of public penance developed—ostracizing the sinner until he had earned his way back into the fold. The fact that all people are sinners and unworthy to be among the elect led to this anathema actually becoming attractive, and soon one could voluntarily become a penitent.

In the 1100s the penitent movement became widespread, with individuals adopting some monastic restrictions while still living in the world. In 1175 the Pope sanctioned the movement and participation became a popular act of religious commitment. The spirit of the movement, absolution of sins, led in 1215 to the institution of annual confession for all believers. This was the time of St. Francis (1181-1226), who began as a penitent and is often taken to be the founder of the movement. In the same period a new literary genre developed, the Confessor's Handbook.

One of the penitent groups was the Humiliati. In 1184 the Humiliati, together with the Waldensians and Cathars, were condemned by the Lucchese Pope Lucius III. The Humiliati were, however, reconciled with the church in 1201, and reorganized into three orders: regular monastic houses, houses of celibates, and married people. The Humiliati were disbanded in 1572 when St. Charles Borromeo's efforts to reform it led to an attempt on his life, but third orders flourished in other mendicant orders, particularly the Franciscans. It was members of this group which acquired the monastery of San Micheletto in 1433.

~

40. San Francesco
St. Francis

Saint Francis of Assisi died in 1226. The earliest known painting of him is by a Lucchese, Bonaventura Berlinghieri, in 1235. Berlinghieri had almost certainly looked upon St. Francis' face.

The Franciscans established themselves in Lucca in 1228, when they were granted an orchard outside the walls on which to build a church and monastery. Within four years a small church was ready, dedicated to Mary Magdalene. It lay just beyond the area known as the *fratta*, the scrublands. The road which leads to the church is still called Via della Fratta.

Donations of land and money continued steadily through the 1200s and by the end of the century a much grander building was complete. The progression of work can be read in the seams along the exterior wall. The final addition, about 1400, was of the rear chapels, probably funded by Paolo Guinigi. The church, directly opposite the Guinigi villa, benefited greatly from the attentions of his family. In 1354 Francesco Guinigi built the annexed Chapel of Santa Lucia for his private use.

In 1859 the Italian State directed that the use of the church was to be given over to the French army, and in the suppression of 1866 the remaining clerics were ordered to find other quarters. The church became a military storehouse and the interior was trashed. Even the bell tower lost its bells, though three of them were later returned.

In 1906, when it was put up for sale, San Francesco's glories were reduced to a dry real estate contract: "ground floor: 1 church, 30 rooms, 3 corridors, two stairways, 1 latrine, 9 porticoes, 3 cloisters, 1 plot of earth..." There were also two more floors;

another 28 rooms, 7 corridors, and 2 latrines. In 1910, after 45 years of alienation, the church and cloisters were returned to the Church. A plaque on the front records this reacquisition.

After the fall of Mussolini in September 1943 the Germans occupied the city. The church remained unscathed until the following September as the Allied front swept through and three artillery rounds hit the building, blowing out all the windows. Other shells fell into the cloister but with minimal damage. The windows were replaced in the mid-50s by **Giuseppe Nenci** of Siena with scenes from the life of St. Francis and a new rose window. To pay for the repairs the order sold a plot of land. In the 70s and 80s they were compelled to sell more land and part of the convent, turning part of a cloister into a government run half-way house for released prisoners.

By the late 1980s, San Francesco, which had weathered 700 years, again let in the elements and threatened to collapse. The bell tower was so compromised the bells could not safely be rung. Rescue funds were solicited from the faithful, the State, and preservationists and disaster averted. Considering its tribulations, one tries not to bemoan what was lost but to be grateful for what survives.

Exterior

The lower façade of the church, below the cornice, was built by the mid-1200s with the typical Lucchesi features of the period, limestone facing with horizontal banding and shallow blind arcades. There is only one front door. Attached to the facade are two sepulchral altars, one dated 1249, the other from the 1300s. The upper part of the facade remained unfinished until 1927 when the fascist government completed the work, adding a fasces to the Christian symbols.

Cloisters

During its thriving centuries the monastic complex of San Francesco housed a large number of clerics, tertiaries, and students. Their life surrounded the three cloister gardens which

40. SAN FRANCESCO

still exist and can be visited at certain times. They contain a number of early sepulchers and frescoes. Among these is one to Bonagiunta Tignosini, dated 1274 which still retains its fresco, one of the earliest surviving in Lucca (restored in 1988). Another, dated 1318, memorializes the daughter of Castruccio Castracani (who is buried in the church). There are several others dating from the 1300s to the 1600s.

Interior

The plaque on the right as you enter records that "This church was built in the 13th century, disfigured in the 17th century....restored 1844." The restoration refers to the work of the architect Giuseppe Pardini, who reopened the bifore windows which had been closed in the 1600s.

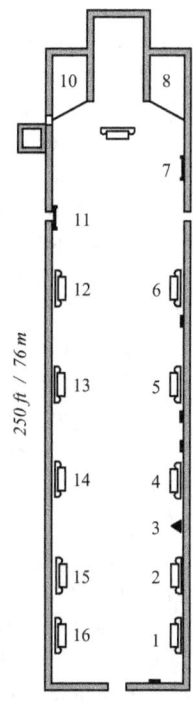

San Francesco

1. (Altar, dated 1675). *St. Bernardino of Siena with Sts. Liborio, Elizabeth of Hungary, and Ludovico di Francia Adoring the Name of Jesus*, anon., 1600s. This altar was not part of the original plan. The coat of arms of the noble Parenti family is on the altar base.

This is a type of painting which is too easily passed over: anonymous 1600s devotional. Even the sign in the church reads only "San Bernardino and other Saints." Other saints. What could less inspire a weary eye? And yet the vision of benefactor and artist were the equal of great paintings by famous artists and eminent patrons. Historically they are of equal interest as insights into their time and place. Bernardino, Liborio, Elizabeth, and Ludovico of France had an intimate significance for someone in the Parenti family. Without some sense of these meanings we can't fully appreciate or appraise the painting.

Elizabeth of Hungary (1207-1231) who appears in the paintings on these first two altars was one of the first, and is one of the favorite, Franciscan saints. She was the daughter of the king of Hungary and was married at age 14 to become a Countess.

Content with her life, in love with her husband, she bore three children and spent her time giving away large sums in alms, establishing hospitals and orphanages. In 1227 her husband went on crusade and died of the plague. When she refused to remarry she was driven from court and became a Franciscan tertiary under the tutelage of her confessor, a famously sadistic taskmaster; he had trained as an inquisitor and mastered its methods. Elizabeth, consigned to tasks such as cleaning the houses of the poor and catching fish to feed them, was content with her austerities and her maltreatment. Nonetheless, three years of such deprivations brought her own life to a close.

Her fame was sufficient to get her canonized within four years of her death, and the construction of a church to house her relics began immediately. It became a popular pilgrimage destination for three hundred years, until a Lutheran ruler dispersed her remains, which assured her a place in Counter Reformation art. She is the patron saint of the Tertiaries, a role well-earned by her sad, short life. (On Tertiaries, or Third Orders, see San Micheletto, church #39.)

2. (Altar, dated 1647). ***Madonna with St. Elizabeth of Hungary and St. Francis*** by **Sebastiano Conca** (1680-1764). The altar is dedicated to "Elizabeth, Queen of the Angels." It bears the crest of the Controni family, a dove on the head of a serpent. St. Elizabeth wears the clothing of a Third Order Franciscan.

3. ***Monument to Giovanni Guidiccioni***, 1500-1541. A wonderful monument, attributed variously to Baccio da Montelupo or Vincenzo Civitali. Both attributions have some problems: Baccio died 6 years before Guidiccioni, and Vincenzo Civitali was only 17 or 18 at Guidiccioni's death.

Guidiccioni was a truly Renaissance cleric: bishop, papal legate, poet, and humanist. It has been suggested that he contributed to the design of his own monument, but given his premature death this seems doubtful.

In the sculpture he is not dead, but dozing; a dreamer who has drifted off after a summer picnic. The plaque records him as "Bishop of Fossombrone, a man of great virtue, culture, and ingenuity, who was Nuncio to the Emperor, and who governed Ancona and Umbria honorably in peace and in war...He lived

40. SAN FRANCESCO

40 years. Cardinal Bartolomeo his uncle, and Antonio his brother, made this."

4. (Altar of St. Francis, 1649). ***St. Francis Receives the Stigmata*** by **Pietro Ricchi** (1605-1675). In poor condition. Ricchi was called "the Lucchese" (not uniquely).

This is perhaps the most historically significant of Lucca's altars. It was dedicated after the revolt of the *Straccioni* by the fraternal order of silk workers. On the altar are their symbols, a *torsella* (bag of raw silk) and crossed spools. The dedication is: "To Saint Francis, lover of the poor, we the University of Silkweavers consecrate this altar, in our poverty."

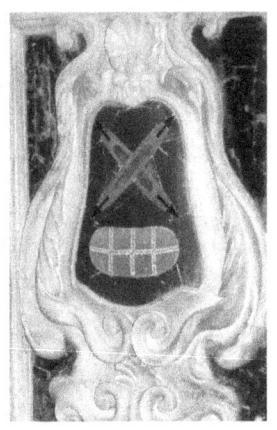

At the top of the altar are sculpted not angels but a workman and his wife. On the column bases there is not the coat of arms of a noble family but the trademark of the society of silkworkers. This altar commemorates Lucca's workers, who labored so hard to create wealth for others and survival for themselves.

To the left of the altar are **Plaques** to Castruccio Castracani.

The top plaque was placed here in 1749.

The lower one ("EN VIVOVIVAMQ...") was written, in the voice of Castruccio, in the early 1500s by Nicolao Tegrimi: "I live on in the feats I accomplished, in the splendor of the Italian military and in the honor of Lucca, jewel of Tuscany. I lived, I sinned, I repented, conceding to the inevitable laws of nature. Pious souls, do good and remember that you also soon will die."Castruccio is buried in this church, wearing the habit of a Franciscan.

5. (Altar) *Coronation of the Virgin with Sts. John, Duns Scotus, Anselm, and Augustine.* A 1700s copy of the popular picture by Francia (1450-1517).

6. (Altar) *Crucifix*, wood, 1800s.

7. *Mary and Jesus*, fresco fragment, about 1400.

Formerly in this area was a monument to Nino Visconti who died in 1288 and is placed by Dante in Purgatory, in the valley of darkness. The Pisan Visconti, at the point of death, asked that his heart be buried in Guelf Lucca, in this church.

8. Pagnini–Baldini Chapel. The loss of the frescoes in this chapel is a tragedy since they had been called the most important frescoes of the 1400s remaining in Lucca. Most were destroyed during the 1746 renovations, but black and white photos of what survived show hauntingly beautiful scenes by one of the masters of the Renaissance. Today these fragments are virtually invisible.

Various attributions have been made, the most attractive and most current is **Baldassare di Biagio**, whose identity and corpus has been reconstituted in recent decades. This would put the date about 1470. Baldassare was an older associate of Matteo Civitali and was the creator of several exquisite works. The main alternative artist is **Borghese di Pietro Borghesi,** dating it about 1450. Berenson thought it likely to be by one of his fabricated personalities, the "Master of the Carrand tryptch." Other suggestions have been Ghirlandaio and Benozzo Gozzoli.

The chapel was originally dedicated by the Pagnini family about 1450.

9. Main altar. The altar is from the 1848 restorations, as are the windows. In the stained glass behind, Volto Santo holds pride

40. SAN FRANCESCO

of place. The beautiful choral seats and lectern, of the 1400s by **Leonardo Marti**, are from Sant'Agostino. They bear the Bernardi coat of arms.

10. Chapel. The original chapel was completely denuded. What you see is the restoration done in 1926, the 700th anniversary of St. Francis' death.

11. Lunette fresco over door, *Madonna and Child*. The arch has been exposed, revealing decorative bricks.

12. (Altar) *Noli me Tangere* (*Touch Me Not*) by **Domenico Cresti (Il Passignano)** (1550-1618), one of the most important Counter Reformation artists. He has two paintings in the Cathedral.

Dedicated to Mary Magdalene, the altar maintains the memory of the Franciscans' first church in Lucca. It was erected in 1610 by the Saminiati family, shown by the inscription and their coat of arms at the column bases: a shield surmounted by an elm with plumes, a vertical band and three diagonals, on white ground.

13. (Altar, dated 1655) *Miracle of St. Antonio of Padua* by **Pietro Ricchi**. Altar erected by the family Martini. Their crest: shield with red cross, black ground, surmounted by plumed elm.

14. (Altar) *Assumption with Sts. Bonaventura, Diego, Ludovico, and Catherine* by **Pietro Ricchi**, painted for this site in 1659. It is unfortunately dark.

Plaque to Boccherini (1743-1805). His remains were moved here in 1999.

Plaque to Francesco Geminiani (1687-1762). Geminiani was a violinist and composer, born in Lucca, died in Dublin. The inscription records that it was placed here "by the fascist commune of Lucca and the Lucchese Academy" in 1932.

15. (Altar, dated 1640) *Nativity* by **Federico Zuccari**, 1596. It replaces an earlier Nativity by Zacchia il Vecchio. The altar was built by the Barsotti family in 1640. Their symbol is an eagle with crown, expressing their tradition as warriors in support of the Emperor.

Plaque to Puccini.

16. (Altar) *St. Salvatore da Orta* by **Domenico (or Giovanni)**

Marraci, about 1635.

The church formerly held paintings by such eminent artists as Deodati Orlandi, Vincenzo Frediani, Michele Ciampanti and his son Ansano.

~

41. San Ponziano

The present appearance of San Ponziano dates from the early 1600s, but by that time the church was already nearly a thousand years old. The earliest document referring to a church on the site is dated 833. Recent excavations have uncovered the foundations of this church, known as San Bartolomeo in Silice, and dated them to the 700s if not earlier. The walls were typical Lombard construction of cut stone layered with river stones arranged in a herringbone fashion. The church had a single nave, almost 50 feet long and 25 wide. It is one of the most significant recent finds in Lucca from the Lombard period and indicates what else might be found if excavations could be carried out in other churches.

By 1100 the church had been acquired by the Benedictines, and in the 1300s by the Olivetans. In 1474 it acquired the relics of St. Ponziano and was rededicated to him and St. Bartholomew. In 1720 the interior was completely renovated, giving it three aisles and luxurious decorations, including works by the Florentine **Giovan Domenico Ferretti**, the Lucchese **Bartolomeo de Santi**, **Giovan Domenico Lombardi**, and **Giuseppe Maria Crespi**. The suppressions of the 1800s resulted in most of these works being lost or dispersed.

The church was reopened for services in 1963 but was later finally closed. It has recently been completely renovated and transformed into an impressive research library.

During the Middle Ages the church was the site of meetings of the Compagnia delle Sette Arti, or Guild of Seven Arts, which included woodworkers, iron workers, carriage makers, and roofers. The street leading to the church is still called the Via delle Sette Arti; the symbols of each of the seven trades can be seen on the buildings along the street.

~

FORMER CHURCHES

1. San Donato
2. San Giorgio
3. Santa Giustina
4. San Luca
5. Santa Maria Filicorbi
6. Santi Pietro e Giovanni Battista
7. Oratorio San Michele del Ghironcello
8. San Lorenzo in Poggio
9. San Sensio
10. Santa Maria della Rotunda
11. Santa Lucia
12. Santa Maria in Palazzo
13. San Pier Maggiore #2
14. San Dalmazio
15. San Pier Maggiore #1
16. Oratorio della Madonnina
17. Oratorio Santa Maria del Gonfalone
18. Oratorio San Giovanetto
19. Oratorio della Croce
20. Oratorio Santa Zita
21. San Pier Cigoli
22. San Gregorio
23. San Quirico all'Ullivo
24. Oratorio dei Poveri
25. Santa Maria in Via
26. San Bartolomeo del Gallo
27. San Donnino
28. Oratorio della Maddalena
29. Sant'Alessandro Minore
30. Oratorio Santa Caterina Orfanelli
31. Oratorio Nome di Gesu
32. Santa Maria Annunziata, dell'Alba
33. San Jacopo alla Tomba
34. San Franceschetto
35. Santa Lucia Chapel
36. Santa Chiara
37. Santa Maria degli Angeli

~

Former Churches

*I*n the following list, when the earliest date is presented as "By (a certain date)", that is the date of the earliest surviving record. The church was often founded considerably earlier.

Many of these small churches were the possessions or headquarters of Confraternities. These were lay religious organizations, formed to honor a particular saint or perform certain benevolent duties.

1. San Donato. Medieval–1531. This venerable church, dedicated to the original patron saint of Lucca, lay outside the medieval walls. It was located where Baluardo San Donato is now and was torn down for the present walls to be built. A new church (#7) was built in his honor, though he now had to share patron sainthood with St. Paolino.

2. San Giorgio. By 899–1810. By the 1000s this already old church, probably of Lombard origins, had a Benedictine monastery which was aligned with Monte Cassino. In the 1500s it became Dominican and the church and monastery were drastically renovated. When the order was suppressed in 1806, the church was destroyed and the other buildings and grounds were converted to a jail, which they remain today. The church lives on only in the name of the street along which it lay.

3. Santa Giustina. 782–1806. This was perhaps the earliest monastery in Lucca, with a royal pedigree. In 753, Desiderio, the last king of the Lombards, established a convent in Brescia. In 782 (eight years after Desiderio was defeated by Charlemagne) Duke Allo of Lucca founded a monastery in Lucca and aligned it with the one in Brescia. In 851 Emperor Lothario I gave these to his wife and daughter. In 997 Emperor Otto granted both the Brescia and Lucca convents to one Abbess Bertha and five years later the convent acquired the precious skull of St. Giustina, who had been martyred in the second century. In the year 1100 the Irish bishop (later saint) Silao died here and was interred under the main alter. In 1175 the convent passed to the direct control of the Pope and during the next few hundred years successive Popes renewed its privileges. In the 1600s and 1700s it continued to host royal visitors and accept their precious gifts, a collection which became extensive. In the 1700s the church and monastery underwent extensive renovations. When it was suppressed in 1806, the relics of St. Giustina and St. Silao were removed, and the gold, silver, and jewel donations of centuries were plundered. In 1808 Princess Elisa had it converted to an orphanage. In 1876 most of it was demolished to create a hospital; today the site houses government offices. Recent excavations have discovered Roman ruins and the crypt of the original church. As does San Giorgio, Santa Giustina survives only as a street name.

4. San Luca. By 1262–1912. The church of San Luca was annexed to the Hospital of San Luca, which was the largest hospital in the State of Lucca, with extensive land holdings and facilities for tending to the poor and sick. From its origin until 1807 the hospital was administered by the Society of Merchants. The hospital complex encompassed the entire present block, south to Via Vittorio Emmanuele II and east to Via del Crocifisso. The church, on the northwest corner on Via San Paolino, was demolished in 1912. Among its possessions were a triptych by Giuliano di Simone and paintings by Lorenzo Zacchia, which today are in the Villa Guinigi Museum.

5. Santa Maria Filicorbi. By 1105–1812. This church was earlier dedicated to St. Ansano, and for a long time this stretch of what is now Via Galli Tassi was called Via Sant'Ansano. When the church was suppressed, several of its possessions were moved to San Paolino, including the statue of St. Ansano by Valdambrino. In 1382 the eminent local artist Angelo Puccinelli did a painting for the church, now lost.

6. Santi Pietro e Giovanni Battista. About 1150–1801. This was the church of the Knights of Malta, and is now incorporated into Palazzo Cavaliere di Malta (#19).

7. Oratorio of San Michele del Ghironcello. The home of the Confraternity of the Ghironcello, so called for the white stripe (*ghirone*) on the cloaks they wore. The date of its founding is lost, but it flourished in the 1500s. The fraternity existed until 1801 when the new democratic government abolished it, finding it a totally secular organization, "too wealthy, and of little or no use to society."

8. San Lorenzo in Poggio. By 1260–ca. 1810. This was the church of the powerful Di Poggio family, where they had their sepulchers. The church survived the expulsion of the Di Poggio family from the neighborhood in 1522, and gave its name to the little courtyard in front of Puccini's house. In 1399 Angelo Puccinelli painted a triptych for it (lost).

9. San Sensio. By 976–early 1800s. Nothing remains of this church, which once gave its name to the piazza which is today called Cocomeri (because it was where watermelons were sold). Though the earliest record of the church is from 976, it is known that the relics of St. Sensio were brought to Lucca by Bishop Giovanni I, who served from 780-801, and the church likely dated to that time.

10. Santa Maria della Rotunda. By 1131–present. The original version of this church was destroyed in the 1370s when Castruccio Castracani's fortress of the Augusta was demolished. It was rebuilt on a circular plan in the 1600s and frescoed by Ippolito Marracci. It was acquired by Maria Luisa who incorporated it into the Ducal Palace. Although nothing sacred remains, it was refurbished and reopened in 2006 as a museum of Italian emigration, well worth a visit.

11. Santa Lucia. By 818–about 1810. Apparently the original building of this little church was already destroyed by 952, but it was rebuilt and gave its name to the charming street of Via Santa Lucia. It was closed under Napoleon, and incorporated into the adjoining building.

12. Santa Maria in Palazzo. By 700s–1810. It was called *in palazzo* because it was within the ducal court of the Lombards. It must have been reconstructed in the medieval period since in 1359 Paolo di Lazzarino was contracted to make a tabernacle for it. The building was destroyed in 1810 as part of Princess Elisa's urban renewal project.

13. San Pier Maggiore #2. 1588–1806. This large church with three aisles, transept, and cupola was built to replace its namesake (#15, below) when that building was demolished to make room for the

Renaissance walls. The new church became the home of the famous fresco the *Madonna of Miracles*, which had been venerated in town for centuries. The altars had paintings by Federico Zuccari, Domenico Passignano, Francesco Vanni, and Pietro Sorri. It was demolished, in turn, by order of Princess Elisa to make room for Piazza Napoleone.

14. San Dalmazio. By 771–early 1800s. St. Dalmazio became a popular saint among the Lombards. He was supposedly a bishop of Pavia, martyred in 304, but his biography was first written in the 600s. After the church was suppressed it was used for storing the royal carriages.

15. San Pier Maggiore #1. By 720–1515. An important basilica, it lay outside the Roman, and later the medieval, walls in the area known as Silice (from silex, indicating a paved road). This was the most important road leading into the city from Pisa, running up to what was called St. Peter's Gate. There were several churches and pilgrim quarters clustered along the route. The church was demolished during the early preparations for the Renaissance walls.

16. Oratorio della Madonnina. 1600s–present. This charming oratorio was erected in memory of the Basilica of San Pier Maggiore #1, which previously occupied the site. The bas-reliefs on the façade are scenes of St. Paolino, St. Peter, and St. Martin. The sculpture above them, of Madonna Enthroned, may have come from the destroyed church. The interior was renovated in the 1700s but retains a fragment of a fresco, perhaps by Borghese di Pietro, an eminent painter active in Lucca in the mid-1400s. It shows the Madonna and Child with Saints Avertano and Romeo, both of whom died in Lucca, but otherwise are entirely obscure. There is also a tomb slab which is perhaps by Matteo Civitali. The oratorio is now the home of the Sagra Musicale Lucchese.

17. Oratorio of Santa Maria del Gonfalone. 1616–1930s. The Confraternity of the Madonna of the Miracles was formed in 1577 in the nearby church of San Leonardo for the purpose of freeing slaves. It later became associated with the fraternity of Santa Maria del Gonfalone in Rome. In 1616 the fraternity built this small church in honor of the Madonna. Although the group was suppressed under Napoleon, it revived and in the mid-1800s the interior of their church was restored. It was still open in 1920 but was closed in the 1930s. It next served as a mortuary, and during World War II as a first aid station for American soldiers. After the war it became a cinema, and has now been converted to shops.

18. Oratorio of San Giovanetto. By 1049–about 1806. The original church, which had a pauper's home attached, was completely reconstructed in 1539 as an oratorio. The vault was frescoed by Coli and Gherardi, 1678-81; ruined by moisture, it was repainted in the 1770s. The oratorio was suppressed under Napoleon and the building became a warehouse. On the exterior there is a small intricate panel, dating from about the 700s, which probably comes from the original building. To its right is a lunette of the Madonna del Soccorso; it is above what was formerly the entrance to a convent administered by the canons of San Frediano, where intimate relations between the nuns and the canons became a problem in the 1500s. (See San Frediano.) The site is presently a bookstore.

19. Oratorio della Croce. 1382–present. The confraternity of the Cross was formed in the late 1200s to comfort the sick and those condemned to death. In 1382 they built an oratorio on this site, with a hospital to fulfill their mission. The church was renovated in the 1500s, and in the early 1600s Paolo Biancucci painted the *Story of the Cross* for the church. In the early 1700s the building was again renovated and the roof raised. The order was suppressed in 1799 and by 1829 their church was being used as stables. It was later revived as a sacred site, but it is once again reduced to being a warehouse, with the barest of remains in the interior.

20. Oratorio of Santa Zita. 1714–present. The fraternal order of Santa Zita was founded in 1675. After a peripatetic period they bought this site which had been the part of the amphitheater which had been converted into a prison. Suppressed under Napoleon, they re-emerged and were still using this oratorio in the mid-1800s. After extended discussions about what to do with the site it was carefully renovated in the 1990s for secular purposes but retained as much as possible of the original structure.

21. San Pier Cigoli. Mid-1300s–about 1860. This once grand and important church traces its origins to a former church of the same name which dated to at least the 900s; it was located to the west of town, outside first the Roman and then the medieval walls. The building was destroyed when the Pisans attacked in 1341 but it was resurrected soon after on the present site under the rule of the Carmelites and, therefore, was frequently called Chiesa del Carmine, which gave its name to the piazza in front of it. The church became a burial site for important families and had an attached convent and cloister. Well endowed, it was richly embellished in the 1400s and renovated in the 1600s and 1700s with valuable art works, now lost or in museums. The cloister area is now a market. The church itself has for long been undergoing renovations which will restore some of its splendor. Among the artists whose works it once contained and which are now in the Villa Guinigi Museum, are Michelangelo di Pietro Membrini, Giorgio Vasari, and Girolamo Scaglia. Attached to the church at one time was the Oratorio of San Rocco, built in 1631 after the great plague; it was demolished in 1936.

22. San Gregorio. 783–1813. It survived for more than a thousand years, but almost nothing now remains. Founded in honor of Sts. Peter and Gregory, it was rebuilt in the 1100s, with a monastery.

23. San Quirico all'Ulivo. By 1031–1808. Though little remains to indicate its prestigious past, San Quirico was once a wealthy church with rich embellishments and burials of important families. Recent excavations have revealed the early medieval church, which measured 65 ft. by 25 ft. Below this were found graves and other Roman remains. The church was rebuilt by 1290, and it flourished in the 1300s and 1400s. In the Villa Guinigi Museum there are two large fresco fragments from the late 1300s and 1400s which give a good idea of the interior decoration of the time. The church was closed under Napoleon and by 1900 it was owned by the Bernardini family. It had fallen into such decay that the family asked permission to demolish the upper part, which was granted. During this work a trove of gold coins was found which appeared to have been buried there when Florence besieged the city in 1437.

24. Oratorio dei Poveri. 1657–1920. The Confraternity of the Holy Name of Jesus of the Poor was formed in 1540 for the purpose of burying paupers and assisting their survivors. It seems that the group flirted with Protestantism in the early days of the infection, during the time of Peter Martyr, but they soon returned to the fold. They bought this site in 1657 and constructed their small oratorio. In 1860 the group joined with the Confraternity of Charity to form the Confraternity of Mercy (*misericordia*—see church of San Salvatore, #13). This oratorio was used until 1920. Later secular renovations have virtually extinguished it.

25. Santa Maria in Via. By 791–1785. The name comes from the church's location on the Via Decumanus, the main Roman cross street. It was demolished, along with many other buildings, to create Piazza Bernardini in the final days of the oligarchy, a time when a family of such eminence, with a palazzo of such grandeur, could arrange the removal of an entire block of historic buildings, including not only this church but also the house and tower of Castruccio Castracani, in order that their home could be more appropriately presented to view.

26. San Bartolomeo del Gallo. By 1100s–? Little is known of this small church, which gave its name to the street and courtyard where it was located, but some intriguing medieval remnants can be seen by peeking in the windows.

27. San Donnino. 790?–present. The first definite reference to this church is in 1043, but it almost certainly dated back to at least 790. The south exterior wall is exposed and shows the typical Lombard masonry technique of herringbone: river jacks arrayed in alternating diagonal rows. The very low door indicates its ancient origins, before the streets were raised in the 1100s. In the interior (now private) there are traces of decorations from the 1200s-1300s. The church was suppressed in 1808 and acquired by the Balbani family, who owned the adjacent palazzi, and was used as a storehouse. In 1882 it was reopened as the site of a lay confraternity, but was closed finally to any sacred use in 1913.

The importance of the church is indicated by its possession of a painted cross by Bonaventura Berlinghieri, dated about 1260. An extremely early and rare work, the cross was still in the church in the 1850s, but it then passed to the Ottolini Balbani family who sold it. In 1921 it went to the Palazzo Venezia museum in Rome.

28. Oratorio della Maddalena. 1536–1923. The Confraternity of Mary Magdalene was formed by 1336 in conjunction with the

Friars of St. Francis. In 1536 they bought the site of this oratorio, which had formerly been the Church of San Pietro in Vinculis (built 801-805). The Oratorio had three altars; on the main altar was a *Crucifixion*, 1595, by Agostino Ghirlanda da Fivizzano, now in the Villa Guinigi Museum. During the 1800s the church went through various tribulations as attempts were made to restore it or change its use. By 1880 there were only thirty members left in the confraternity and they had little money. It was closed for good in 1923. During World War II the building was put to use by the military, and after the war the owners were the Lazzi brothers, who used it as the station for their bus business and made various renovations. The town considered the piazza of the Cathedral an inappropriate location for such an operation and so the bus station was moved to Piazzale Verdi, where it is today. The building was bought by the Banca del Monte di Lucca, and has undergone considerable restructuring, being used today as a conference hall.

29. Sant'Alessandro Minore. By 1000–? This church, although long closed, can be discerned from the front, where there is still the central door with a lunette. By the early 1000s there were two churches dedicated to St. Alexander in Lucca; this, being the much smaller one, was referred to as *Minore*. Both were the possessions of the pope, and in 1045 he gave this one to the canons of the Cathedral. The larger one was given in 1060 to Bishop Anselmo, who would become Pope Alessandro II the following year.

30. Oratorio Santa Caterina Orfanelli. 1348–1852. In Piazza Santa Maria Forisportam a hospital was founded in 1079 to take care of pilgrims, orphans, and widows. In 1348 an oratorio dedicated to St. Catherine was built next to the hospital. The oratorio went through various changes of administration and uses over the centuries, until it was finally closed in 1852. Its most precious surviving possession is a triptych by Angelo Puccinelli of the *Mystical Marriage of St. Catherine with Sts. Peter, John, Gervasio, and Protasio*, the last two being the patrons of the nearby medieval gate. The painting is today in the Villa Guinigi Museum. On the façade of the oratorio, overlooking the piazza, a fresco of the *Madonna of the Poor* can still be seen.

31. Oratorio Nome di Gesù. 1580–1808. This was the home of the Confraternity of the Holy Name of Jesus of the Circumcision. After the order was suppressed under Napoleon, the building was demolished. The interior had been decorated by the well known painter Jacopo Ligozzi, who frescoed the ceiling and did the paintings for the altars. His *Circumcision* for the main altar is today in the sacristy of the Cathedral. For the side altars he painted a *Name of Jesus* and a *Baptism of Christ*, the latter now in the Guinigi Museum.

32. Santa Maria Annunziata, dell'Alba. 1372–present (closed late 1800s). This very small church was built to house and to honor a fresco of the Annunciation which had been painted on the medieval gate in 1342 and was considered miraculous. The church and the confraternity it hosted was the work of essentially one man, Vituccio di Turello. When the miraculous fresco was threatened by military improvements to the gate in 1372 he formed the Confraternity of the Annunciation and built this church to rescue the fresco. Most of the construction was completed by the time of his death in 1396. One hundred years later, 1493-96, the building was enlarged and provided with a columned portico of two rows (larger than today). Interior improvements continued in the 1500s, and in the 1600s a new marble altar was installed, replacing a wooden one by Masseo Civitali. In 1742 the ceiling was vaulted. In 1808 the confraternity was suppressed, the oratorio closed, and part of the portico torn down to facilitate traffic flow in the street. With the Restoration the oratorio reopened and became the home also of the Confraternity dell'Alba (of the dawn), which had also been suppressed and whose home had been destroyed. This confraternity had existed since 1684, their purpose being to pray for the dead. They acquired their name from their habit of rising early Sunday morning, one of their members walking, before dawn, from house to house, ringing a bell and calling out "Praise be to Jesus, let us pray for the souls in Purgatory." Although admirable, this practice was not universally popular with the neighbors and it was discontinued in 1863.

By the later 1800s the church had severely deteriorated. Many proposals were made regarding its destiny and in the early 1900s much it was almost demolished, the portico about to be torn down. In 1907 demolition work actually began, but was called off after a few days, due to protests. In 1914 the Archbishop drastically renovated the structure, reorienting and reducing the church area, and turned the nave into a school of religious instruction for girls. In the early 2000s it was readapted for use as a hotel and conference hall. These last renovations were carefully done, preserving and exposing what was possible of the earlier sacred structure.

The building retains its inspirational fresco, which has survived many tribulations. The original was a fairly mediocre artistic achievement, and in the 1390s it was touched up, adding the figure of the church's founder and his confraternal brethren. In the 1400s it was completely frescoed over by a much more accomplished artist, perhaps Giuliano di Simone. Restoration work in the 1830s exposed some of the original fresco, and then in the 1980s the 1400s work was removed by the process of strappo, and the original is now again revealed, but devoid, apparently, of its former powers.

33. San Jacopo alla Tomba. By 1260–1808. The old alternative name is San Giacomo. Remarkably little is known about this church, considering its long and locally significant history. It was a pilgrim church, and it apparently had a tomb which was an object of veneration. It lay outside the medieval walls, along one of the main roads into town, so it was the first church to which many pilgrims came, often on their way to Campostela. It had a convent attached and a hospital for pilgrims. Though it is not certain, it appears that the church had a painting by Angelo Puccinelli of the *Assumption of the Virgin*, now in the possession of Santa Maria Forisportam. When the church was closed, the site was turned into a paper factory and nothing remains.

34. San Franceschetto. 1309–present. Founded in 1309 as a private chapel of the Fondora family. Marco Paoli considers it the earliest example of a private, aristocratic chapel. In the 20th century it became a movie theatre, and was later acquired by the town for use as a half-way house.

35. Santa Lucia Chapel. 1354–present. This was the chapel of the Guinigi family, and their burial spot. The first stone was laid by Francesco Guinigi with his own hands, on the site of a destroyed oratorio dedicated to Santa Lucia; the building was completed by Francesco's death in 1358. It has entrances on either end. The Guinigi continued to make donations to the church, including a painting by Agostino Marti for the main altar. Over the years it housed various confraternities.

36. Santa Chiara. About 1400–late 1800s. This was the church and convent of the Franciscan Poor Clares, near the church of San Francesco, built on land donated by Paolo Guinigi, whose family was closely associated with the Franciscans. After the Napoleonic suppression the church and cloisters were occupied by the Capuchins until 1866.

37. Santa Maria degli Angeli. 1610–1808. At one time this church housed the Berlinghieri cross which is now in the Villa Guinigi Museum. The cloister can still be visited, though the structures have all been drastically renovated.

Church not shown on the map:

Santi Gemignana e Ginese. By 1200, later incorporated into Palazzo Burlamacchi (#12) in the 1500s.

~

The Palazzi of Lucca

Palazzi

For entries followed by (F) the family is dealt with in the Family section.

1. Palazzo Moriconi—Reconstructed in the 1500s on medieval houses and the remains of the Roman theatre. The entranceway with a lovely iron lunette is very similar to the nearby Palazzo Fanucci (#7). Evidence of Guelph windows can be seen on the piano nobile. *(F)*

2. Palazzo Boccella—One of the grandest and most interesting mansions. It was built in the 1500s and 1600s by the extremely wealthy Boccella family in the Manneristic style of the great Tuscan villas. It is an extravagance in conservative Lucca and was looked on somewhat askance when it was built. The exterior has a profusion of fantastic *mascheroni* (grotesque masks), an imposing main entrance, and excellent detailing on the wood eaves. The interior was once elaborately painted and the salon is still in excellent condition. The themes of its paintings are somewhat uncertain, portraying what looks like Pope Julius II but is perhaps Paul III, who visited Lucca in 1541. (The Boccella family had long and close ties with the papacy.) Another painting portrays a victory over the Turks, and others show familial scenes and banquets, all done in a vibrant Mannerist palette. The *stemma* (coat of arms) over the main door is that of the Bernardini, who were its later owners. *(F)*

3. Palazzo Ottolini—Today best known as Palazzo Poschi Meuron. Along Via San Giorgio it has a typical Lucchese façade of the 1500s, understated but with a grand entrance door. Reconstructed on buildings of the 1200s, the remains of a tower are still evident on the west side. Originally belonging to the Busdraghi family, it was sold in the 1600s to the Ottolini and in the early 1800s to the Meuron family, who intermarried with the Poschi. *(F)*

4. Palazzo Parenzi—Constructed in the early 1500s on houses and towers of the 1200s. It originally had extensive gardens in the rear, where there is now a parking lot. The entrance on Via Santa Giustina leads through a vaulted passage into the former gardens, and a large carriage entrance is on Via della Colombaia. Today the building belongs to the town. Many of the furnishings were transferred to Palazzo Mansi (Museum #1) after a marriage between the Parenzi and Mansi families. *(F)*

5. Palazzo Diodati—One of the greatest Lucchese palazzi. It is commonly known as Palazzo Orsetti, for the family which lived there from 1661 until 1963. It is now owned by the Commune and can be visited. The rooms which were remodeled during the Napoleonic period are well preserved and are a popular site for weddings. There is also a small collection of paintings, among them *Death of Wallenstein* by Paolini.

The understructure of the palazzo dates to the 1200s when it was owned by the Rolandinghi (or Rolandini) family, who gave their name to the courtyard in the rear (now Piazza G. Leonardi) and thence to the church of Santa Maria Corteorlandini. In 1332 the palazzo was sold to the Saggina family; in the exposed decorative brick on the rear their initial "S" can still be seen. In 1399 it was bought by Alessandro Diodati, a doctor and merchant, whose descendants would live there until 1661.

The exterior has two equally important facades, each with a stunning doorway, the most impressive in Lucca. They may have been made for the visit of Emperor Charles V and Pope Paul III in 1541, during which the Diodati hosted the Emperor's daughter. John Milton was a later guest. The walled garden across the street to the east, now open to the public, formerly belonged to the Orsetti family. *(F)*

6. Palazzo Minutoli-Tegrimi—The present incarnation of the building dates to the 1600s, but underneath are the medieval walls and tower of the Tegrimi family who owned it in the 1200s. The remains of their tower can be identified on the southeast corner, on Piazza San Salvatore. The Tegrimi later merged with the Minutoli family, who owned the palazzo until recently. The building is now best known for housing the Trattoria Da Leo, one of the most popular eateries in town.

In the 1200s there were three towers on this corner of Piazza San Salvatore. The one which still exists, known as *Torre del Veglio*, the Watchtower, is one of the few towers which remain in nearly original state. *(F)*

7. Palazzetto Fanucci—This is only a palazzetto, almost just a house, but an interesting one. It has a large entrance door for such a small building. The ground floor is impressively high, given the overall dimensions, and is what elevates it above the status of a house. The structure is best known for retaining its Guelph windows. The underlying structure dates from the 1200s, the present building from the 1500s. The name is somewhat arbitrary: the Fanucci family owned it in 1725. In 1200 it was the site of the Narducci house and tower, of which nothing remains.

8. Palazzo Massoni—An excellent example of a 1500s Lucchese palazzo. The reconstruction at that time reoriented the entrance from the narrow Via Santa Giustina to the broader Piazza San Matteo, permitting a small flight of entrance steps. The noble Massoni family owned it in the 1700s. In the 1200s the Olivieri family owned the underlying structure. *(F)*

9. Palazzo Malpigli—This grand palazzo dominates this stretch of Via Santa Giustina. The coat of arms over the door is that of the Malpigli and bears the date 1506. The impressively extended façade is substantially intact, though the windows were altered (eliminating Guelph windows), as were the entranceways, in the 1700s.

The grand carriage entrance leads to a colonnaded portico which extends to the large garden in the rear. This is a reminder of the gardens which once graced the interiors of many palazzi, and some of which, hidden, still do. A lovely (but frustrating) iron gate separates us from the garden. The columns of the portico were made when the Civitali were the sculptural masters of Lucca and reflect their aesthetic.

The great poet Torquato Tasso (1544-1595) was a friend of the Malpigli and stayed in the house. He wrote of the *grandissima* quantity of books in all languages and all sciences, all bound in silk, of many paintings, maps, globes, and celestial charts, crystals to restore the sight, mathematical instruments, and so on.

The slightly undulating façade is a product of the medieval buildings which provide the underlying structure. We know who owned it in the 1200s—the Paruta family who transferred it to the Malpigli, itself a family dating to the 1000s.

The carriage entrance on the east leads to a separate, smaller palazzo and garden (not shown separately on the map). This portion belonged to the Controni in the 1700s, and later to the Giannini family, who married into the Orsetti family.

10. Palazzo Dipinto—The name literally means the "painted palace," so called for the frescoes which at one time covered its façade. They were done by Agostino Ghirlanda in the 1500s for the De Nobili family, who rebuilt the palazzo. Fortunately they preserved the medieval brickwork on the west side, which has some of the best examples of decorative brick in the city, a panoply of arches and the ghosts of former windows. With enough patience you can decipher renovations spanning centuries and imagine the building's previous incarnations. On the front there is one remaining Guelph window.

11. Palazzo Garbesi—This small palazzo of the 1500s was built not by nobility or wealthy merchants, but by a family of bakers and millers. The first record of the family is in 1460. By 1599 they were listed 40th on the tax roles; it seems they had very recently improved their lot.

12. Palazzo Burlamacchi—Built in the early 1500s by the Burlamacchi, it comprises an entire block and incorporates medieval houses as well as the church of Sts. Gemignana and Ginese, which existed by the year 1200. The palazzo has two important facades, though the main entrance is along Via Burlamacchi, where one Guelph window survives.

Among those who lived here was the Dominican Friar Filippo Burlamacchi who was long regarded as the first biographer of Savonarola, though the author is now known as Pseudo Burlamacchi. Filippo was, however, well acquainted with Savonarola and led the way in welcoming his followers to Lucca after the Florentine preacher's unfortunate demise. The most famous Burlamacchi was Francesco, who was born in this house. It is his statue which stands in Piazza San Michele. A plaque on the southeast corner of the house records that in 1548 he was "decapitated in Milan for desiring Liberty" (of Tuscany from the Medici tyranny). *(F)*

13. Palazzo Cittadella/Orsetti—This vast palazzo has been occupied since the 1200s, at which time it had a tower at each corner on Via San Paolino. It was given its present appearance in the 1600s when it passed to the Orsetti family. Notice the ornate carving on the eaves, and the grand carriage entrance on the east side. It was later owned by the Cittadella family, whose coat of arms is over the entrance on Via Burlamacchi and who gave their name to the piazza in which Puccini sits. One of their former houses was directly behind the Puccini statue. The piazza was formerly named for the Di Poggio family before their downfall and the razing of their houses in 1522. In 1896 the palazzo was inherited by the Mazzarosa family, after the death of the last Cittadella. Befitting the wealth of its owners, the interior is still sumptuous. *(F)*

14. Palazzo Sardi—The base of a tower from the 1200s is still evident on the corner along Via San Paolino. The present palazzo was begun by Filippo Sardi in 1637 and enlarged by one of his descendants in 1726 who added the large carriage entrances along the courtyard. The wavy wall along Via Burlamacchi is a good example of newer buildings incorporating previous houses. In the 19th century the interior was redecorated in the style of the day, and the palazzo had a wealth of art and rare furnishings.

15. Palazzo Sesti—Built in the early 1500s on towers and houses from the 1200s, which explains the off-center entrance door. In the early 1700s it belonged to the Sesti family, and looks today much as it did then. Nearby was the church of Santa Maria Filicorbi, later called Sant'Ansano (former church #5).

16. Palazzo Bottini—A fairly arbitrary family attribution, it is one of the lesser of many residences of the Bottini during their years as one of Lucca's preeminent families. Yet they had arrived late in the city; they became citizens only in the late 1400s. The Malpigli family, who went on to much grander palazzi, had already been in Lucca for centuries when they owned the building in the 1200s.

The present incarnation of the palazzo dates from the mid-1500s, though the first floor windows are later, and certainly inharmonious, but they are typical of the street level windows omnipresent in Lucca—functional. Still, it is a pleasantly symmetrical palazzo, with three steps up to the front door, a Lucchesi acknowledgement of the idea of an entrance stairway. (F)

17. Palazzo Boccella—Not being very attractive on the façade, it seems appropriate that today it serves as a bureaucratic office, the Notary Archives. It retains, however, a stately colonnaded courtyard, almost a secular cloister, with capitals from the workshop of Nicolao Civitali. The coat of arms of the Boccella is woven into one of these. The palazzo was rebuilt in the early 1500s. The odd arrangement of the front windows and door reflect the underlying structure from the 1200s. (F)

The palazzo which lies to the north bears a plaque commemorating Lorenzo Nottolini, Lucca's great 19th century hydraulic engineer. He lived and died there.

18. Palazzo Bernardini—(Not the famous Palazzo Bernardini, #65.) The palazzo has an elevated section which was built before 1561, when it was already owned by the Bernardini. In that year, the Sanminiati family bought adjoining houses, and the two families reached an agreement to not raise their houses higher than they were at the time. This agreement was to remain in effect in perpetuity. The elevated section retains its Guelph windows of the early 1500s. The carriage entrance is just to the west. The Bernardini sold the palazzo in 1871. (F)

19. Palazzo della Magione dei Cavalieri di Malta—This was the home in Lucca of the Knights of Malta, to whom passed the wealth of the Templars after a papal bull banned that order in 1312. The Templars had been in Lucca since 1143, about 20 years after their founding in Jerusalem. In 1799 Lucca banned the Maltese Knights and confiscated their property. During renovations in 1637 remains of the Roman wall were discovered. The building underwent extensive renovations in the 1700s and refacing in the 1800s. On the east side of the palazzo there was a small church dedicated to Sts. Peter and John the Baptist which dated to the 1200s and was the church of the Knights.

20. Palazzo Santini—In the Middle Ages this site was on the north edge of the open quarter of town, so there were no medieval houses or towers to constrain the palazzi which were built later. The area was taken over in the early 1300s by Castruccio Castracani to build his fortress, the Augusta, which when later demolished furnished a great deal of building material. The present structure was built in the late 1600s by the Santini family. It later passed to the Bondacca and the Parenzi families, after multiple renovations. Behind it were extensive gardens.

21. Palazzo Mansi—This lovely palazzo, set back from the street, almost like a small villa, was one of many which belonged to the Mansi family. It had a garden along the boundary with the Ducal Palace but when Maria Luisa had Nottolini rebuild the northern wing, a good part of the Mansi estate and its gardens were appropriated. Eventually it was inherited by Ascanio Mansi, minister and State Secretary to Maria Luisa. The front was completely restructured after 1820. *(F)*

22. Palazzo Pfanner—A rare opportunity to enter a palazzo. It is best known for its garden in the rear, with the tower of San Frediano looming over it. The iron lunette over the main door is one of the best in town. On the western exterior, where brick is exposed, it can be seen that the underlying structure is medieval, with remains of arches over the windows.

The original palazzo was built by the Moriconi family, but was extensively renovated in the late 1660s by Domenico Controni, at great expense. It was bought in 1860 by the Swiss Felice Pfanner, to live in and to build a brewery. The license to do so was granted with the provision that it be "a good German brewery." The ground floor was open to customers who could enjoy their beer at tables in the great hall and garden; it operated until 1929. The palazzo passed to Pfanner's son Pietro, a well known doctor, mayor of Lucca, and local benefactor. It is closed to visits in the winter.

23. Palazzo Lucchesini—The present structure is a 1700s remodeling of a 1500s building, as shown by the remains of Guelph windows. There is a lovely external staircase and courtyard which can be seen from the wall and the Palazzo Pfanner garden. The palazzo was acquired by the Bourbon in 1819, and turned into a school. Today it serves as the Liceo Classico Niccolò Macchiavelli.

24. Palazzo Fatinelli—The Fatinelli were the masters of Santa Zita, and the fountain and sculptures on the façade celebrate her, but this is not actually where she lived. Zita died in 1278. The palazzo was built probably in the late 1200s but the Fatinelli did not take possession until 1370. The family certainly lived nearby, however, only a short distance from San Frediano. The palazzo was renovated, with a new door and windows, in the 1500s though it still keeps much of its late medieval atmosphere. *(F)*

25. Palazzo Andriani—A fairly plain building, but with an imposing entrance which constitutes almost the entirety of the decoration and utterly dominates the façade. It was constructed in the early 1700s on medieval buildings. Remains of the Roman wall have been found in the basement, providing evidence of a bulge in the wall to accommodate the theater.

26. Palazzo Orsucci—A wonderfully unique palazzo, which occupies an entire block and has a coherent design all the way around. The 2nd floor windows are surmounted by niches with large shells. It has an elaborate entrance door with crowded carvings and grotesque masks somewhat similar to those on Palazzo Boccella (#2). Note the mask on the SE corner, with an exquisite lantern attached to it. The carriage entrance is in the rear. Also in the rear, note a small room jutting out,  originally perhaps a lavatory. In the street directly below there is a small round "manhole"—could it be that originally a pipe went straight down into it? Built on medieval structures, the present palazzo was commissioned in the 1700s by Lorenzo Orsucci, who is responsible for the upgrade of the façade but not the underlying building; this dates to at least the 1500s, when it was owned by

Francesco Cattani. The Town in 1558 banished him for being a Lutheran, and confiscated this palazzo.

27. Palazzo Sardini—A plaque on the west side records that Giacomo Sardini restored the palazzo in 1795. The underlying structure is late medieval (1300s), with obvious tower remains, with corbels and putlog holes for wooden porches. Note the battlements on top with a Poseidon-like face and the sad faced Liberty era mask below the plaque. The battlements are meant to conceal the octagonal rooms on top. The large entranceway on the piazza looks like a carriage entrance, but leads directly to a stairway. On the south side at ground level between the tower pilasters is the arch of a medieval door. There are many chisel marks indicating the chipping off of the plaster which once coated the surface.  The three towers incorporated into the palazzo belonged to the Arnolfini. They sold it in 1587 to Davino Sardini, who had become very wealthy as a merchant with the Buonvisi in Flanders. The Sardini family died out in the early 1900s. The palazzo was restored, with care and sensitivity, in the late 1900s, by Count Minutoli Tegrimi. *(F)*

28. Palazzo Conti/Boccella—Generally considered one of the most beautiful late Renaissance palazzi. To see why, walk through to the inner courtyard if the door is open. There is an intricate iron gate and colonnade. The palazzo was restructured on three medieval residences in the 1500s, originally with Guelph windows on the piano nobile. The palazzo is known by various names. In the 1300s it belonged to the Micheli family. Having suffered financial reversals they sold it to the Gualanducci about 1620, who sold it to the Conti about 1750, who in turn were soon forced to sell it to the Boccella. In the early 1900s it was bought by Diego Sani, a successful exporter of olive oil to America, and is today generally known as Palazzo Sani. It is now the site of the Commercial Association of Lucca. *(F—Boccella)*

29. Palazzo Onesti—The plaster which once covered the façade has been removed, exposing the underlying brick, which allows us to appreciate the typical medieval structure, although the arched openings have long been filled in. The high arches of the ground floor originally opened to merchants' shops. The next two stories would have been used as warehouses and the small upper floor as living space. When the building was converted to a palazzo, probably in the 1300s, the 2nd and 3rd floor arches would have had mullioned windows installed. *(F)*

30. Palazzo Tucci—In the 1300s here stood the house and tower of the Guicciardi family, the tower being on the northwest corner. Beginning in 1751 the palazzo was radically transformed by Joseph Tucci, work being completed by 1779, the date inscribed on the extravagant front door surmounted by a balcony—an unusual feature in Lucca. The eaves are of stone and flow all the way around. The interior was lavishly decorated, much of which remains. The rear side retains its sinuous medieval brickwork, although with replaced windows, the originals evident but bricked up. It is a good spot to mentally reconstruct the original architecture. A plaque records that here was born the operatic composer Alfredo Catalani in 1854; there is a monument to him on Baluardo San Paolino. The palazzo remains in the Tucci family.

31. Palazzo Santini—This grand palazzo today houses the offices of the Commune of Lucca, so you may enter to admire the remains of the frescoed vault ceiling and grotesques on the street level. As is evident from the size and sumptuousness of the palazzo, the

Santini were one of the wealthiest families in Lucca. It is their coat of arms over the main entrance on Via del Moro. Even the eaves of the building received exceptional attention. The present building was begun in the 1630s by uniting several medieval structures. The passageway, still a convenient short cut, was an alley in the Middle Ages.

When the Grand Duke of Tuscany visited Lucca in 1775 he was lavishly received here. Unfortunately, little of the interior splendor remains, having been reduced to bureaucratic functionality.

32. Palazzo Trenta—This is the old Trenta palazzo, much more modest than their new one (#50). Along the street it retains much of its medieval appearance. It was constructed in the early 1300s by combining two structures of the 1200s, the renovations including mullioned windows (most of which have been altered). The palazzo was acquired by Federico Trenta in 1361 and included the courtyard in the rear, entered from Via del Moro. By 1450 it was called the "old palazzo" of the family. In the 1640s they sold it to the Marchiò family, by whose name the courtyard is still known. On the front is the Trenta crest, with three bull heads. *(F)*

33. Palazzo Cenami—One of the lesser residences belonging to the eminent Cenami family. The building dates to the 1400s but underwent renovations before being bought by Felice Cenami in the latter 1600s. It has an interior column-lined courtyard from the 1500s. The carriage entrance, which is often open, is greatly decayed but retains remnants of its frescoed vaults. *(F)*

34. Palazzo Decanato/Cenami—This extensive building, stretching almost the entire length of the block, was designed by Francesco Marti, a noted goldsmith and sculptor, this being his only attributed work as an architect. The previously existing buildings had for centuries belonged to the church of San Michele and had also been the home of the Anziani (the supreme governing council of Lucca). In 1501 the eminent Silvestro Gigli, who was not only deacon of San Michele but also Bishop of Worcester, made a deal with Nicolao Cenami in which it was agreed that Gigli would provide for the demolition of the buildings while Cenami would raise the funds to pay for the new construction. Cenami would take possession of the lower floors to rent out to merchants, as well as the upper level, while the piano nobile would be used by the deacons (*decanato*) and the priests of the church. With the death of Cenami his heirs contested the will, leading to a conflict with the Deacon of San Michele, Martino Gigli, who ultimately acquired the building in 1560.

The palazzo has been significantly altered since that time. A view of the original building is offered in the masterly intarsia by Ambrogio and Nicolao Pucci, which can be seen in the Villa Guinigi Museum; dated 1529, it shows the merchant shops of the day and the Guelph windows typical of the architecture of the time.

35. Palazzo Vanni [identified as Baldassari on map]—The corrected attribution of this palazzo was made by Marco Paoli. The Vanni family owned it as early as 1404. The present building existed by 1529 since it appears in the intarsia by the Pucci, mentioned above (#34). It has been significantly renovated by new shops and the replacement of the original Guelph windows. The family crest over the entranceway, with a dragon, is that of the Vanni, not the Baldassari.

36. Palazzo Ghivizzani—This was the most important residence of the Ghivizzani family. This lovely section of Piazza San Michele thankfully retains a good deal of its look from the 1300s, including the row of mullioned windows with gothic trefoil arches. The underlying structures are older, not surprisingly. It is likely that some of the foundations are Roman, as this was (probably) one side of the Roman forum. In the 1200s there were a row of 5 towers here, separated by the houses of various important families. The towers were later incorporated into the new palazzo. On the far left of the block, as early as 818 was the small church of Santa Lucia, which gave its name to the street leading north out of the piazza. (*F*)

37. Palazzo Arnolfini/Cenami—One of the most imposing palazzi in Lucca, it was built by the Arnolfini in the 1500s, though exactly when, and by which member of the family, is a matter of dispute, as is the architect, though it is usually attributed to Nicolao Civitali. Whatever its origins it is an exceptional display of wealth right in the center of town. It has decidedly Florentine influences, particularly the stonework of the ground floor, the upper windows, and the interior courtyard with a portico on all sides. Notice the very fine iron work of the lunettes over the two entrance doors. The palazzo was bought by the Cenami in 1605; at the time they were the second wealthiest family in town and the Arnolfini were fourth.

The interior retains its original decorations which, as is to be expected, are exceptional, but most of it is not open to the public. Fortunately the ground floor can be visited. It still belongs to the Cenami family. *(F)*

38. Palazzo Fivizzani—Piazza San Giusto, the high point of town, has been one of the most prestigious areas since Lombard times, when it was the site of the royal court. In the 1500s most of the palazzi were completely renovated, but underlying them are the medieval structures. Within Fivizzani there is a former tower, evidenced by the exceptional width of an interior wall.

Along Via Cenami there are other medieval remnants, including decorative brick which survived by being plastered over for many years, and several smaller Renaissance palazzi.

39. Palazzo Gigli—A milestone in Lucchese architecture because, with Palazzo Bernardini, it is the oldest example of a palazzo with interior courtyard. It is generally considered the most beautiful example of 1500s civil architecture in Lucca. The project was probably begun about 1500 by Matteo Civitali and completed by his son Nicolao about 1525. The Guelph windows, which had great influence on subsequent architecture, may have first been used on this palazzo.

The Gigli family died out in the 1700s and the palazzo passed through several hands until, in 1893, it became the home of the *Cassa di Risparmio di Lucca* (Lucca Savings Bank). The first such benevolent bank was formed in Vienna in 1819 and the idea soon spread to Italy. By 1837 the bank in Lucca was operational, dedicated to returning its profits "to the poor who were friends of our Lord." The organization still funds many cultural works, restorations, books, conventions and much more. *(F)*

40. Palazzo Paoli—This grand building is now the home of Hotel Napoleone.

41. Palazzo Franciotti—This palazzo lies on what was the outskirts of the Ducal court in the 800s and 900s and it may lie on the site of the royal mill. The present building has its origins in the 1300s when it was perhaps already owned by the Franciotti family. It underwent extensive renovations in the 1500s and 1600s, by which time it had passed by marriage to the Arnolfini. In the late 1600s the palazzo was extended to the east, into the area which was previously the garden. *(F)*

42. Palazzo Mansi—One of many palazzi belonging to the various lines of this ancient and eminent family, it is representative of the palazzi built "from scratch" beginning in the later 1500s, when this area of town was created by the new walls. The new land was subdivided into rectangular lots which were sold by the city to help fund the wall construction. The new palazzo did not need to adapt to previous structures and so could be designed rationally, with a functional elegance, the rooms arranged around a central courtyard. The ground floor has been degraded somewhat by the opening of shops, and the top floor is a later addition. The main entrance door with the crest of the Mansi has maintained its dignity. Notice the lanterns at the corners, each unique. *(F)*

43. Palazzo Antelminelli—The façade of this expansive palazzo has remained relatively unmolested since it was constructed in the early 1500s; the rather simple doorway and the ground floor windows are typical of that period. The upper windows were originally Guelph crosses, which are still discernible. The entire structure has a severity and lack of ornamentation appropriate for its time, when the Savonarolan ethic was dominant in town.

The palazzo was built by Bernardino Antelminelli (of the family of Castruccio Castracani). He was the father of Baldassare, who in the mid-1500s did much to restore the good name of the family. The treacherous ambitions of his son unfortunately led to the line's final downfall. The palazzo then passed through several hands. It became the last residence of the Count and Countess Guinigi-Magrini, by whose name the palazzo is commonly known. In their day it was lavishly decorated, with an impressive art collection, now dispersed. Today the palazzo belongs to the town. *(F)*

44. Palazzo Buonvisi, the new or **Summer Residence**—In the 1600s this stretch of Via Fillungo was known as the Street of the Buonvisi because their two grand palazzi dominated the thoroughfare. This residence was built in the 1580s by unifying medieval structures, evident in the gentle curve of the façade. It was probably built by Buonviso Buonvisi, who was made a Cardinal in 1599, the same year his family was ranked the richest in Lucca, with more than twice the wealth of the 2nd ranked Cenami. The palazzo reflects their standing. It is the only one in the city with two interior courtyards, each at a different level,

being from separate original buildings, though this difference is disguised on the exterior. The northern section had previously been owned by the Burlamacchi. It is recorded that in the early 1700s this palazzo was used as the summer residence of the Buonvisi, the older one, nearly opposite, being the winter quarters. In the early 1800s the palazzo was not only luxuriously furnished but had an extensive library and a collection of more than 200 paintings. Later in that century the possessions were sold by Prince Poniatowski, one of the heirs, to pay his extensive debts. Today the building houses the town's art school, so you can step in to look at the lovely courtyard. *(F)*

45. Palazzetto Buonvisi—A small, charming residence, built about 1600. It was set back to allow the carriageway to the rear of the neighboring palazzo to remain open. In the late 1700s it apparently had a very fine garden in the French style. *(F)*

46. Palazzo Cenami (Mansi)—One of the best located palazzi, facing onto Piazza San Frediano. The Cenami lived here in a grand house as early as 1405, though it was rebuilt in the 1500s. In the middle of that century it was sold to Gerolamo Menocchi, the richest merchant of leather in the city, who had offices throughout Europe. It later passed to the Mansi family, through marriage. *(F—Menocchi)*

47. Palazzo Busdraghi—A great hodge-podge of a palazzo created from a number of pre-existing buildings, evident in the erratic interior rooms. Along Via Fillungo is a unique entranceway with Doric columns, an early 1500s iron lunette, carved wood door, grotesque reliefs, and the Busdraghi crest. This oversized palazzo was once another of the Buonvisi palazzi, but was bought by the Busdraghi in 1630; the contract was signed in the Oratorio of San Giovanetto, across the street (former church #18). The main façade of the palazzo is on Via Busdraghi, where there is also a large garden. On Via Fillungo there is an excellent survival of decorative brick. Notice also the eaves. The palazzo is also known as Brancoli-Busdraghi. The Brancoli family was in Lucca as early as 1305. In 1877 they were permitted to join their name and crest to the Busdraghi, of whom there were no members surviving.

48. Palazzo Buonvisi, the old or **Winter Residence**—This extensive palazzo, hardly identifiable as a single residence, was the old Buonvisi palazzo. When it was severely damaged during the *Straccioni* uprising in 1531, the family built the more suitable "summer" palace across the street. The entire façade along Via Fillungo retains its medieval aspect. Whether the family actually retired here during the winter is uncertain.

49. Palazzo Moriconi—This architecturally unique palazzo is a solid Florentine presence along Via Fillungo, superimposed on ancient structures, including the Roman amphitheatre. The palazzo was built by Lando Moriconi in the late 1300s by  uniting buildings which had long been in his family. Although it was refaced with stone about 1500 the medieval aspect was preserved, the mullion windows of the upper stories still plainly evident. *(F)*

50. Palazzo Trenta—This is the new, grand palazzo of the Trenta family, built at the height of their eminence and wealth. In 1412 Lorenzo Trenta began acquiring the property, at the same time as he was employing Jacopo della Quercia to work on the Trenta chapel in San Frediano. The palazzo was probably completed by Lorenzo's heirs in the mid-1400s. It established a new style of construction in Lucca, the first definitive alternative to *Trecento* (1300s) style; instead of brick it had stone facing, and substituted mullion windows with large, closely spaced rectangular ones. The great stone portal opened for carriages into an interior courtyard. The family crest still adorns the façade. It is reported that Charles VIII of France stayed here briefly in 1494, as he passed through on his way to claim the throne of Naples, thereby commencing the Italian Wars. *(F)*

51. Palazzi Bartolomei—In the 1500s all the palazzi surrounding Piazza San Pietro Somaldi were owned by various members of the Bartolomei family. The largest, to the right of the church, later passed to the Spada and Cenami families. The most beautiful, on the north side of the piazza, has a unique large garden on the second story overlooking the piazza. It has a lovely columned loggia and originally had mullion windows in the main building, attesting to its medieval foundations. *(F)*

Piazza San Pietro Somaldi, which lay outside the Roman walls, was in ancient times the slaughterhouse center of the town. This was closed down when the medieval walls incorporated the area into the town proper. In the first stage of gentrification it became the area where many artists had their workshops. By the 1500s, with Lucca's economic expansion and a need to open new real estate for the wealthy, the piazza became transformed into the luxurious living area it remains today.

The plaque on the westerly palazzo commemorates Carlo del Prete, a famous aviator who, among other accomplishments, in 1928 broke the world distance record by flying non-stop from Rome to Brazil. He died a few weeks later in a plane crash, at age thirty-one. He lived here, as do his descendants.

52. Palazzo Spada—This lovely palazzo, recently restored, holds a commanding site at the corner of Via Nuova, Piazza San Pietro Somaldi, and Via della Fratta. Its irregularity is the result of being adapted in the 1500s to the underlying medieval structures. It was one of several palazzi owned by this ancient family, which was aligned by marriage with the Bartolomei, who owned all the other palazzi on the piazza. The interior decoration, with beautiful ceilings, is from the 1630s. *(F)*

53. Palazzo Bottini—A representative palazzo along what is still commonly known as Via Nuova—New Street—the descriptive name by which it was known in the 1400s, after the medieval walls had been built; this road ran just outside where the Roman wall had been. When the area was incorporated into the city proper many of the newly rich, lacking hereditary homesteads, bought up the lots to build their houses. The Bottini family built one of the most beautiful, with a columned courtyard and rear garden; it is the Bottini crest we see over the entrance and in the courtyard. The palazzo was built in the late 1500s; the interior renovations were complete by 1607. It today houses the rooms of hotel La Magnolia, so it can easily be enjoyed. *(F)*

54. Palazzo De Nobili—A truly impressive residence, comprising an entire block, appropriate for such an ancient and noble family. The De Nobili family had lived in the vicinity since early times, but when they became aligned by marriage with Pope Nicholas V (1447-1455) their already significant fortune increased substantially. Pope Nicholas visited the city in 1447. The next year the De Nobili began buying the houses where this palazzo now stands. It was reconstructed in the mid-1500s, the north side having for its foundation the Roman wall and one of its gates. It has undergone subsequent renovations but the exquisite principal entrance on Piazza del Carmine is original. Old catalogues reveal that it once housed an impressive array of paintings, silks, and objets d'art. The size, grandeur and structural independence of the palazzo later made it a suitable home for the Bank of Italy. *(F)*

55. Palazzo Saminiati—One of the many palazzi of this very wealthy family. It was one of their residences by at least the 1500s, but the building was radically transformed in the 1730s when the façade along Piazza Guidiccioni became the front of the building. It was obviously inspired by, and meant to rival and complement, the opposing Palazzo Guidiccioni. It became the seat of public offices during the Bourbon period of the early 1800s. *(F)*

56. Palazzo Guidiccioni—The Guidiccioni family lived on this site since at least the 1200s, making it the palazzo which was continuously inhabited by the same family for the longest period of any residence in town. On the rear you can see the remains of the medieval building's arches and pilasters. In 1539 Cardinal Bartolomeo Guidiccioni wrote that the building was in great disrepair and threatened with collapse. Rehabilitation began soon after, but it seems that most of the work was done after the 1560s, in conscious imitation of the work of the architect Bartolomeo Ammannati (designer of the Pitti Palace) who was in Lucca at the time working on the Palazzo Pubblico. The two palazzi show similarities, especially in the lower windows. Vincenzo Civitali has traditionally been credited with some of the work, but this seems not to be the case. It also appears that architectural tweaking went on until the 1700s.

In 1822 the building became the State Archives, which it remains. They are famous as the most extensive civic archive in Italy. *(F)*

57. Palazzo Mei—Reconstructed about 1500 on existing buildings. *(F)*

58. Palazzi Guinigi—These two palazzi of the Guinigi family are the most beautiful, and best preserved, gothic palazzi in Lucca. And, of course, there is that 130 feet high tower with trees on top. The Guinigi family lived in the neighborhood since at least the 1200s; at that time they had a tower, though not the one we see today.

Both palazzi were built about 1375. The one on the east was probably built first, by Francesco Guinigi, *"padre della patria,"* on the foundations of medieval buildings and the Roman wall. There are observable remains of the medieval stone arches at ground level though the ground floor was altered in the 1500s when the series of arches was filled in and new rectangular windows installed. The upper floors are well preserved originals, with gothic lobed arches on the mullion windows. In 1401 the building was divided among the three sons of Francesco: the first floor went to Paolo, who had just made himself Lord of Lucca. Baldassare took the second and Giovanni the third. After the fall of Paolo Guinigi his part went to the Commune. By about 1530 the whole building was in the possession of the powerful and rich Vincenzo Guinigi (1504-1551). After the great bankruptcy of the Guinigi partnership in 1574 the palazzo was sold, but Tommaso Guinigi, Francesco's son, was able to repurchase it in 1588 and at his death in 1615 it passed to his son. This line of the Guinigi died out in 1816.

The other palazzo, with the tower, was built slightly later by the sons of Nicolao Guinigi: Dino, Lazzaro, and Jacopo. It is a more imposing building, with a higher ground floor and wider mullion windows harmoniously continued around both facades. The ornamentation which was characteristic of Trecento architecture was brought to an elaborate conclusion. The tower was something of an anachronism, built at a time when most wealthy families were tearing them down. It was erected on the foundation of a medieval tower of the Benettoni family. This palazzo remained in the Guinigi family until it was acquired by the town in 1956 from Count Arturo. *(F)*

59. Palazzo Controni—This large, beautiful palazzo was built in the 1690s by Giovanni Controni, who had bought the property from the Guinigi family. It is the most grand and beautiful of the palazzi built outside the medieval city, unconstrained by underlying structures. The façade is relentlessly symmetrical, with a long row of high arched windows on the piano nobile. It is self-consciously grand, even employing street side balconies, which are very unusual in Lucca. In the mid-1800s it was bought by the Massoni family, which was well connected with the Bourbon court. They sold it off piecemeal during the 20th century. *(F)*

60. Palazzo Franciotti (or **Gentili**)—This lovely palazzo is one of the best preserved examples of late Trecento domestic architecture. It has often been called the most beautiful in Lucca. It dates approximately to the same period as the Guinigi palazzi, but notice the different treatment of the windows, here surmounted by regular curves, whereas the Guinigi has gothic lobes. The irregularity of the front on the piazza is the result of the underlying earlier buildings, which in the 1200s included a tower. At one time the palazzo, as with virtually every other building in Lucca, was plastered over, but this covering was removed in the 20th century. The oversize mullion windows, or *pentafore* (five openings), are the only such ones remaining in Lucca. In 1404 the palazzo was the main house of the Gentili family. In the mid-1400s they sold it to the Franciotti, a family related to the Della Rovere popes. It is their crest mounted on the east side, and it was apparently they who added the stunning doorway on Via Sant'Andrea, which is often attributed to Jacopo della Quercia, though the dating makes this difficult.

The Gentili family can be traced back to the 1100s. Their family chapel in San Frediano has their tombs, dated 1336; they were obviously wealthy by that time. The line died out in 1560. *(F)*

61. Palazzo Altogradi—This Cinquecento palazzo with its harmonious and regular front, a grand central door surmounted by iron balcony, and flanked by unique and stately windows, is built on medieval structures which are evidenced in the irregularity of the rest of the building. *(F)*

62. Palazzo Vannulli—Reconstructed on medieval foundations in the first half of the 1500s by the Vannulli family. The entrance on Vicolo delle Vantaglie still bears their crest. As late as the 1700s the area which is now Piazza dell'Arancio was the garden of the palazzo, filled with orange (*arancio*) trees.

63. Palazzo Fatinelli—The Fatinelli were living here by the year 1200, when they had their tower on the northeast corner. The family built the present grand palazzo in the early 1500s, combining several estates. It is very large but not decoratively extravagant, save for the main door on Via Fatinelli. In the mid-1800s it passed to the Sardi family by marriage. In the early 2000s it underwent extensive renovation into separate domiciles.

The palazzo just to the south, opposite the church of San Quirico, belonged to the Saminiati family, and bears their crest over the entrance. *(F)*

64. Palazzo Calandrini/Lippi—The structure we see today was unified by the Lippi family in the 1600s. It is now home to the music academy *Istituto Boccherini*. The northern portion was, in the 1500s, the home of the Calandrini family; it was confiscated by the Republic when the family was condemned as Lutherans in 1568. *(F—Calandrini)*

65. Palazzo Bernardini—This truly impressive palazzo was commissioned in 1517 by the greatest of the Bernardini, Martino. Its design, in a somewhat archaic Florentine style, is commonly credited to Nicolao Civitali. The piano nobile originally had *bifora* windows. The main door is superb, with its iron lunette and original lanterns. The piazza in front of the building was opened in 1785 by the demolition of several houses and the church of Santa Maria in Via. At this time the palazzo was lengthened on the sides (where there are no benches) but the integrity of the building was maintained.

The window to the right of the door, where there is a stone jamb which has curled away from the wall, has its place in local folklore; it is called the miraculous stone or the devil's stone. At this spot on the original building there had been a sacred image. When the palazzo was built the spirits rejected the defamation and tried to expel the stone. More prosaic explanations have also been proffered.

In the late 1800s the palazzo still retained most of its magnificent furnishings: Roman and medieval sculptures in the courtyard, extravagant interiors, armor, and paintings including a Fra Bartolomeo. These were all sold when the family died out. The building was acquired in the later 1900s by the Industrial Association of Lucca. *(F)*

66. Palazzo Burlamacchi—The underlying structure of this palazzo is medieval. The removal of plaster has brought some of this to light, including the remains of the tower on the southeast corner, which in the 1200s belonged to the Allucingoli family *(F)*. It was here that Pope Lucius III was born (Ubaldo Allucingoli); he is commemorated by a plaque on the front.

The palazzo was reconstructed in the 1500s and renovated again in the 1700s. The Burlamacchi purchased it in 1600s and it remained in the family until they died out in the early 20th century.

The crest of the Burlamacchi is over the door on Piazza Suffragio. Notice the lovely carved eaves. *(F)*

67. Palazzo Penitesi—It was built in the 1500s but has later alterations, including the addition of an upper floor. It has two entrances; the one on Via dell'Angelo Custode, where the family crest can be seen, leads into a courtyard. The palazzo seems to be a source of literary inspiration. Montaigne stayed here for two weeks in 1581 and wrote insightfully and favorably about the Lucchese Republic. In the 1600s it was the home of the doctor and scholar Francesco Fiorentini who wrote *Memoirs of Mathilda of Canossa*. In the 20th century it was the home of Augusto Mancini (1875-1957), author of a standard *History of Lucca*. *(F)*

68. Palazzo Spada—Occupied since the 1200s; the tower on the northeast corner can still be seen from Piazza dei Servi. There are also remains of medieval arches and decorative brick. In 1507 a Spada bought the easterly portion of the house and upgraded it; looking at it from Via Santa Croce, this was the portion with the door and two windows on each side. In 1547 the Spada bought the adjoining house from the Santini and unified the entire structure, which compromised its symmetry. *(F)*

69. Palazzo Mazzarosa—Certainly one of the most prestigious and best preserved palazzi in the city, notable for both the refined building and the objects within. The underlying structure dates at least to the 1200s when it was the home of the attorneys' guild. In the 1400s it was the residence of the Minutoli family, who sold it to the Mazzarosa in 1597. In the early 1600s the Mazzarosa transformed it into the building we see today, with its elegantly symmetrical façade. Above the main door is a large seal with Volto Santo and the family coat of arms.

The furnishings and art within the palazzo date to the 1600s, although the collection was increased over the centuries, with notable additions by Antonio Mazzarosa in the 1800s. By the mid-1700s the wealth within the house was great enough for the owner to ask permission to install iron doors, which were forbidden in town. The right was granted.

Among the articles reported to be in the palazzo are Romanesque sculptures, most notably a lintel signed by Biduino (see church of San Salvatore, #13), the *Entrance into Jerusalem*—a truly stunning private possession. A brief catalogue of the rest: Etruscan, Roman, Romanesque, and Gothic sculptures and reliefs; ceramics, crystal, tapestries; paintings by Rubens, Dürer, Michelangelo di Pietro Membrini (Maestro del Tondo Lathrop), Tintoretto, Ligozzi, Paolini, Carracci, Pietro Testa, Marracci, Lombardi, and much else. *(F)*

70. Palazzo Boccella—One of many palazzi owned by the Boccella family. It was reconstructed in the later 1600s on ancient foundations, including the eastern gate of the Roman wall. It has a stately, if not original, presence. *(F)*

71. Palazzi Balbani—Two palazzi belonging to the same family; the one on the west is very narrow. The large palazzo on the east, today a bank, was the main residence of the family when they were among the wealthiest and most powerful in the city. It was built in the 1500s on medieval foundations, which explains the rather sparse placement of windows on the first floor. On the floors above it retains Guelph windows, though those on the front are restorations. The plaque on the corner records that here (in what is now the piazza) was the home of Castruccio Castracani.

This area was for so long the center of the family that it was known as the Balbani neighborhood. Their earliest known sepulcher, 1375, is in the little church of San Benedetto (#32).

The Balbani produced some of the most famous local heretics during the Reformation. The loss of the westerly, smaller, palazzo was one of the prices they paid; it was confiscated by the Republic in 1558. *(F)*

72. Palazzo Tegrimi—This large palazzo, overlooking Piazza dei Servi, was reconstructed on medieval buildings by the Tegrimi family in the early 1500s. The family died out in 1761, by which time the building was occupied by the Hospital of San Luca, which resulted in considerable renovations. *(F)*

73. Palazzo Tegrimi/Mansi—A beautiful palazzo with a garden. The irregular shape is the result of the underlying medieval buildings. It is the only palazzo in town which retains any fragments of exterior frescoes, an embellishment which was once popular; they can be glimpsed from Via del Battistero. The elevated connection with palazzo #74 is known as the Vault of the

Mansi, famous as the place where the murder of Lelio Buonvisi took place in 1593, in the affair of Lucrezia Buonvisi.

Gerardo Mansi, who should know, has pointed out that there is scant evidence the Tegrimi ever owned the palazzo, and that the Mansi bought it from the Di Poggio in 1565. *(F)*

74. Palazzi Saminiati—By the 1400s the Saminiati (also Sanminiati) family had a palazzo on the west side of this block. Along the westerly wall the medieval remains are evident. In the 1500s they either built or reconstructed a palazzo on the right and united the two with a shared garden. The palazzo on the right was bought by Ludovico Mansi in 1572. He soon connected it to the palazzo he already owned on the north side of Via del Battistero by an elevated walkway, the locally well-known, for infamy, *volta dei Mansi* (see above, #73). In 1583 he bought the palazzo on the left, after it had passed briefly to the Antelminelli. Notice the superb iron lanterns on the corners. In Piazza Antelminelli, in front of this palazzo, there were, in the 1200s, the houses and tower of the Antelminelli, the family of Castruccio Castracani. When in the early 1300s the Guelphs took over the city the houses of the Ghibelline Antelminelli were razed to the ground. *(F)*

The fountain in the piazza was built in 1832, designed by Nottolini.

75. Palazzo Bernardi/Micheletti—Perhaps the loveliest palazzo in Lucca when viewed from the Cathedral steps, nestled against San Giovanni, softened by the greenery and protective walls of its oversized garden, with the brick dome of the Baptistery and the imposing bell tower overlooking it. The palazzo complex was built in the late 1570s for Giovanni Battista Bernardi and was, almost certainly, designed by the architect Bartolomeo Ammannati, who was in town working on the Palazzo Pubblico. Bernardi, of the great Lucchese family, was Bishop of Aiaccio. It is his family's coat of arms, crossed battle axes, which are over the unique doorways into the garden.

By the 1700s, as can be seen in engravings, the ground floor of the palazzo had two shops opening onto the piazza, where the windows now are. In the 1800s the desirable property passed into the hands of Duke Ludovico Bourbon, and later to the Micheletti family. Your author plans to purchase it some day. *(F)*

76. Palazzo Bernardi—This palazzo was reconstructed on medieval foundations before 1535 by Cristoforo Bernardi, who wrote in his will that he had acquired and rebuilt it at great effort and expense. He noted that it was frescoed on the exterior. These paintings, by Zacchia da Vezzano, were still evident in 1833 when they were described as large paintings of "Roman stories with lovely caryatids and the war of the centaurs." By 1877 only fragments remained, and today nothing. Cristoforo took such pride in his home that he declared it could not be sold by the family for at least 4 generations. In this palazzo lived and died the magistrate and literary figure Luigi Fornaciari (1798-1858), who is commemorated by a plaque. *(F)*

77. Palazzo Boccella—This exquisite palazzo, with its commanding position and its villa-like dual entrance stairs, was built in the mid-1500s directly on top of the medieval wall, which was in the process of being torn down. It was most likely built by the Boccella family, which still owned it in the 1700s. In 2009 it became the home of a museum of contemporary art. *(F)*

The following three palazzi are all in the area outside the Roman wall, just inside the medieval gate. When the new walls greatly expanded the town to the east, this area became a desirable residential neighborhood. Though not remarkable, at least in their present state, they provide a snapshot of the urban renewal in the later 1500s. They are recorded by Velia Bartoli in *Lucca: Guida alle Architetture*.

78. Palazzo Ghilarducci—This palazzo and the following one were previously owned by the Sardini family and had extensive gardens in the rear. This one, reconstructed about 1600, later went to the Ghilarducci. The underlying medieval structure is revealed by the irregular spacing of the doorways.

79. Palazzo Orsucci—Bought by the Orsucci but later renovated when the building was subdivided.

80. Palazzo Bondacca—Though not one of the old wealthy families—they ranked 182nd in 1599—the Bondacca made some very good marriages into the 1800s. They lived here since the early 1600s and renovated it in the mid-1700s.

81. Palazzo Sirti (or **Mansi**)—This imposing palazzo, dominating the piazza of Santa Maria Forisportam, is best known, justifiably, as one of the great palazzi of the Mansi family. It was built about 1600 and bought late in that century by the Sirti family. It then passed to one line of the Mansi family, which had split and left their ancestral home in Via San Pellegrino. It became the residence of Ascanio Mansi (1773-1840) who enlarged and enriched it. Ascanio was one of the most important political figures of his time, serving as First Minister and Secretary of State during the Napoleonic and Bourbon periods. He also became fantastically wealthy through inheritance and by marrying one of the two Arnolfini sisters, who were the last of their line. In the palazzo he assembled an impressive art gallery, with paintings by Bellini, Fra Bartolomeo, Ghirlandaio, Carracci, and many others. His wealth eventually passed to his granddaughter, who was married to a Burlamacchi. The crest on the façade is of the Mansi; it is often mistaken for the Medici crest.

The following three palazzi are built in an area opened up by the present walls. The town laid out the new land in regular lots, which it sold off to help finance the immense construction project. Well-to-do families bought several contiguous parcels, which they merged to erect their new palazzi.

82. Palazzo Poggio—In 1522 some members of the large, ancient, and powerful Di Poggio family conspired to overthrow the government of Lucca, stormed the Palazzo of the Elders (*Anziani*) and assassinated the Gonfaloniere. Their punishment was swift and severe: seven family members were decapitated, the houses in their traditional neighborhood were destroyed, and the family was dispersed throughout the city. Their wealth survived, however: in 1599 they were still the fifth richest family.

With the building of the new wall, which made available new areas for development, the family purchased an entire block, ten lots, to build this grand new palazzo. It was certainly an impressive undertaking, and is an excellent example of the mid-1500s style, unconstrained by pre-existing structures. It was originally decorated on the exterior with frescoes by Agostino Ghirlanda da Fivizzano. *(F)*

83. Palazzo Arnolfini—When this block of lots was sold the Balbani family bought the southern four lots to build a fairly modest palazzo. The Arnolfini bought the other eight, but when they started construction is uncertain. In the mid-1600s they acquired the Balbani palazzo and integrated it into the unified structure we see today. Aside from the ground floor entrances and windows, it is a remarkably plain building, an aspect which is reinforced by the later renovations and placement of modern functional windows. Its most distinguishing feature is the oversize interior courtyard with portico. *(F)*

84. Palazzo Garzoni—This block was originally purchased by the Antelminelli who began construction of an immense palazzo, in keeping with the ambitions of the family, the descendants of Castruccio Castracani. The project was probably incomplete when, in the 1590s, the family was convicted of conspiring against the Republic; the males were executed and their property confiscated. In 1603 their palazzo was bought by the Garzoni family, an appropriate acquisition as the Garzoni had been supporters of Castruccio three hundred years earlier.

The palazzo originally had a very large garden on the southern portion; when sold in 1791 it had a large grove of orange trees. Later functional renovations destroyed much of this portion, though it still retains an interior courtyard.

85. Palazzo Marchiò—Lunardo Marchiò bought the lots here to build this rather austere palazzo, part of it on top of the medieval walls. On the rear there was originally a loggia overlooking a garden, which is now destroyed. It is a good example of a later 1500s palazzo built from scratch, not on a medieval skeleton.

86. Palazzo Mungai—Also built over the medieval wall in the 1500s, for a newly rich merchant.

87. Villa Buonvisi, or Bottini—A classic example of Lucchese Renaissance villas, unique for being in town rather than in the hills. It was built by the brothers Bernardino and Paolo Buonvisi in the 1570s, when the Buonvisi were the richest family in Lucca. The interior frescoes were finished in the 1590s. The architect is uncertain but the doors into the garden have been attributed to Vincenzo Civitali. The villa remained in the Buonvisi family until they died out in the Napoleonic period; it was acquired by Elisa Baciocchi, Napoleon's sister and Grand Duchess of Tuscany. After the fall of Napoleon it passed to the Marquis Lorenzo Bottini when he married Marianna Motroni. She was an accomplished musician and composer who turned the villa into the site of her famous salon. It passed to the State in the mid-1900s and is now used to host conventions.

Palazzo Pretorio (Palazzo del Podestà)—In July 1492 the town council voted to begin construction of a new residence and offices for the chief magistrate of the republic, the podestà. Construction began in 1494 and was probably finished about 1510. The result was perhaps the most beautiful Renaissance building in Lucca. It is generally believed that Matteo Civitali was involved in the design and that after his death in 1501 the work was carried on by his son Nicolao. There is no documentary evidence to support this, but it is impossible to believe that the pre-eminent artist in Lucca and his workshop were not responsible for such an exquisite building.

The new palazzo had a ground floor loggia, an unusual feature in Lucca. This was the space where the podestà and the chief of police would conduct many of their public duties. The ground floor also had rooms for the residence of the chief of police and the officials of the podestà, a few jail cells, and attorneys' chambers.

On the *piano nobile* were the residences of the podestà, the sindaco (mayor) and the councilor and, above the loggia, the *sala grande* for State functions.

In 1588 the loggia was extended further into the building, doubling its size. The work was entrusted to Vincenzo Civitali, son of Nicolao. Other than this change the building largely looks as it did when originally built. The square windows on the upper story replace what was originally a series of large oculi. The clock dates from the late 1800s.

In the center of the loggia today is a statue of Matteo Civitali. Along the walls are busts of eminent Lucchesi, including:

Carlo Piaggia (1827-1882) who explored the Nile, the Sudan, and Ethiopia and discovered Lake Kyoga in Uganda;

Augusto Passaglia (1837-1918) sculptor;

Vincenzo Consani (1818-1887) sculptor who did the monument to Matilda in San Giovanni and the lovely Madonna over the side door to Sant'Alessandro.

Tito Strocchi (1846-1879) who fought with Garibaldi and led an assault on Rome in 1870.

Palazzo Pubblico—Palazzo Pubblico, as it was called when Lucca was a free republic, was later referred to as Palazzo Ducale when Lucca became an appendage of royalty. It is now properly referred to as Palazzo Provinciale since it is a possession of the Province of Lucca.

Underlying the present building are remains of the Augusta, the fortress built by Castruccio Castracani about 1320. The Augusta was a fortified camp within the city walls and occupied the entire southwest quarter of the city. This area had been left as open space since Roman times, providing room for livestock, storage, and agriculture within the security of the walls.

Castruccio used two sides of the recently completed medieval walls for his fortress, and then fortified the other two sides, probably utilizing existing buildings. The Augusta provided space for barracks, horses, weapons, supplies, and a large parade ground for his army of several thousand men. It is widely believed that Giotto was hired by Castruccio to design the palatial part of the fortress, which is a reasonable but unsubstantiated conjecture. After Castruccio's fall the Augusta was used by a succession of

Lucca's foreign rulers for the next forty years. The last of these, the Pisans, were the most resented. When they were expelled in 1369 the Augusta was demolished, with fervor. A small section along the eastern wall, where Castruccio's main palazzo probably was, was preserved and transformed into the first Palazzo Pubblico, the seat of the restored republican government. It served as such for only thirty years, until 1400, when Paolo Guinigi made himself Lord of Lucca. He took over the palazzo and began improving and enlarging it to serve as his own residence and offices. With his fall in 1430 it once again became the public's palace, and would remain so for 350 years.

For a century after the fall of Guinigi little seems to have been done on the building. In 1540, at the same time as construction of the new city walls was beginning, extensive renovations were started on the palace. It was a period of growing prosperity and self-confidence as Lucca was the only independent state in Tuscany to resist a Florentine takeover. By 1578 ambitions had grown and Lucca hired the eminent Florentine architect Bartolomeo Ammannati (1511-1592) to design a suitable palazzo. He had already spent over ten years supervising work on the Palazzo Pitti and had designed Ponte Santa Trinita in Florence. His plan was grandiose: twin palazzi with courtyards, their joint façades extending 600 feet. Such a huge complex revived visions of the Augusta. Ammannati worked on the palazzo for about four years, but he and his successors brought only a small portion of his plan to fruition. The southerly half of the building, including the entranceway and the north side of the *Cortile degli Svizzeri*, is his work although the façade has been renovated. (The *Cortile degli Svizzeri* is so-called because it was the barracks of the Swiss Guard which protected the rulers of the Republic.)

After Ammannati almost no work was done on the palazzo for more than one hundred years. In 1706 a rising architectural star, Filippo Juvara (1678-1736), was asked to prepare new plans for its completion. These were nearly as grandiose as Ammannati's and, although Juvara was familiar with several of the ruling families and visited Lucca in succeeding years, his plans languished, too extravagant to be carried out by the small republic. In 1724 Juvara was commissioned to prepare a new, scaled down plan, concentrating on completing the north side of the palazzo.

Although he was now famous as the foremost exponent of baroque architecture his plans for the palazzo were restrained, continuing the more sober vision of Ammannati. Overseeing much of this work was the Lucchese architect Francesco Pini. Work proceeded efficiently and by the death of Juvara the northeast section of the palazzo and much of the interior courtyard were completed but a great deal of finishing work, the upper storey and interiors, were left undone and work ground to a halt. In 1743 Pini would lament that "all is open to the air, all is falling apart." So it remained, ever deteriorating, until the arrival of Princess Elisa in 1806. Although Elisa preferred to stay at her villa in nearby Marlia she took an ambitious interest in the city and her new palace. She cleared a large piazza in front of it, ravaging the ancient government center—the ten storey high tower of the palazzo, the mint, the prison, the post office, the salt warehouse, the church of San Pietro Maggiore and many other buildings. To clear such an expansive space Elisa must have had large ambitions for her new home but she reigned for only six years.

In 1817 Maria Luisa of the Bourbon dynasty became the hereditary ruler of Lucca and it was she who finally completed the palazzo, tying together the disparate pieces, harmonizing the façade and transforming the interior into the elegant rooms we see today. The work was overseen by the eminent Lucchese engineer Lorenzo Nottolini (1787-1851) who was appointed the royal architect in 1817. He had previously worked, in his early 20s, on Elisa's villa in Marlia. He also oversaw the renovation of the piazza of the amphitheatre and built the exquisite aqueduct of 400 arches which carried water from the Pisan mountains into Lucca.

In the early 2000s the palazzo was extensively renovated. It now houses the provincial tourist office and hosts exhibitions and concerts so it can easily be visited. The *Sala delle Guardie* is perhaps the most impressive room, extravagantly frescoed in classical themes by **Luigi Ademollo** in 1819. Other rooms were decorated at the same time by **Gaspare Martellini** and **Domenico Del Frate**.

~

The Families of Lucca

The Families

The patricians of Lucca valued ancient roots even more than wealth; the most prized status was to be declared an original citizen. Tracing a family's genealogy often led to an overly ambitious assertion of antiquity. Although records survive beginning in the 700s, it is by rare chance that they contain a family name, usually in connection with a bequest to, or of, a church, since the best preserved records are those in the Archbishop's archives. These survived both the great conflagration of 1314, when the Pisans sacked Lucca, and the fire of 1329 which consumed the town hall and its records.

Remarkably, one civic document survived. It was from the important communal statutes of 1308, which established the form and ambitions of the popular government which had arisen after 1300. Among its sections, the most revolutionary was the list of those families which were forbidden to hold positions in government; it was a list of the established powers, the old guard, the *magnati*. Many of these families left Lucca rather than live in subservience (many settling in Venice), and they took the capital and production secrets of the silk industry with them. It was the end of Lucca's monopoly over the silk trade. Many exiles returned to Lucca after 1314, when the popular government was overthrown by the Pisans and Castruccio.

The list was lost and not discovered until 1536, so it is subject to some suspicions of later additions, attempts by families to prove their early presence in town. Being among the once banned had become a prized status symbol. The names of families which would dominate Lucca in following centuries leap out—Cenami, Fatinelli, Guidiccioni, Malpigli, Burlamacchi, Mansi. This 1308 list is our best source for establishing the antiquity of Lucca's noble houses.

When Lucca regained its independence in 1369, the patricians were in control; it was they, after all, who had paid the city's ransom. The families which were prominent at this time would continue to be the rulers of the Republic of Lucca until it joined the Kingdom of Italy, and they still today assert a powerful influence on the city's identity. The dominance and self-identity of this patrician class grew over time. In 1556, after various uprisings and plots, they asserted their prerogatives and officially became an oligarchy. By 1628 they felt it necessary to produce an authoritative list (commonly known as the *Libro d'Oro*) of the noble families and the crest (*stemma*) to which they were entitled, a matter which had too frequently been a bone of contention. From this date their ranks were to be closed to new entrants.

As their world slipped away in the late eighteenth century, it became even more important to declare their privileged status. In 1787, as their demise was almost in sight, the rulers drew up another list of the "original families and noble personages" of the Republic of Lucca.

The disaster to the old order wrought by Napoleon put an end briefly to the historical role of the aristocracy, but not their pretensions. In 1826 one more list of the patricians of Lucca was promulgated by the State, which at this time belonged to the Bourbon. For the first time it was simply called the *Libro d'Oro*. To appreciate the mindset of present day Lucca it is helpful to remember that these families did not disappear in the nineteenth century; many remain in town.

It should also be remembered that the patricians were not simply a complacent aristocracy, they were merchants and bankers; their wealth was made in commerce. Industriousness was one of the characteristics which had to permeate such a society for it to maintain its independence; fortitude, self-reliance, and a certain pugnacity were others.

In the (yet another) list which follows, only the most prominent families are included.

In this section the office of Gonfaloniere is often referred to. The *Gonfaloniere di Giustizia* was the most honorable position in the Republic and the number of times a family held the office is the best indicator of an individual's family status and personal eminence. The Gonfaloniere was elected by the College of Elders (the *Anziani*) and by the Council of Thirty-six plus eighteen invitees. (The plural is gonfalonieri.)

In 1599 a great census of wealth was taken for tax purposes; a family's rank on this list is often given in the accounts that follow. The Buonvisi were by far the richest—over 900,000 scudi. The Cenami were 2nd with 407,000, the Mansi 3rd with 150,000, followed closely by the Arnolfini, Di Poggio and Guinigi.

The words *Anziani* and Elders are used interchangeably. They were the ruling council of twelve, elected for two year terms by the outgoing *Anziani* and the Council of Thirty-six.

~

Families

Allucingoli

The Allucingoli were one of the oldest families in Lucca. In 900 they granted to the bishop a church which was on the site where Santa Giulia (#31) is today. The remains of the family tower can still be discerned on the southeast corner of Palazzo Burlamacchi (#66). On the front of this palazzo is a plaque recording that here was born Pope Lucius III (Ubaldo Allucingoli). Born about 1100, he was Pope from 1181-1185. During these four years Lucca was, naturally, a special recipient of papal attention. His reign was dominated, however, by a dispute with the Emperor over the disposition of lands which had belonged to the great Countess Matilda. On her death in 1115 she had left her domains to the church; the Emperor thought they should be ceded to him but the Pope refused and the issue became one of the early causes of the Guelph-Ghibelline dispute.

On one thing Pope Lucius and the Emperor agreed: the need to stamp out heresy. In 1184 Lucius issued a bull inaugurating the medieval inquisition. It was directed against the Cathars, the Waldensians, and others; they were condemned by both Church and Imperial powers, leaving them nowhere to turn for protection.

Altogradi
Palazzo #61

The Altogradi had a slow but ultimately very successful climb up the social ladder of Lucca. In the 1200s they were wine merchants, and later became meat merchants. Paolo Guinigi made them citizens in 1417 but it was not until the 1500s that they adopted the name Altogradi, to reflect their acquired status (literally, high grade). They first appear in the Council of Elders in 1532. By 1599 they were one of the wealthiest families, ranking 25th, thanks to the wealth of Giuseppe who was a famous jurist, writer, and antiquarian. He passed his intellect on to his son, a writer, and his grandson Lelio, who bought the second floor of palazzo #61 in 1642. Lelio famously pled the case for the Town Elders in their dispute with Bishop Franciotti, which had led to a papal interdict against the city. His brief in defense of the secular power was so brilliantly written that it was soon being read throughout Italy and the Pope finally prohibited its publication. Nonetheless, Lelio was ultimately successful, the interdict was lifted, and Bishop Franciotti was banished. Lelio's son married a Mansi and his grandson finally became the first of the family to hold the post of Gonfaloniere in 1719. He served in the same position twice more, and his son served four times.

Antelminelli
Palazzo #43

The Antelminelli was the family of Castruccio Castracani. They were probably in Lucca by the 900s but they are first documented in the early 1100s. As leaders of the White (Ghibelline) faction they were banished from the city in 1301 and their houses were razed. After the coup by Castruccio the family returned to glory, but their glory died with him. The family was powerful enough to remain and play a reduced role in the city, though rarely in high civic positions. In the 1500s Baldassare Antelminelli began to restore the family honor. He was the only member to serve as Gonfaloniere, a post he held five times, between 1548 and 1573. His son Bernardino had unfortunate ambitions of grandeur; he sought to reclaim Castruccio's possessions and plotted with the Grand Duke of Tuscany against the Republic. He was arrested in 1596 along with his sons and under torture they revealed their plot. They were all executed, their property was confiscated, and the family was finished.

Arnolfini
Palazzo #37, #83

The Arnofini had arrived in town by 1080, bearing title of nobility, yet they were not expelled in the purge of the *magnati* in 1308. They seem to have survived quite well the turmoil of Castruccio and even the Pisan occupation, establishing trading houses throughout Europe during this period. They were wealthy enough to help purchase Lucca's independence in 1369. From this date on they were leaders in the government, constantly served in the Elders and held the post of Gonfaloniere 88 times, more than any family except the Guinigi. In 1434 Jan Van Eyck painted the merchant Giovanni Arnolfini and his bride Giovanna Cenami in one of the most famous northern panel paintings of the fifteenth century. The Arnolfini wealth and eminence is amply demonstrated by their palazzo on Via Santa Croce (#37). They served as ambassadors, as ecclesiastics, and as soldiers, but always foremost as merchants. The name died out in the 1800s when the surviving females married other Lucchesi nobility. At one time the family also owned palazzo #27 and #41.

Balbani
Palazzo #3, #71

The Balbani may well descend from Lombard nobles of the 700s. In the 1100s they were feudal lords but threw in their lot with the newly formed Commune, granting it their castle in Balbano in 1194. After independence in 1370 they became a dominant force in the government, providing more than seventy Gonfalonieri over the next four hundred years. In the 1500s and 1600s they established one of the widest commercial networks in Europe, and financed the Kings of Spain and France. Markedly innovative in business, they were major players in the new field of maritime insurance and they speculated heavily in silver from the New World.

They are also credited with introducing Lutheranism into Lucca in 1525. In the succeeding religious and civic crisis, many family members were exiled and their possessions confiscated. Nonetheless, the family ranked as the 12th richest in 1599.

Bartolomei
Palazzi #51

The Bartolomei family had two main lines. One, which died out in the 1400s, was famous for making very large loans to the Archbishop of Canterbury and King Edward of England in 1339. They were also instrumental in purchasing Lucca's liberty in 1369.

The second line, which built and inhabited several palazzi, could trace their local origins back to the early 1300s, at which time they were already living in the neighborhood of San Pietro Somaldi. They were active in government, holding the post of

Gonfaloniere fifteen times between 1433 and 1743. By the 1400s their wealth was sufficient to allow them to buy up all the houses on Piazza San Pietro Somaldi and by the 1500s to have them all renovated in modern style. The family made excellent marriages with other great families, including the Spada who later owned several of these palazzi.

Bernardi
Palazzo #75, #76

The Bernardi arrived in Lucca from Florence about 1200 and are credited with introducing the art of goldsmithery to their new town. In the 1400s and 1500s they were a dominant force in the government. Due to their prominence in both Church and State they were employed, successfully, in preventing the Inquisition from being established in Lucca. They acquired a large fortune in the 1500s and built two prestigious palazzi on the piazza of the Cathedral. For #75 (perhaps the loveliest palazzo in Lucca when seen from the Cathedral steps) they were apparently able to waylay the great architect Ammannati, who was in town working on the Palazzo Pubblico. The family slowly died out in the 1700s.

Bernardini
Palazzo #18, #65

The Bernardini trace their origins back to a Lordship in the year 1000. The family remained always at the pinnacle of Lucchese society. In the early 1200s one of them negotiated a truce in the social war between the *popolo* and the *magnati,* and oversaw the construction of the new city walls. The family became Paolo Guinigi's consiglieri in business and politics, yet after his fall their eminence only increased. Martino, married to a Guinigi, was the most influential man of the 1500s. He rallied the nobles during the Poggio revolt of 1522, and again for the Straccioni revolt in 1532. In 1556 he instituted the Martinian laws (named after him) which excluded from government any family not an "original citizen," that is, without an impeccable pedigree. These laws formally established the oligarchic form of government, which remained in place until the end of the Republic. Martino Bernardini built the family's great palazzo (#65), employing Vincenzo Civitali.

In 1599 the Bernardini were the 11th richest family in Lucca. Their fortunes continued to increase and by the arrival of Napoleon they were positioned to align themselves closely with the Baciocchi court. The family lasted into the 20th century.

Boccella
Palazzo #2, #17, #28, #70, #77

The Boccella can be traced back to about the year 1200. They were at the center of Lucchese society for the next seven hundred years, as diplomats, jurists, and very wealthy merchants. They served as tax collectors under Castruccio, which significantly increased their wealth. They assumed the post of Gonfaloniere as soon as it was re-established upon independence in 1370 and they held it fifty more times, until the very end of the Republic. In 1370 they provided the ambassador to the papal court in Avignon. In 1599 they ranked 28th in wealth, a very respectable sum. In 1625 the Boccella built the Oratorio of the Madonna del Sasso in Sant'Agostino. In the same century they consolidated their social position with a series of optimal marriages. They owned several of the most prestigious palazzi in Lucca. The last survivor of the house, Cesare, was an advisor to the Duke in the 1800s and in 1849 was called upon by Leopold II to reform the educational system in Lucca.

Bottini
Palazzo #16, #53

The Bottini came to Lucca from Como in the 1300s. They acquired citizenship about 1500 and first entered the Council of Elders in 1555. Originally smiths, they turned to trade and became very wealthy, by 1599 the 7th richest family in the city. In the early 1600s they made an exorbitant loan to the King of Spain who proved unable to repay it. The family pursued the debt for more than 300 years. When a Bottini became a Cardinal in the 1800s he employed the aid of the Pope in his collection efforts, but to no avail. The King of Spain formally defaulted on the loan in 1921.

In the early 1600s a Bottini operated a famous merchant house in Nuremburg, which went bankrupt in 1629. Nonetheless, the family grew and prospered, often by making marriages with the cream of Lucchese society, and by attaining prestigious positions within the Church. Filippo was the first to be elected Gonfaloniere, in 1749. He also introduced Boccherini to the world by sponsoring his first cantata, written for the annual Tasche (the civic celebration of the Republic) in 1765. In the next century the Marquis Lorenzo Bottini married Marianna Motrone who was an accomplished musician and composer; she performed at the court of Elisa Baciocchi under the direction of Paganini. To the marriage she brought the Villa Buonvisi where she presided over a noted musical salon.

Buonvisi
Palazzo #44, #45, #48, #87

The Buonvisi were for a long time the greatest Lucchese family, in terms of wealth and influence. They could trace their presence in Lucca back to the 1100s. They were not among the banished magnates in 1308, but did serve Castruccio as Chancellor. Although a Buonvisi was counselor to Paolo Guinigi, it was the Buonvisi, with the Cenami, who overthrew him in 1430. The next year a Buonvisi became Gonfaloniere for the first time.

In the 1300s the Buonvisi were silk merchants in Bruges. By 1400 they were also bankers with branches in London, Paris, Nuremburg, Genoa, and Venice. By 1500 they were at the pinnacle of Lucchese society, leaders in government, and making the best marriages in town. In 1511 they erected their ornate chapel in San Frediano, where they buried three cardinals. One of them, Girolamo, was bishop of Lucca for 20 years and was very nearly elected Pope; he was blocked by the French because Lucca at the time was too friendly with Spain.

The extent of the Buonvisi wealth is shown in their three greatest palazzi: #48, their old 1400s palazzo on Via Fillungo, which became known as the Winter Palace; #44, the new or Summer Palace, built in the 1500s almost opposite the old one (this stretch of Via Fillungo was known at the time as Via Buonvisi, it was so dominated by these palazzi), and; #87, their in-town villa, built in the last decades of the 1500s just outside the medieval gates, in the area opened up by the new walls.

During the revolt of the Straccioni in 1531 the Buonvisi were greatly threatened and it appeared that they might restore order by declaring themselves Lords, in the manner of Paolo Guinigi. But prudence on their part prevailed, as did their cause—the suppression of the workers—and the establishment of an oligarchy wrote finish to the threats from below.

In 1599 the Buonvisi were by far the wealthiest family in Lucca—907,000 scudi, versus the Cenami in second place with 407,000, and the Mansi in third with 150,000.

In 1629 the Buonvisi company collapsed in the greatest bankruptcy in Lucca's history. They brought many down with them and the merchant class never fully recovered; after this event, inherited glory increasingly replaced wealth as the cynosure of Lucca's elite.

The family died out about 1800.

Burlamacchi
Palazzo #12, #66

The Burlamacchi were an ancient and very distinguished family. They left their castle and moved to the city about the year 1200. Later in that century they were listed as patrons of the church of Santa Maria Filicorbi (former church #5) and in 1308 they were among those families banned by the popular government. It was a brief setback. They returned six years later with Castruccio and prospered greatly during the 1300s, becoming among the wealthiest merchants in Lucca. In 1387 they were elected Gonfaloniere and would hold the post 72 more times, until the very end of the Republic. In 1599 they were the 14th richest family.

Perhaps more than for commerce the Burlamacchi had a predilection for politics. In 1436 one of them was exiled for his part in the Di Poggio conspiracy. Francesco, the most famous of the family, served as Gonfaloniere twice, but then conceived and conspired to create a Tuscan Union of Lucca, Siena and (horror!) Pisa. The main nemesis of the project was Cosimo de Medici, but the Lucchese town fathers were also displeased. Francesco was placed under arrest by the Emperor and beheaded in Milan on February 14, 1548. In the mid-1800s he was rehabilitated as one of the first martyrs of Italian nationalism and rewarded with a statue in the center of town, in Piazza San Michele.

Among other notable members of the line—

Fra Pacifico Burlamacchi (1465-1519) was an intimate of Savonarola and was for long credited with writing the first biography of the Florentine friar, though the text shows the emendations of later hands. It was Pacifico who gave us our first account of the Bonfire of the Vanities, an act of which he thoroughly approved. He was a leader in welcoming the followers of Savonarola to Lucca when they were driven out of Florence. One of the Burlamacchi palazzi (#12) was directly across from the church of San Paolino which was designed by another Savonarolan follower, Baccio da Montelupo. The family's more prestigious palazzo (#66) in Piazza Bernardini, remained in the family until the 20th century.

Michele Burlamacchi was born in 1531. He became wealthy working abroad for the Buonvisi. He returned to Lucca to marry a Calandrini, one of the foremost Lutheran families. In 1570 he was declared a heretic (the only one of his family) and fled to France, and then to Geneva where he joined the expanding community of Lucchesi Protestants. His son Filippo settled in England where he became a citizen and influential enough to arrange loans for the king during the Thirty Years War, using his contacts among Lucchese exiles. The financial straits of the English king (he had dissolved Parliament, which held the purse strings) led to Burlamacchi's bankruptcy in 1635. In 1633 the family in Lucca had lent a very large sum to the King of Spain, which also was never repaid.

Giovan Giacomo (1694-1748), of the line established in France in the mid-1500s (he is therefore known as Jean-Jacques), was one of the greatest jurists of the 1700s. At age 26 he ascended to the chair of natural and civil law in Geneva, and traveled extensively in Europe. His works were translated into several languages, were appreciated by Rousseau, and were known in America; his influence is detectable in the Declaration of Independence and the Constitution.

Francois-Charles Bourlamaque was born in Paris in 1716 and became a captain in the French army. In 1759 he was third in command under Montcalm at the Battle of Quebec and was instrumental in the French victory. The town of Bourlamaque in southwestern Quebec is named for him.

Calandrini
Palazzo #64

Although they were exiled as heretics in 1568 the Calandrini family's orthodox credentials had formerly been impeccable. Giarente Calandrini was the second husband of the mother of Pope Nicholas V (1447-55). They had four children. One of them, Filippo, was made a Noble of the Republic of Lucca in 1447 and two years later he became a cardinal. A grandson, Giovanni Matteo, who was a Roman Senator and Papal notary, moved to Lucca in 1466 and easily acquired full citizenship, a rare honor which probably involved the intervention of the Pope, who had been born in nearby Sarzana. Giovanni's son married a Buonvisi and prospered in the family company. He was one of the first Lucchese to invest heavily in the business of livestock. He served as Elder thirteen times, was ambassador to Florence, and played a pivotal role in putting down the uprising of the Straccioni in 1532. His children married a Buonvisi, a Burlamacchi, an Arnofini and, crucially, Giuliano married a Balbani—the family credited with introducing Reformation ideas into Lucca. When Giuliano proclaimed his conversion publicly, he and a brother were banished from the city. His sons and other family members followed his example and suffered his fate.

One of the descendents of these exiles foreswore the family heresy. His son Filippo, born in 1661, returned to Lucca and re-established the honor of the family.

Cenami
Palazzo #33, #34, #37, #46

The Cenami are one of the oldest and wealthiest families in Lucca. They trace their origins to before the year 1000, when they were feudal lords with a castle. In 1197, when the Society of the Army of the People was formed in opposition to the Society of the Towers, the Cenami had two important towers in town and were also tax collectors for the Emperor. They were conspicuously Ghibelline. In 1308 they were among the families banned from political office; they took up residence in Venice where they continued their silk business and maintained offices in Paris and Bruges, which gave rise to a French line. Their hearts, however, never left Lucca; during their exile in Venice they were patrons of the Fraternity of Volto Santo.

The Cenami helped purchase Lucca's liberty in 1369. In 1376 a Cenami became Gonfaloniere. Members of the family would hold the position a notable 75 times.

In 1430 Pietro Cenami led the coup against Paolo Guinigi and was granted the honorific *Padre della Patria*. Six years later he was himself murdered, stabbed 22 times in an attempted coup by members of the Di Poggio family. The conspirators had expected popular support, but were instead condemned and decapitated.

The Cenami continued in positions of eminence. They also developed close business ties with France. By 1599 they were the second richest family in Lucca, after the Buonvisi, with whom they were aligned by marriage.

During the rule of Napoleon's sister, Bartolomeo Cenami was made Senator of the Republic and, judging by the honors bestowed on him, was not only a favorite but an intimate of Elisa. Over the centuries the Cenami owned some of the most prestigious palazzi in Lucca. The family survives.

Cittadella
Palazzo #13

The citadel which is the origin of the family name was built by Paolo Guinigi, using part of the Augusta, Castruccio Castracani's fortress. The first known member of the family was the citadel's captain of the guard. When Guinigi was overthrown the family had the wisdom to hand over the citadel keys to the Elders and was rewarded with the privileges of citizenship and the new, noble, name Cittadella.

The family held the post of Gonfaloniere for the first time in 1470, and again in 1475, but curiously, not again until 1606. After this they held it 29 more times, the last in 1796.

The Cittadella were not notable as merchants but they filled many eminent political posts, mastering a profession which they continued after the arrival of Napoleon. One of them was Secretary of State under Elisa, even though he had once been accused of plotting to overthrow the government. Another Cittadella was the representative of Lucca to the Council of Vienna in 1814 and was later Secretary of State under the Bourbons, who granted him the hereditary title of Marquis. He married a Burlamacchi, and his son a Mazzarosa. The family's grand palazzo (#13) overlooked the piazza which bears their name (and hosts the statue of Puccini).

Controni
Palazzo #22, #59

Of humble origins, the Controni were late arrivals to Lucchese society but they prospered greatly. The family made their fortune as silk merchants in the 1600s, in company with the Mansi with whom they owned the largest production facilities in the city. They were involved in numerous ventures abroad, particularly in Poland. Their entrance to these opportunities were propitious marriages with other established and emerging families, such as the Orsetti, Boccella, and Bernardini.

In 1651 the government of Lucca was in severe financial straits, in part due to the cost of the just completed walls. To raise money the Republic offered for sale positions in the nobility. A limited number could afford to purchase the honor. Among those so ennobled were the Controni, who were granted the status of "original citizens."

It was Domenico Controni (1616-1685), progenitor of the family wealth and nobility, who reconstructed the exquisite palazzo (later bought by the Pfanner) where in 1692 the Controni entertained the young prince of Denmark. (See Palazzo #22.) As quickly as the family emerged into prominence, they faded from view.

De Nobili
Palazzo #10, #54

Their very name is an assertion of nobility. In 1299 they sold their feudal lands to the commune, moved to the city, and became citizens. In the 1400s they married into the family of Pope Nicholas V; he came to visit them in 1447. That same year he appointed the De Nobili to be patrons of the pilgrimage church of San Pellegrino in Alpe; they commissioned Matteo Civitali to sculpt a marble *tempietto* to house its saintly relics. (A trip to view this out-of-the-way masterpiece is well worth the steep journey.)

Members of the family held positions as diverse as Treasurer of Perugia and Governor of Spoleto, and they were granted the title Counts Palatine by the Emperor. For many centuries the De Nobili were part of the backbone of Lucca, one of the most stable voices in its government. They served as Gonfaloniere 45 times and provided endless Anziani. In 1599 they were the 15th wealthiest family.

When the future Empress Josephine arrived unannounced at the gates of Lucca in 1796, seeking refuge while Napoleon warred in Austria, she was befriended by Eleonora Bernardini, née De Nobili, which laid the basis for the close relations between Lucca and the future Emperor.

The family's most stunning, truly grandiose, palazzo (#54) was on Via Nuova; it was later used by the Bank of Italy. In the 1600s, for another home (#10), they commissioned the exterior paintings which gave Palazzo Dipinto its name.

Diodati
Palazzo #5

The Diodati arrived in town in 1347 as doctors. During the 1400s they became increasingly rich and married into the heights of society. By the 1500s they had reached the pinnacle, intermarrying with the Buonvisi. In 1541, when the Emperor and the Pope arrived together in Lucca, the Diodati hosted the Emperor's daughter and the Pope baptized a new Diodati son, Carlo (the Emperor Charles was his godfather and namesake). Despite such orthodox beginnings, Carlo grew up to become an ardent Calvinist and was exiled in 1567 with other family members. The heretics settled in Geneva and transferred their money out of Lucca, sending the remaining family into a slow decline. Nonetheless, in 1599 they were still the 9th richest in Lucca. By 1661, however, they were compelled to sell their stunning palazzo; it is today a State office, open for visits, and a popular site for marriage ceremonies.

Fatinelli
Palazzo #24, #63

In a society where the quality of a family's marriages was one of the best indicators of its status, the Fatinelli made a fine art of matrimony; over time they aligned themselves with virtually every important family in town. Yet they were not among the wealthiest merchants. Their status arose from their ancient feudal origins and from their having been the employers of Santa Zita in the 1200s, an association which they cultivated diligently.

Their palazzo on Via Fontana (#24) is a lovely well-preserved medieval residence, but it was not built until after the death of Zita, and the Fatinelli did not buy it until about 1370. Nonetheless, it preserves her memory on the façade, with a fountain erected in the 1600s purporting to be the site from which she drew water for those who thirsted. The Fatinelli paid for Zita's tomb in San Frediano and subsequently constructed their chapel around it. In 1410 they were allowed to place their family crest there, and to use it for family burials, closely tying their name to the city's most famous saint.

In the 1500s Pietro Fatinelli conspired to overthrow the ruling mercantile oligarchy in Lucca, whom he considered upstarts; he thought they had replaced wealth for nobility as the criterion to rule. Pietro was arrested and tortured as a matter of course, though it seems his confession was inspired more by pride in his venture than by duress. He was hanged in 1543. The rest of his family was not implicated, nor did they suffer great loss of prestige.

The Fatinelli served as Gonfaloniere 24 times between 1470 and 1796, though never once between 1500 and 1623. They survived to serve under the Bourbons. One of the last members initiated the first gas street lights in town. The family also owned the very large palazzo (#63) on Via Sant'Andrea, which in the early 21st century was converted to apartments.

Franciotti
Palazzo #41, #60

The Franciotti came to Lucca from Carrara in the early 1300s. Their rise to power began in 1481 when Giovan Francesco married the niece of Pope Sixtus IV, of the extremely powerful Della Rovere family. Their son became Bishop of Lucca in 1503, appointed by his uncle Pope Julius II. Three other Della Rovere were to hold the See of Lucca until 1517. The crest on the Franciotti palazzo (#41) is that of the Della Rovere.

A Franciotti once again became Bishop in 1637, serving simultaneously as a cardinal. He had the audacity to challenge the rather dictatorial governance of the city fathers, which led them to appeal their case to the Pope. Accused of nepotism, the Bishop's brothers were jailed and he was driven from the bishop's seat in 1645, though he remained a cardinal. He lived another twenty-two years during which time Popes and their opinions of him changed; he was ultimately considered to be the more virtuous actor in the affair and became a counselor to the papacy.

By 1600 the Franciotti were the 10th richest family in Lucca. They served as Gonfaloniere 15 times, though in 1660 one of its members was disruptive enough to get himself exiled. The family died out in the early 1700s.

Ghivizzani
Palazzo #36

Originally from Ghivizzano, the family emigrated to Lucca about 1240. They first appeared in the Council of Elders in 1391 and as Gonfaloniere in 1438. Wealthy but apparently frugal, they were instrumental in drawing up the severe sumptuary laws of 1440 which forbade ostentatious displays of wealth in dress, jewelry, and weddings. As with most such laws the objects of restraint were the women of the household; lavishing money on the man's castle was still appropriate. The Ghivizzani were generous to the Church. They paid for the stained glass windows in the Cathedral, not neglecting to include in them the family crest. In the 1500s they made matrimonial alliances with the most eminent families in Lucca, which dispersed most of their wealth. The remaining bearer of the family name was far down on the tax list of 1599.

Gigli
Palazzo #39

The first Gigli came to Lucca, probably from Hungary, before 973. By the 1200s the family was prominent as jurists and notaries, professions in which they continued to excel in later centuries. They prospered under the Pisan domination in the 1300s, were instrumental in restoring the Republic in 1370, and continued to be active in the government in the 1400s and later. In 1497 Giovanni Gigli became Bishop of Worcester, England. When he died he was succeeded by Silvestro Gigli who held the seat for more than twenty years, serving Henry VII and Henry VIII as their ambassador to Rome. Silvestro was buried in San Michele in a grand tomb by Baccio da Montelupo, of which only a fragment remains.

Palazzo #39 was owned by the Gigli since at least 1324, at which time the men of the family agreed that it would not be sold without their or their heirs' unanimous consent. The present building was commissioned by Paolo Gigli, who had gone to England as a merchant and returned with great riches (he was the brother of Bishop Silvestro). In 1599, though still wealthy, the family ranked 51st on the tax roles.

Guidiccioni
Palazzo #56

The Guidiccioni family traces their roots in Lucca to the year 780, just after the fall of the Lombard kingdom. They were banned in 1308, but soon returned and in 1331 swore their fealty to the Emperor. As soon as Lucca obtained its freedom in 1370 the Guidiccioni appear as Elders in the government and active as merchants in Bruges and other cities. In the 1500s their wealth increased dramatically, ranking them 32nd in 1599, and they became constant figures in the government. The first became Gonfaloniere in 1457 and the family held the position another 40 times, the last in 1796. They attained their greatest eminence, however, in the church. Giovanni (1500-1541), papal nuncio to Spain and bishop of Fossombrone, was an eminent humanist. His tomb in San Francesco is one of the loveliest monuments in Lucca. It was commissioned by his uncle Bartolomeo, who was made a cardinal in 1539 and from 1546-1549 was bishop of Lucca. He was succeeded as bishop by his grandnephew Alessandro who held the post for 51 years. Alessandro renounced the seat in 1600 in favor of his nephew, Alessandro II, who held the position until 1637. A Guidiccioni, therefore, held the See of Lucca continuously for more than 90 years, through the difficult period of the Reformation and the Counter Reformation.

The family's grand palazzo (#56), which had been in their hands since the 1300s and was thoroughly renovated in the 1500s, is now the home of Lucca's famous archives.

Guinigi
Palazzo #58

Guinigi is the best known family name in Lucca, thanks to their tower with the trees on top, which has replaced Volto Santo as the symbol of the town.

The family's origin, though disputed, is ancient. They were certainly present in town in the late 900s, but they may well be descended from a Winizio who is recorded in the early 800s. More ambitious genealogists have tried to trace them back to the Lombards, or even the Romans. At the turn of the millennium they were already one of the most important families in town and by the 1200s their residences and towers defined the *Contrada Guinigi* (Guinigi neighborhood). Banned in 1308, they soon returned and continued an inexorable rise to the pinnacle of Lucchese society.

Francesco Guinigi orchestrated the purchase of Lucca's independence in 1369 and was rewarded with the honorific *padre della patria*. In 1385 his nephew Giovanni served as Gonfaloniere; it was he who was the progenitor of the two main lines of the family. It was Francesco's son, Paolo, who became the most famous, or infamous, Guinigi. In 1400 he managed to take control of the town, abolished representative government, and proclaimed himself *Signore*, Lord. He ruled until 1430 when he was deposed by other nobles led by Pietro Cenami, who was declared the new *padre della patria*. Whatever his sins, we can thank Paolo for commissioning Jacopo della Quercia to sculpt the tomb of his wife Ilaria del Carretto, the most sublime work of art in town. He also built the villa outside the walls which now houses the museum.

The two grand palazzi (#58), built in the late 1300s, bear witness to the wealth and status of the family at that time.

Despite the ignominious downfall of Paolo, his relatives (though not Paolo's descendants) went on to great political and financial success. They provided a total of 93 Gonfalonieri, the most of any family; the last was in 1790. (There were 15 between 1371 and 1399, then none until 1460.) In the 1500s the Guinigi headed one of the major mercantile and banking houses in Lucca, with offices throughout Europe. Despite two severe bankruptcies, in 1520 and 1574, on the tax list of 1599 the Guinigi were the sixth wealthiest family.

Mansi
Palazzo #21, #42, #73 and what is now museum #1

The Mansi are one of the most ancient and successful families in Lucca. They were already notable by the 1000s, were prominent in the commune formed in 1162, and nurtured their status during the 1200s. They were among those banned in 1308, but they quickly returned and continued to prosper. They were late in entering commerce but eventually acquired an immense fortune as international merchants. The family split into several lines which owned many palazzi in the city over the centuries. The greatest of these is now the Mansi Museum. The family produced 66 Gonfalonieri.

In 1599 the Mansi were already the third richest family, and the 1600s proved immensely profitable. Among the steady flow of worthy citizens which the family provided the Republic, perhaps the best known is Ascanio, ambassador to the Congress of Vienna. He was the beneficiary of large bequests, including that which came from his marriage to Anna Arnolfini who, with her sister, was the last of that house.

The Mansi family survives with vitality today. Among its members is Gerardo Mansi, the author of the comprehensive and authoritative books *I Patrizi di Lucca* and *I Palazzi di Lucca*, and to whom I offer a profound appreciation.

Massoni
Palazzo #8

The Massoni arrived in Lucca in the 1300s; in the 1400s they are identified as spinners and weavers. By the 1500s they owned a good deal of real estate and were marrying into the lesser nobility. Their true rise in wealth began in the early 1500s. By the middle of that century they were becoming active abroad, especially in France. Their increasing wealth is demonstrated in the extravagance of their dowries. By the mid-1600s they were active in politics in the General Council and by 1700 they were finally admitted to the Elders. They remained active in political life in the 1800s under the Bourbons, ultimately attaining the title of Marquis.

Mazzarosa
Palazzo #69

Although not among the ancient nobility—one of the early members was mentioned in 1487 as a stone-carver working with Matteo Civitali—the financial and social ascent of the Mazzarosa in the 1500s was remarkable. They became citizens in 1525. In mid-century Alessandro married the wealthy Chiara Guidiccioni and together they bought palazzo #69. Their son Francesco married an Orsucci and thereby acquired an even greater hereditary fortune. Succeeding generations made ever more profitable marriages among the local patricians. When the male line was about to die out a rigid family rule was made that a male marrying into the family would take the name Mazzarosa, to perpetuate their wealth and honor. The first to do so, in 1732, was Tommaso Nieri, scion of another ancient house. His son had no heirs but before his death he adopted Antonio Mansi, who acquired the Mazzarosa name, palazzo #69, and a villa in Segrominio. Antonio had an illustrious career as writer, agronomist, Senator under the Baciocchi principate, director of the Liceo Universitario, and finally a Senator of the Kingdom of Italy and a leader of the Risorgimento in Lucca. He also assembled much of the art and antiquities collection which still resides in their palazzo. He married an Orsucci and had three sons, one of whom married a lady of the court of the Grand Duchess of Tuscany. His son served for many years as Director of the Cassa di Risparmio di Lucca. The family has continued, and flourished.

Mei
Palazzo #57

The Mei family had a checkered career in Lucca. They first became citizens in 1391. During the 1400s they became increasingly wealthy merchants and prominent in government but in 1490 one of their number was accused of treason and beheaded. The other members do not seem to have suffered. In the 1500s the family made several prestigious marital alliances. Biagio Mei was especially respected, serving the Republic as ambassador to the Pope, the Emperor, and Venice. His son, however, committed the double sin of going bankrupt and becoming a Lutheran; he fled to Geneva, managing to escape his debtors with a fair amount of his wealth intact. In 1558 he was officially condemned as a heretic and his palazzo was confiscated by the State. His son remained in town and managed to prosper, obtained absolution, and became Gonfaloniere in 1621.

Menocchi
Palazzo #46

The Menocchi family made their wealth in the leather trade. In the early 1500s they were not yet numbered among the nobility, but their close ties to the Burlamacchi family facilitated their social rise. By mid-century they were active in government and present in many of the great merchant houses. They assured their position during the revolt of the Straccioni in 1531. The revolt, inspired by the discontent among the silk workers, threatened to become a general class conflict, but the Menocchi managed to maintain the allegiance of the leatherworkers, weakening and ultimately defeating the social revolution. The family soon, however, began to suffer reversals; a company they set up in Sicily to dominate the grain trade suffered a disastrous bankruptcy. By the 1600s they were forced to sell much of their property.

Meuron
Palazzo #3

The Meuron were latecomers to Lucca. Jean Paul, a brilliant engineer of bridges, had been a close associate of the Bonapartes in Corsica and he went on to serve as an engineer in the French army, helping to organize Napoleon's expedition to Egypt. He later became close to Elisa Baciocchi, settled in Lucca and bought a very fine palazzo (#3) from the Ottolini. The Meuron later intermarried with the Poschi family who were originally Pisan nobility; they took up habitation in the Meuron palazzo, where descendants still live.

Minutoli
Palazzo #6

Arriving in Lucca in the 1200s from Naples via Florence they immediately became active in government, though they did not become citizens until the restoration of the Republic in 1369. The marriages made by the family in the 1500s comprise a list of distinguished matches with such families as the Antelminelli, Orsucci, Bottini, and Bernardini. By the end of the century they ranked 49th in wealth, a comfortable and honorable position. In the later 1700s the family merged with the Tegrimi when the last of that line died without issue. In the 1400s the Minutoli owned Palazzo #69 (Mazzarosa).

Moriconi
Palazzo #1, #49

The Moriconi were one of the earliest known families in Lucca; they have been traced back, perhaps somewhat ambitiously, to the year 742. One member was among the High Commissioners in the 1100s, and in the 1200s they served in the Council of Elders. Their landholdings in town were extensive, including, of course, towers. They remained wealthy into the 1600s when Frediano Moriconi established businesses in Poland. He became a good friend of the Grand Treasurer of Lithuania, to whom he made a large loan to enable King Casimiro to pay his army. With the untimely death of the Treasurer the loan was never repaid, but

Frediano was granted a feudatory income and his son Scipione married into the local nobility. In the mid-1600s most of the line in Lucca had died out and finally in 1678 the remaining member fled precipitously to Poland to escape his debts. The Controni family bought his real estate from his debtors.

Onesti
Palazzo #29

The Onesti were an important merchant family, known to be doing business in Paris and London by the late 1200s. They have two tombs in the cemetery of St. Catherine (along the north side of San Frediano) dated 1340; Marco Paoli has suggested they were the patrons of the fresco *Pietà with two mourners* which can still be seen there.

Ottolini
Palazzo #3

The Ottolini were one of the least ancient noble families. Originally from Castelnuovo Garfagnana, they first appear as citizens of Lucca in 1447. Though originally of little wealth, in the early 1500s Paolo Ottolini created the family fortune by dealing in silk, and by 1599 they were one of the wealthiest families in Lucca. Their position was helped by a series of marriages with the noblest of families. The Ottolini did not provide a Gonfaloniere until 1712, but they served frequently after that. They bought the wonderful palazzo #3 from the Busdraghi in the 1600s and sold it to the Meuron in the early 1800s.

Parenzi
Palazzo #4

The Parenzi first appear in the 1300s as members of the great Ricciardi merchant banking firm, who were financiers and paymasters to the King of England. In succeeding years the family prospered sufficiently for its bankruptcy in 1542 to shake the entire merchant class, many of which had invested with the firm. One of the results of this great bankruptcy was the creation of limited liability corporations. In the 1600s the Parenzi recovered spectacularly, becoming one of the major merchant houses in northern Europe. When the daughter of the last male of the line married a Mansi in 1792 it was the sensation of Lucchese society since it united the city's two richest families. The furnishings of Palazzo #14, which had been in the family since the early 1500s, were transferred to Palazzo Mansi. At one time the Parenzi also owned palazzo #5.

Penitesi
Palazzo #67

The Penitesi (or Pinitesi) were probably in Lucca as early as the 1200s but they did not become citizens and enter the nobility until the mid-1400s. They served often in the government and were also among the town's intellectual elite. In 1581 they entertained Montaigne in their palazzo.

Di Poggio
Palazzo #82

The most troublesome family in Lucca, the Di Poggio were also one of the oldest, dating perhaps to the 700s, certainly to the 900s. The sources of their success were clannishness, aggressiveness, pride, and fecundity. The family clustered around and dominated the area where Puccini later lived, Piazza Cittadella. As one of the most powerful old families, the Di Poggio were banned in 1308. They did not accept the domination of Castruccio and conspired against him, not as populists but as old guard with their own claims to supremacy. As soon as Castruccio died the Di Poggio aspired to take his place. In March 1329 the Di Poggio fought the Castracani in the streets, compelling the Emperor to restore order. In the tumult a fire broke out in the Di Poggio neighborhood, spread towards San Michele and the palazzo of the *Anziani*, where it consumed what civic records had survived the Pisan inferno fifteen years earlier. The Di Poggio were exiled again, briefly.

In 1436 two members of the family entered the palazzo of the *Anziani* and stabbed to death Pietro Cenami, the celebrated *padre della patria* who had overthrown Paolo Guinigi six years earlier and restored the Republic. The motive for his assassination was, typically for the Di Poggio, a family feud more than considered ambition: Cenami had offended their honor by forbidding a marriage.

Despite this despicable act the Di Poggio were permitted to remain in town. They became increasingly formidable in the later 1400s, when the saying was prevalent *quando Poggio poggiava, tutta Lucca tremava*, "when it rains Poggio, all Lucca quakes." The Di Poggio were Gonfaloniere a total of thirty-nine times, most of these in the latter half of the 1400s. They last held the position in 1522, the year they conspired to overthrow the Republic. The immediate cause of their discontent again seems petty, a dispute over control of the church of Santa Giulia, but it inspired them to attempt another coup, breaking once again into the palazzo of the *Anziani* and assassinating the Gonfaloniere. This time they had overreached. Seven members of the family were executed and the rest were dispersed around the city, forbidden to live in their hereditary enclave.

They were never again a political force, but they managed to hold on to their money. In 1599 they were the fifth richest family in Lucca, able to build an immense palazzo (#82) in the new development on the southeast side of town. The family is recorded until the 1800s.

Sanminiati
Palazzo #55, #74

The name is also spelled Saminiati. A large family, they were in town since at least the 1300s but did not become citizens until the 1430s. By the 1500s they were one of the pillars of Lucchese mercantile society. When the company Cenami, Parenzi, Sanminiati failed in 1552 it was the greatest bankruptcy in town up to that time. The Sanminiati were scrupulous about paying their debts, which they were able to do by selling many of their properties. With that remarkable ability to withstand apparent ruin which was a trait of the oligarchy, the Sanminiati at the end of the 1500s were still the 13th richest family in town. The family continued to flourish and contribute much to their city. Giovanni Sanminiati served as Elder and wrote a distinguished history of Lucca as well as works on agriculture. He was a friend of Montaigne, who visited Lucca in 1581. Benedetto Sanminiati directed work on the Palazzo Pubblico after the departure of Ammannati.

Sardini
Palazzo #27

Arriving in Lucca in the latter 1300s, by the 1400s the Sardini were attaining influence and in the 1500s and 1600s were important members of the ruling class. They were the 17th richest in 1599. Scipione (1526-1608), merchant and soldier, was prominent in the royal courts of France, England, and Spain. Several members of the family were famous as diplomats, a profession at which the family excelled. Others were merchants, one of whom did well enough in partnership with the Buonvisi to buy the stunning palazzo #27. The family had their black sheep: one was convicted of mishandling tax collections and another was exiled for his role in murdering a Di Poggio, but generally the Sardini were pillars of society into the 1800s.

Sbarra

The Sbarra had a pedigree as fine and ancient as any, traced back to a Count in the 900s. In the 1200s and 1300s they were among the most prominent merchants and were living in the area on Via Roma around Corte Sbarra, which can be easily entered to view their houses. They retained their position until the end of the Republic, being Gonfaloniere 46 times.

Spada
Palazzo #52, #68

The Spada settled in Lucca by 1230, though they could trace their lineage back to about 1000. In the early 1300s they were still not among the local potentates, but later in that century they became familiar figures in the government. It was not until the 1500s that they became very wealthy and began a series of important marital alliances. During the papal conclave of 1670, during which the French and Spanish cardinals feuded for five months, Cardinal Giovan Battista Spada came within a hairbreadth of becoming pope, losing out to Emilio Altieri, who had not wanted the job and so was the perfect compromise.

Tegrimi
Palazzo #6, #72, #73

The Tegrimi were one of the most ancient families and one of the most respected though never one of the richest, yet they managed to build a number of impressive palazzi. It is possible that they arrived in Lucca as knights of the French King Pepin in the 700s. The first sure documentation is in the early 1300s when they were bankers and money-changers. After the fall of Paolo Guinigi they became active in government and began a long family career of serving the State, holding the post of Gonfaloniere thirty-four times. It was a Tegrimi who in 1550 was the representative of Lucca to Rome, defending the city against charges of irreligion; he managed to keep the Inquisition out of the city. In a town of merchants the family is barely represented in that undertaking. Besides the three palazzi shown on the map, they also (after the family merged with the Minutoli) owned Palazzo #27.

Trenta
Palazzo #32, #50

Although the Trenta family claims to have hosted Saint Richard in the 720s, they do not appear in records until 1331. Nonetheless, they quickly became one of the wealthiest and most influential members of Lucchese society. As soon as Lucca was liberated in 1370 they provided a Gonfaloniere, a post they held another 60 times, the last in 1729.

In 1361 Federico, the founder of the line (as best we know), bought the palazzo on Via San Giorgio (#32) which still preserves many of its medieval elements. One of his sons, Lorenzo, became extremely wealthy and began buying properties along Via Fillungo which became the basis for the family's grand palazzo (#50). Lorenzo also constructed the family chapel in San Frediano and was able to commission Jacopo della Quercia to sculpt its exquisite altar and the tomb slabs of Lorenzo and his wife. (Paolo Guinigi was della Quercia's other local patron.)

Stefano Trenta was Bishop of Lucca from 1448 to 1477 and served a succession of popes on important diplomatic missions. He also restarted work on the Cathedral, which had long lain dormant, and commissioned Matteo Civitali to transform the interior over the following decades.

Of the women of the line, Maria Maddalena is famous for having won the heart of the young prince of Denmark when he visited Lucca in 1692 and stayed in the palazzo of the Controni (#22). The religious differences made the romance impossible and the prince's father whisked him back to Denmark to a more appropriate marriage. Maria retired to a convent. When the prince became king he returned to Italy in 1709 and managed to have a few hours conversation with his lost love.

~

The Streets of Lucca

The Streets of Lucca

Via Sant'Andrea—This was one of the original Roman streets, long and straight. In the early Middle Ages it ran through one of the tanning districts in town and had a canal in it which carried away the waste. It is today the best approach to Palazzo Guinigi, especially at night when the tower is lit.

Via degli Angeli—Street of the Angels, named in honor of the angels who appeared to Santa Zita. It ran along the outside of the Roman wall where it curved out to accommodate the Roman theatre.

Via Anguillara—An ancient street which lay at the heart of the *borgo* (neighborhood) of San Frediano. This *borgo*, which lay outside the Roman walls, was important since at least the 600s when Bishop Frediano was expelled by the Lombards and erected a new church where San Frediano now stands. In the medieval period it was also the Jewish quarter. It has some of the earliest examples of decorative brick and a wonderful old feel to it. An *anguillara* is an eel breeding ground and this was once a swampy area, but the street is probably named after the family Anguilla who lived in the area in the 1200s. They were banished in 1308 but returned soon after.

Via dell'Arancio—"Street of the oranges" for the orange orchard of Palazzo Vannulli (#62), which once occupied Piazza dell'Arancio.

Via degli Asili—Site of the first secular elementary school (*asilo*) in Lucca. Antonio Mazzarosa, Director of Public Education, proposed such a school in 1836 but the idea came under attack from conservative forces, who thought it would become a breeding ground of liberalism. Duke Lodovico finally allowed it to be established, so long as the course structure was strictly regulated by the State.

Via del Battistero—"Street of the Baptistry." A well-preserved and charming medieval street, it is now the antiques center. Spend some time here, looking closely.

Via Buia—Literally, "Dark Street," for obvious reasons. It has some of the best examples of early decorative brick and many superb iron lunettes. Boccherini was born in the house on the corner with Via Fillungo and for a time the street was called Via Boccherini, but Via Buia is the original and present name.

Via delle Conce—On the outskirts of the main tanning district, the name recalls the process of *concia,* tanning. In the Middle Ages it was called Via dei Pellegrini because it was the main Pilgrim (*pellegrino*) entrance to town and led to the church of San Pellegrino.

Via Fillungo—This is Lucca's Main Street, the shopping center and the thoroughfare for the Sunday *passeggiata*. In Roman times Via Fillungo was the *Cardus Maximus*, the central north-south street. It ran straight north from its intersection with the *Decumanus Maximus* to the north gate and then angled northeasterly up to the bridge across the Serchio. You can spend quite a while here, shopping and deciphering the last one thousand years of Lucca's history in the architecture of its buildings. The name of the street probably derives from the castle of Fillongo in the Garfagnana which belonged to the Falanbrini family, who lived at the south end of the street about the year 1000.

If you can take your eyes off the items in the store windows there are many other details to notice. The lower end of the street, up to the bend, gives a glimpse into the medieval world. It is an array of high, wide, ground floor archways, today filled with glass storefronts, but which in the Middle Ages were open to the street. Inside were cavernous rooms with vaulted ceilings, some of which are still maintained. Above this was the main living floor of the merchants, the *piano nobile*, which had arched windows separated by graceful white columns. A few of these windows remain, some have been restored, and the outlines of many more can be detected where later plastering has been removed.

In recent years a good deal of decorative brick has been exposed. Some are early, fairly crude examples, simple geometric designs, others are later, more refined floral patterns, some quite elaborate. There are also many samples of fine iron lunettes which in the Renaissance became an important decorative element of doorways.

Walking up the street from the intersection with Via Roma

and Via Santa Croce, some things to notice are—

On the right hand corner is the house of Giovanni Sercambi (1348-1424). He was an invaluable chronicler of his turbulent times, the author of a book of stories which rivals Boccaccio's *Decameron*, and he was Paolo Guinigi's consigliere. He had a grand medieval house, with a tower on the corner, large entrance archways, and large mullioned windows, which have been filled in though the outlines of most can still be discerned.

Just up on your left, opposite the church of San Cristoforo, is a medieval house which was lovingly recreated (more than restored) in the 1920s; the beautiful crest is that of the owner (Stefani) in the early 1400s. On its north side is a fairly well preserved tower, called *"del Travaglio"* (tower of troubles). If you step into the alleyway you get a good idea of the tower's extent and construction. In the building just opposite the alleyway is the house on Vicolo San Carlo (completely modernized) in which Lucca's greatest sculptor, Matteo Civitali, lived, as noted by a plaque.

At the next corner on your right is the *Torre delle Ore*, the clock tower, the lower portion dating to about the year 1000. It is worth the small expense to climb it, though you might want ear plugs when the hour strikes. On the opposite corner is another restored late medieval house, Casa Barletti, with exquisite decorative brick on the gothic arches of the windows and the oculi. On its north side is the Barletti family tower.

A little further up is the Piazza and Palazzo dei Mercanti, the ancient home of the merchants' association. It has been completely, but faithfully, restored.

Do not pass by Caffè di Simo without going in. It remains as it was when Puccini liked to spend time there with his friends and it is still the most pleasant place for afternoon tea. The hot chocolate is famous; it provides a remarkable jolt of energy.

The Deutsche Bank on the corner of Via Streghi has beautiful decorative brick, but they are modern recreations. This was the northern extent of the Roman city; the city gate was a few steps beyond, where the angle in the road is. The next stretch was the road running out of town; from ancient times it ran through a busy suburb. On the left was the San Frediano neighborhood. On the right a large amphitheater was built in the first or second century.

By the time of the Lombards, in the 600s, the huge structure was already being converted to living and storage areas. Much of the Roman work can still be seen along the outside, especially on the north side. Well into the 20th century the interior was used as an open air market, but today it provides a pleasant place to rest in the sun at a café, contemplating everything or nothing, with equal pleasure.

The stretch of road just past the amphitheater has several of the grandest palazzi in Lucca, most of which were at one time owned by the Buonvisi family; in the later Renaissance this part of Via Fillungo was called the street of the Buonvisi. It ended at the medieval gate, one of two which remain. Here Via Fillungo veers off to the left into Piazza Santa Maria, where the old bridge into town used to be.

Via Fontana—In ancient times one of the main aqueducts ran along here. Today the street has the fountain (*fontana*) from which Santa Zita supposedly drew water. The present fountain dates, however, to the 1800s. This was one of the main streets of the neighborhood of San Frediano.

Via San Giorgio—This was one of the original Roman streets, which ran directly in front of the Theatre. It is named for the church of San Giorgio which was destroyed in 1810. Though much of the street has been modernized it has several examples of decorative brick.

Via San Paolino—This traces the western end of the *Decumanus Maximus*, the central east-west road of the Roman city. The original pavement has been discovered about 8 feet below the present. After Via Fillungo it is the busiest street in town, down which groups of tourists first penetrate the city. I cannot walk down it without thinking of Caesar, Pompey, and Crassus walking the same route. The western Roman gate was where Via San Paolino crosses Via Galli Tassi. Here today is the small Piazza dei Malcontenti (the malcontents) where at one time convicted criminals met their fate. A little further along is Piazza Citadella where a statue of Puccini holds court. His house, now a museum, is just behind him to the right. Just beyond is Piazza Cocomeri, where watermelons were once sold. The street exits into the central piazza of the city, which in Roman times was the site of the forum. The *Decumanus* continued on to the east gate, along what is now Via Roma and Via Santa Croce.

Via Pelleria—In the center of the old tanning district, the *pelleria*, this street is still evocative of the Middle Ages. The floral decorative brick at #32 is one of the oldest examples in the city, from the late 1100s. Before the medieval wall was constructed in the 1200s, the *pelleria* had its own wall to protect it from not only invaders but the River Serchio which ran along its northern edge.

Corte delle Pesce—The fish market was located here for many centuries.

~

The Walls of Lucca

The Walls of Lucca

Lucca has always been a walled city. The Etruscans had fortified the little bend in the river, though not sufficiently well to prevent the Ligurians from taking it in 584 BC. The settlement was, however, well enough defended to require a long siege by the Romans before they finally conquered it in 250 BC. In 218 BC, when Hannibal invaded Italy and defeated the Roman army in the Po valley, the Romans fled to the safety of Lucca because its walls made it the nearest defensible place. When Rome made Lucca a colony in 180 BC, all such colonies being armed camps, they set to work to build walls which would last, and last they did. In 56 BC Lucca was the southernmost town of Caesar's dominion of Cisalpine Gaul, just outside the border of Rome proper. He judged it secure enough for him to summon there Pompey and Crassus, to form the so-called 2nd triumvirate, soon to dissolve into civil war and the end of the Roman Republic.

The Roman Walls

The creation of a city was a religious no less than a civic endeavor and by the time Lucca was founded in 180 BC the rituals were well established. After the surveyor had established the center of the future city, oriented himself to the points of the compass and laid out the main streets, a furrow was dug where the wall was to be built. The plow was pulled by a white heifer and a white bull. The excavated soil was piled on the city side of the ditch and where the plow was raised the city gates would be built. Where the surveyor had set his center stake a hole was dug, called the *mundus*, which opened into the underworld. To protect the city a slab was placed over it. This covering would be removed three times a year, on which occasions all business stopped, the city being exposed to the spirits of the dead.

Quite a few remnants of Lucca's Roman wall have been unearthed. The only exception is the western wall, but that almost certainly followed the course of what is today Via Galli Tassi and Via San Domenico. The streets were laid out in a regular grid which still defines the *centro storico*. The survival of this pattern of streets is the best evidence we have for the uninterrupted exercise of civic rule in Lucca since its origin. Without a vigilant government the streets would have fallen into disrepair and buildings would have gradually encroached onto the public space, as happened in almost all other Roman cities.

At the center of the city was the forum. It was in the space now occupied by the piazza and church of San Michele, which has been known since the Middle Ages as *San Michele in fora*. The size of the original forum was probably larger than the present piazza; it is thought to have extended east to Via Fillungo and north to Via Buia. The forum would have been flanked by merchant shops and on one side there would have been a large columned basilica with an apse in which the magistrate sat. There would also have been a curia hall for the local Senate.

The Roman walls traced a rectangle of about 2,150 ft. on the north and south, and 1,750 ft. on the east and west. On the northwest there was a bulge to accommodate a theatre. The area of the town was about 90 acres. Although population figures are always guesstimates, by the early Christian era there were probably about 10,000 people living within the walls.

The walls themselves were 9 feet wide and 23 feet high. The lower rows used large blocks of limestone; the upper levels used lighter but very strong travertine.

Over time suburbs began to arise just outside the walls. The tanning district (*pelleria*) on the northwest of the city may well date from Roman times, since such a foul activity was best performed outside the densely inhabited area. The river Serchio almost lapped at the northern wall, providing an additional defense against attackers but also a constant danger of flooding. Another branch of the river flowed along the east wall and then turned to run along the south. It was these branches of the river which undoubtedly had determined the original size of the city.

Considering how well the streets were maintained as the Roman Empire fell apart, the walls must have been equally well preserved. They had certainly deteriorated little by 552 when the Byzantine army led by Narses undertook a three month siege but never succeeded in breaching the walls. During the Lombard rule (570-774) the Dukes of Lucca certainly made maintenance of the walls one of their priorities.

With the general political decline of the 800s and 900s, however, the walls began to suffer from neglect. Decrees prohibiting the dismantling of them to acquire building materials indicate that this was happening. Buildings were also constructed against the inner and outer faces of the wall, utilizing it as a ready made side for the new structure. The churches of Santi Simone e Giuda and Sant'Anastasio Minore both used the city wall for one of their sides.

When the Marquis of Tuscany moved his residence to Florence about the year 1000 the defenses of Lucca became less important to the seat of power. Marquis Boniface II, who ruled from 1027 to 1052, treated Lucca almost as an enemy territory. The city was virtually independent, was strong enough to engage in constant battles with Pisa, and threatened to become a challenge to the Florentine court. Boniface consequently began to dismantle sections of the Roman wall and to tear down towers.

The only place where a substantial section of the original wall can be seen today is the west side of the church of Santa Maria della Rosa.

The Medieval Walls

With the death of Boniface and the virtual end of any centralized political authority, Lucca was able to assert its independence. In 1050 Lucca attacked Pisa, razed one of that city's most important castles and sufficiently threatened the seaport for the emperor to intervene, though to no avail. The conflict continued for eight years. It was probably during this time that Lucca began erecting new defenses, the first stages being somewhat hastily built walls around the suburbs.

When the emperor came to Lucca in 1081 he was welcomed by the Ghibellines, who were currently in control. He rewarded them for their loyalty by granting a number of privileges and immunities. He also forbade anyone to demolish the town walls, "either the old or the new," which shows that by this time Lucca was already in the process of building new walls, though the Roman ones still remained.

In the early and mid-1100s war with Pisa became endemic. In 1154 Pisa began construction of new city walls, starting on the north—the Lucca—side, which prompted Lucca to work in earnest on their own new ring of walls. By 1209 the project was well underway, though in that year the Emperor again issued a decree which stated that the old Roman wall was not to be demolished. Only in the 1220s did the systematic demolition of the Roman wall begin as the medieval wall became viable. The new wall was substantially complete by 1265. By that time the Roman wall had probably disappeared above ground, its stones being reused in the construction boom which was going on in that century.

The new wall enclosed substantial portions of what had been the suburbs. The expansion was greatest on the north where the large borgo of San Frediano and the amphitheater were brought into the town proper. The city was pushed out about 500 feet on the east and west, but only about 100 feet on the south, where it incorporated what is today Corso Garibaldi, which in the Roman period had been the *Decumano Centuriale*, the military road which ran just outside the wall.

The new wall almost doubled the size of the city from about 90 acres to about 180; the average population increased from perhaps 10,000 to 15,000.

The Renaissance Walls

In 1453 the Turks assaulted Constantinople with a barrage of cannon fire. The strongest walls in Europe fell and at long last the Roman Empire fell with them (in Gibbon's view). The lesson of the effectiveness of artillery was transported to Italy when King Charles VIII of France invaded in 1494. His cannons easily dispatched any medieval wall they encountered. The thinness of these walls made them doubly deficient: not only were they easily brought down by artillery, they were so narrow they could not accommodate cannon for defensive fire.

There was no simple solution. Retrofitting the walls was impossible. If Lucca was to survive as a viable state it would have to erect an entirely new set of walls, a daunting and almost impossibly expensive enterprise.

In 1504 a new department was created to study the situation, the *Offizio delle Fortificazioni della citt*à *e dello Stato*. In 1513 preliminary work was started. The first step was to clear away all of the buildings which had been erected outside the walls so a defensive perimeter could be maintained. This was known as the *tagliata*, the cut-down zone. Every building and every tree was cleared within a distance the length of a cannon shot. What suburbs were to remain would have to be incorporated into the new ring of walls. By 1521 seven substantial new circular towers were erected at strategic points on which cannon could be installed; you can see the remains of these on Baluardo San Colombano, Baluardo Santa Croce, and just inside Baluardo San Salvatore. They were a massive but hastily installed stopgap measure. Along the southeast, the most poorly defended side, a new temporary wall was erected.

By 1550 sufficient preparations for permanent walls were complete and provisions for financing made. It must have taken a long time for the scope of the plans to sink in and for the nay-sayers to be convinced of the possibility of carrying the project to fruition. It was not an easy period for the State. In 1522 there had been an uprising which was barely put down by the authorities. Dissension in the ruling class had erupted in the Fatinelli conspiracy of 1544. Lutheranism was rampant in town and threatened the unity of government. Florence was becoming ever more powerful; they occupied much of Lucca's environs and by 1550 they threatened to finally subdue the city itself. Lucca's nobility circled the wagons. In 1556 they established an oligarchy and in 1558 banished the Lutherans. They were determined to maintain their rule and independence.

Construction of the walls would take one hundred years; they were finally completed in 1650. Only an exceptionally stable ruling class could maintain such an impetus over several generations. Since there was to be nothing outside the wall the city had to be enlarged to accommodate future development; it increased in size by about 90 acres (the size of the Roman city) to 270 acres. The main expansion was on the east where there were several monasteries with extensive grounds, the largest being San Francesco and San Micheletto.

The new wall was a massive earthen structure, 100 feet wide at its base, 60 feet at the top, 23 feet in height. There were only three gates into the city, one on the north for crossing the Serchio into the Garfagnana, one on the west leading to the sea, and one on the south leading to Pisa. There was no gate on the east, the most vulnerable, Florentine, side. Plans changed during construction, of course, as the science of fortification developed. The form of the new bastions would be regularized only in the 1600s, carefully designed to allow raking fire in all directions. On the north a section of the medieval wall could be reused; this is the only section with stone on its outer face. The rest of the wall was faced in brick—what a quantity of brick! On the west the medieval wall was also retained at first, with a new bastion built at the gate of San Donato. The last work to be done was to push this west wall out a little and build new bastions according to the design which had been gradually developed. Inside these bastions were cavernous arched rooms to accommodate the soldiers, horses, war material, and provisions for the guard. From them there were sally ports, narrow passageways which allowed defenders to exit but which would be almost impossible to storm. The most accessible of these for the present day visitor is under Baluardo San Martino, though others are open at times.

Outside the walls was an elaborate series of V-shaped earthen platforms, called half-moons, from which snipers provided the initial defense against attack. From these the ground sloped slowly away so that any attack would have to be made uphill through a barren landscape. Between the wall and the outworks there was a moat, though this proved difficult to maintain, tending to turn into a stagnant pool, and it slowly diminished in size. Originally 25 feet wide, within one hundred years it had shrunk to twelve feet; today it remains only as a narrow, shallow ditch. The three gates were accessed over drawbridges. The gates were closed at sunset and opened at sunrise. Foreigners had to surrender their weapons to the guards before they could enter the town.

Once the walls were completed, anyone assaulting Lucca faced formidable odds. Along the wall were placed about 130 artillery pieces: long range culverins, medium range cannon and bombards, and mortars which could rain stone and debris down on attackers as they closed in. The artillery and gunpowder were made in town.

By the time of the Napoleonic wars, however, the walls no longer provided a viable military defense. In 1799 the Austrians confiscated all of the artillery. In 1811 Princess Elisa opened a new gate on the east side, leading to Florence. Under the Bourbons any semblance of military character disappeared as the top of the wall was transformed into an elegant tree lined promenade.

As did all fortifications, the walls of Lucca passed in ownership to the Kingdom of Italy in 1862, and were put up for sale. In 1870 they were sold to the Commune of Lucca, which then had to decide what was to be done with them. The cost of maintenance would be considerable, and would be spent on something which no longer performed any practical purpose. Whereas the walls had once provided security they now threatened to suffocate the town.

The barren zone outside the walls was by the 1870s simply unproductive land. Gradually buildings began to appear and in the 1880s planning for new roads and developments began. The moat was reduced to a ditch. A railway station was built in the 1840s. Later in the century a tramway was built and a passage through the wall was opened to allow the trams into the city, with a track up to Piazza Santa Maria. The outworks began to disappear. In 1911 a new gate, Sant'Anna, was opened in the southwest wall, and in 1931 the small Porta San Jacopo was built on the north.

Today the walls are one of the great prides of Lucca. Ascend them and you have suddenly left the cramped world of the city behind and feel almost as if you are in the country.

~

Index of Artists

The *patria*, or birthplace, is given when known.

Ademollo, Luigi (Milan 1764–1849) 319
Allori, Alessandro (Florence 1535–1607) 200
Ammannati, Bartolomeo (Florence 1511–1592) 306, 313, 318, 328, 347
Ardenti, Alessandro (doc. 1539–1595) 71, 117, 228, 255, 256
Aretino, Spinello (Arezzo 1350–1411) 164, 165, 215, 217
Aspertini, Amico (Bologna 1474–1528) 148, 160
Auriperto (mid-700s) 209

Balducci, Giovanni (Florence 1560–Naples 1631) 229
Baratta, Giovan Domenico (Carrara 1670–1747) 155
Barbieri, Giovan Francesco called *Il Guercino* (Bologna 1591–1666) 255, 256
Bartolomeo, Fra (Prato 1472–1517) 84, 85, 199, 309, 314
Bartolomeo, Martino di (Siena ca. 1367–ca. 1435) 254
Batoni, Pompeo Girolamo (Lucca 1708–1787) 65, 78
Berlinghieri, Berlinghiero (Lucca died 1232–1236) 142, 285
Berlinghieri, Bonaventura (Lucca active 1230s) 265, 281
Biagio, Baldassare di (Lucca ca. 1430–1484) 77, 195, 270
Biancucci, Paolo (Lucca 1596–1650) 136, 138, 196, 205, 229, 279
Biduino (later 1100s) 110, 112, 113, 310
Bonodito (1190s) 212
Borghese di Pietro (Pisa 1397–1463) 243, 270, 278
Boselli, Matteo (Lucca 1593–1668) 219, 220, 228, 229, 247
Brandimarte, Benedetto (Lucca ca. 1550–after 1614) 238
Brina, Francesco del (Florence fl. 1540–1585) 83
Brugieri, Domenico (Lucca 1678–1744) 65, 93, 97, 217, 224, 243, 258

Cassiani, Fra Stefano called *Il Certosino* (Lucca ca. 1640–1714) 76
Castellotti, Lorenzo (Lucca 1718–?) 61, 65, 78, 84, 155
Catene, Gian Gherardo dalle (Modena ca. 1482–ca. 1542) 117

Cecchi, Francesco Antonio (Lucca 1717–?) 83, 161, 165
Cecchi, Giovanni 160
Chiari, Enrico 93
Ciai, Camillo (Lucca, mid-1600s) 82, 156
Ciampanti, Ansano (Lucca ca.1474–ca. 1535) 148, 178, 272
Ciampanti, Michele (Lucca ca. 1440s–after 1511) 148, 151, 272
Civitali, Matteo (Lucca 1436–1501) 31, 55, 84, 126, 130, 155, 160, 165, 169, 187, 195, 197, 198, 200, 242, 243, 245, 257, 278, 300, 316, 317, 335, 342, 350
Civitali, Masseo (Lucca fl. 1484-1514) 157, 283
Civitali, Nicolao (Lucca 1482–1560) 72, 78, 243, 293, 299, 300, 309, 316
Civitali, Vincenzo (Lucca 1523–1597) 72, 160, 198, 255, 306, 316, 317, 328
Coli, Giovanni (Lucca 1636–1681) 51, 52, 97, 169, 187, 199, 279
Colonna, Michelangelo (Ravenna 1604–1687) 95
Conca, Sebastiano (Naples 1680–1764) 212, 268
Consani, Vincenzo (Lucca 1818–1887) 131, 177, 256, 317
Coppola, Giovanni Andrea (Puglia 1597-1659) 85
Costantino, Luca di 228
Crespi, Giuseppe Maria called *Il Spagnolo* (Bologna 1665-1747) 273
Cresti, Domenico called *Il Passignano* (Florence 1559-1638) 84, 194, 195, 271, 278
Cybei, Giovanni (Carrara 1706–1784) 65

Dinelli, Filippo 220
Diotisalvi (Pisa mid-1100s) 167

Ferretti, Giovan Domenico (Florence 1692–1768) 273
Ferrucci, Giovan Domenico (Fiesole 1619–after 1669) 53, 82, 136, 151, 258
Francesco, Cecco di 238
Franchi, Antonio called *Il Lucchese* (Lucca 1634–1709) 52, 133, 134, 156, 211, 220, 243
Franchi, Tiberio (Lucca ca. 1600–1664) 212
Frate, Domenico del (Lucca 1765–Rome 1821) 319
Frediani, Vincenzo di Antonio (Lucca ca. 1455–1505) 196, 201, 272

INDEX OF ARTISTS

Gherardi, Filippo (Lucca 1643–1704) 51, 52, 75, 97, 169, 187,199, 229, 279
Ghino, Antonio di (Siena doc. 1465–1477) 195
Ghirlanda, Agostino, da Fivizzano (later 1500s) 282, 291, 315
Ghirlandaio, Domenico (Florence 1449–1494) 196, 198, 314
Giambologna (Bologna 1529–1608) 199
Gigli, Giuseppe 84
Gimignani, Giacinto (Pistoia 1606–1681) 78, 89, 90
Giordano, Luca (Naples 1634-1705) 95
Giovanni, Bartolomeo di (later 1400s) 196
Grammatica, Antiveduto (Rome 1571–1626) 93
Guarnerio, Pietro d'Angelo (Siena doc. 1370–1422) 74, 191
Guidetto, also Guido master mason (active ca. 1190–1210) 60, 91, 120, 135, 163, 167, 182, 210
Guidotti, Paolo (Lucca ca. 1560–1629) 78, 83, 93, 130, 154, 155, 178, 245

Landucci, Nicolao (Lucca 1801–1868) 212
Lazzarino, Paolo di (Lucca doc. 1320–1385) 73, 186, 216, 233, 242, 277
Lazzoni, Giovanni (Lucca 1618–after 1687) 65
Lembi, Stefano 131
Ligozzi, Jacopo (Verona 1547–1627) 56, 196, 199, 228, 283, 311
Lippi, Filippino (Florence 1457–1504) 132
Locatelli, G. 178
Lombardi, Giovan Domenico (Lucca 1682–1751) 74, 78, 84, 220, 223, 224, 273, 311
Lomi, Aurelio (Florence 1556–1622) 158
Lunardi, Giuseppe 206

Magni, Salimbene (Lucca mid-1500s) 75
Manetti, Rutilio (Siena 1571–1639) 84
Mannucci, Gaspare (Florence 1575–1642) 95, 117, 157, 206, 211, 256
Mannucci, Pier Filippo (Lucca 1601–1669) 220, 258
Marcucci, Michele (1846–1926) 76, 95,
Marracci, Giovanni (Lucca 1637–1704) 56, 61, 96, 136, 178, 205, 213, 256, 258, 311
Marracci, Ippolito (Lucca ca. 1650–early 1700s) 277

Martellini, Gaspare (Florence 1785–1857) 319
Marti, Agostino (Lucca 1482–after 1540) 77, 132, 285
Martinelli, Domenico (Lucca 1650–1718) 165, 223
Martini, Gaspare 160
Membrini, Michelangelo di Pietro (doc. 1484–1525) 90, 148, 213, 280, 311
Merli, Giulia 78
Montelupo, Baccio da (1469-1535) 67, 68, 131,165, 196, 332, 339
Montelupo, Raffaello da (1504-1566) 133, 243

Neroni, Bartolomeo (Siena 1500–ca.1572) 71
Nocchi, Bernardino (Lucca 1741–1812) 161
Nocchi, Pietro (Rome 1783–1854) 258
Nottolini, Lorenzo (Lucca 1787–1851) 107, 293, 294, 312, 319

Oddi, Muzio (Urbino 1569–1639) 199
Orlandi, Deodato (Lucca ca. 1260–ca. 1315) 212, 272

Paggi, Giovanni Battista (Genoa 1554–1627) 200, 201
Paolini, Pietro (Lucca 1603–1681) 83, 90, 94, 130, 154, 155, 229, 243, 258, 289, 311
Passaglia, Augusto (Lucca 1837–1918) 206, 317
Passignano see Cresti, Domenico
Pini, Francesco (Lucca active 1720s–1761) 61, 65, 319
Pinotti, Pompeo (Lucca) 69, 73
Pisa, Giuliano da 151
Pisano, Giuliano da 190
Pisano, Nicola (ca. 1220–ca. 1284) 189
Pucci, Ambrogio and Nicolao (Lucca late 1400s–early 1500s) 299
Puccinelli, Angelo (Lucca doc. 1379–1407) 73, 128, 134, 256, 276, 277, 282, 284

Quercia, Jacopo della (Siena 1367–1438) 30, 71, 159, 160, 191, 195, 217, 304, 340, 349

Reni, Guido (Bologna 1575–1642) 95, 212
Ricchi, Pietro called *Il Lucchese* (Lucca 1606–1675) 269, 271
Ridolfi, Michele (Lucca 1793–1854) 107, 195
Robbia, Andrea della (Florence 1435–1528) 150

Robbia, Luca della (Florence ca. 1400–1482) 130
Rosselli, Matteo (Florence 1578–1650) 93, 242, 243

Santi, Bartolomeo de (Lucca 1701–1764) 65, 83, 84, 273
Scaglia, Girolamo (Lucca ca. 1620–1686) 74, 136, 156, 196, 219, 220, 247, 254, 280
Scorsini, Pietro (Lucca 1659–ca. 1720) 93, 97
Simone, Giuliano di (Lucca doc. 1383–1397) 128, 151, 162, 178, 276, 284
Sorri, Pietro (Siena 1556–1622) 155, 157, 199, 258, 278
Stagi, Stagio (Pietrasanta 1496–1563) 115

Testa, Pietro called *Il Lucchesino* (Lucca 1612–1650) 72, 84, 311
Tintore, Francesco del (Lucca 1645–1718) 154
Tintoretto (Venice 1518–1594) 194, 311
Tofanelli, Stefano (Lucca 1752–1812) 115, 161, 198, 199, 212
Trenta, Banduccio (Lucca 1588–1644) 118

Unti, Giovanni (Lucca 1786–?) 116

Valdambrino, Francesco di (Siena ca. 1375–before 1435) 71, 191, 217, 276
Vambré, Giovanni, *il vecchio* (Flemish, active Lucca 1671–1714) 95
Vambré, Giovanni, *il giovane* (Lucca 1705–ca.1781) 61, 132, 198, 255
Vanni, Francesco (Siena 1563–1610) 78, 84, 90, 96, 278
Vanni, Giovan Battista (Florence 1599–1660) 242
Viola, Domenico (Naples ca. 1615–1696) 83

Zacchia da Vezzano, *il vecchio* (1490s–1561) 90, 116, 211, 313
Zacchia, Lorenzo, *il giovane* (Lucca 1524–1587) 74, 116, 228, 247, 276
Zanobi, Domenico di (Florence doc. 1460–1481) 197
Zuccari, Federico (ca. 1540–1609) 194, 271, 278

The Wanderer's Map of Lucca

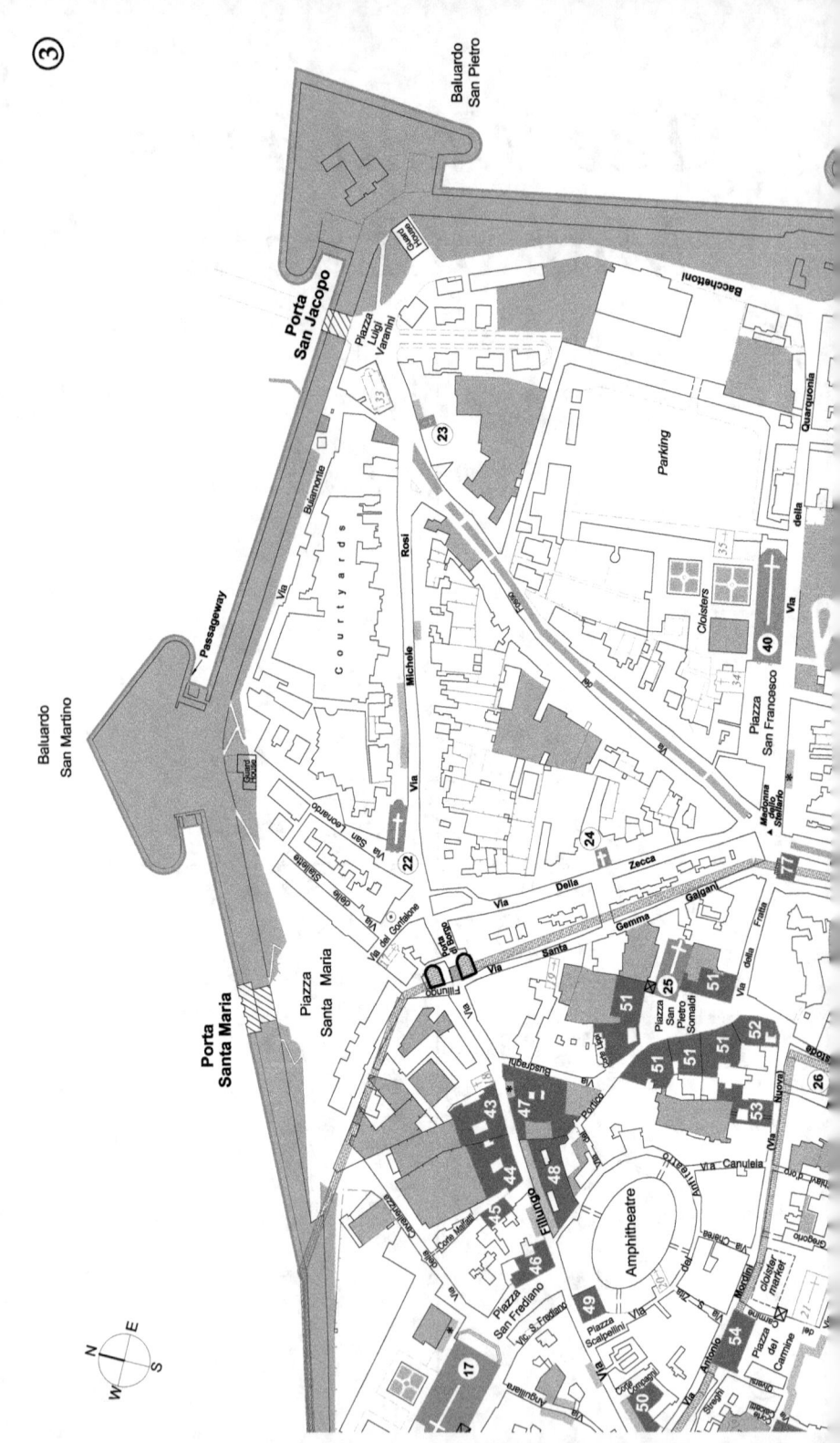

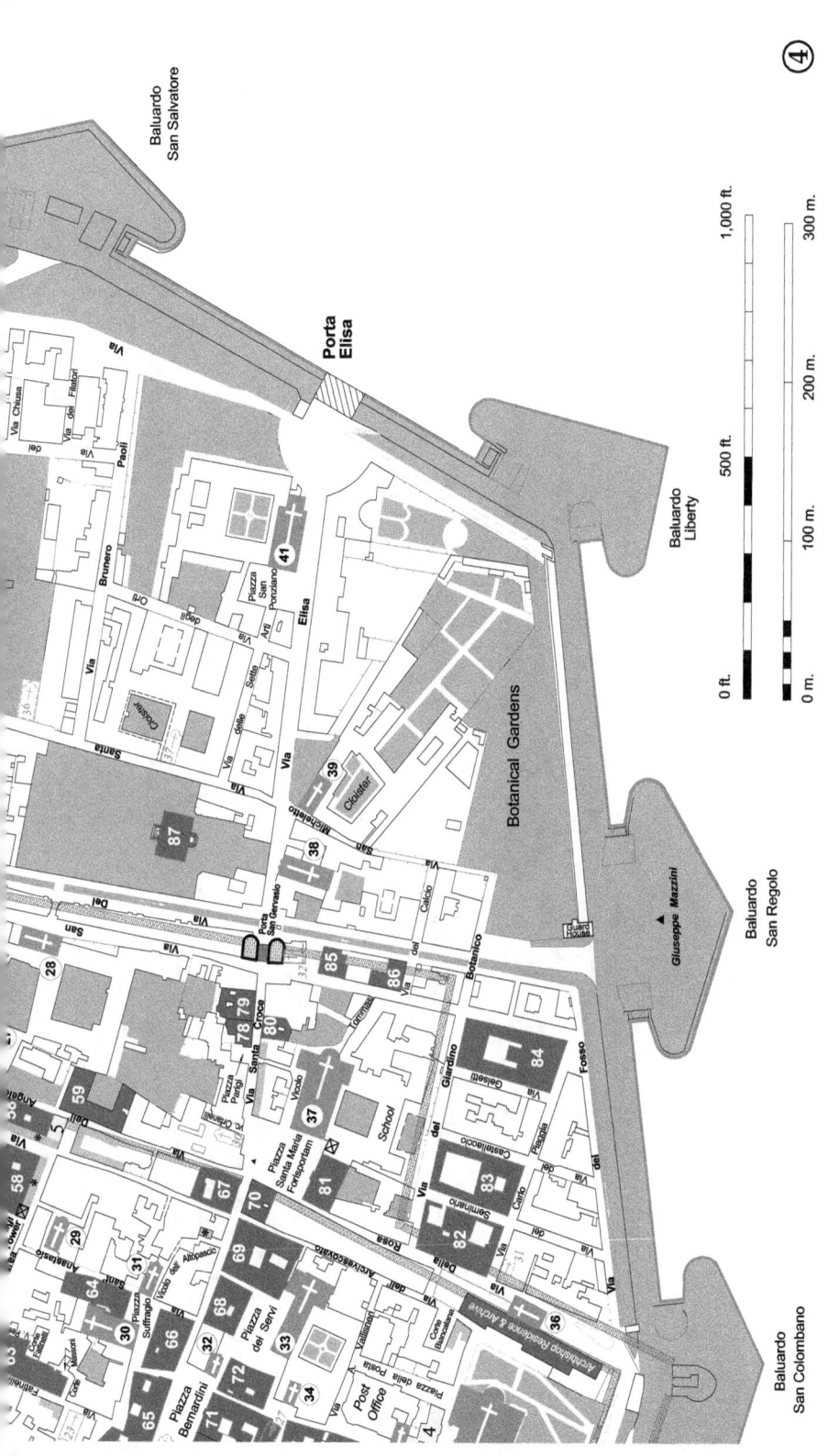

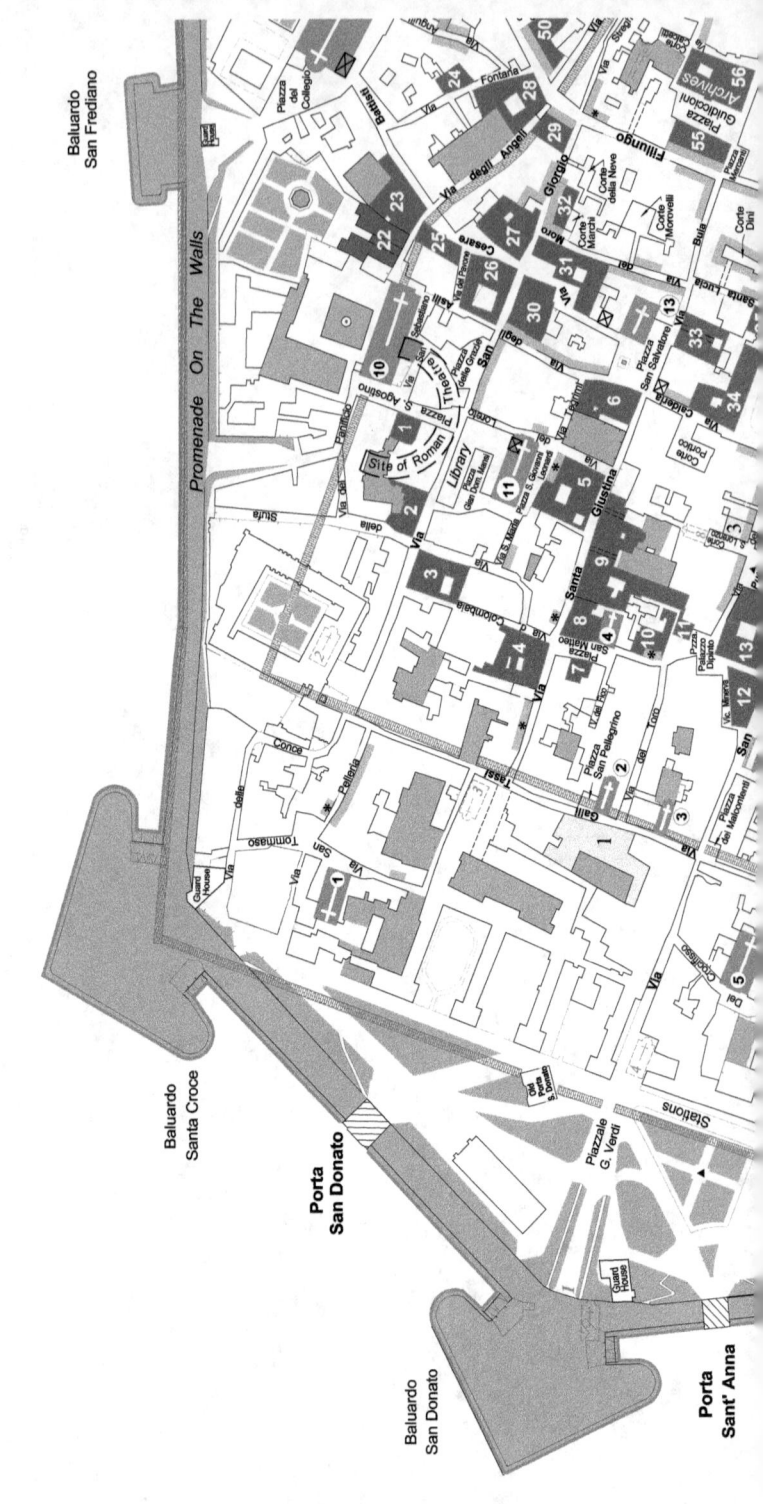

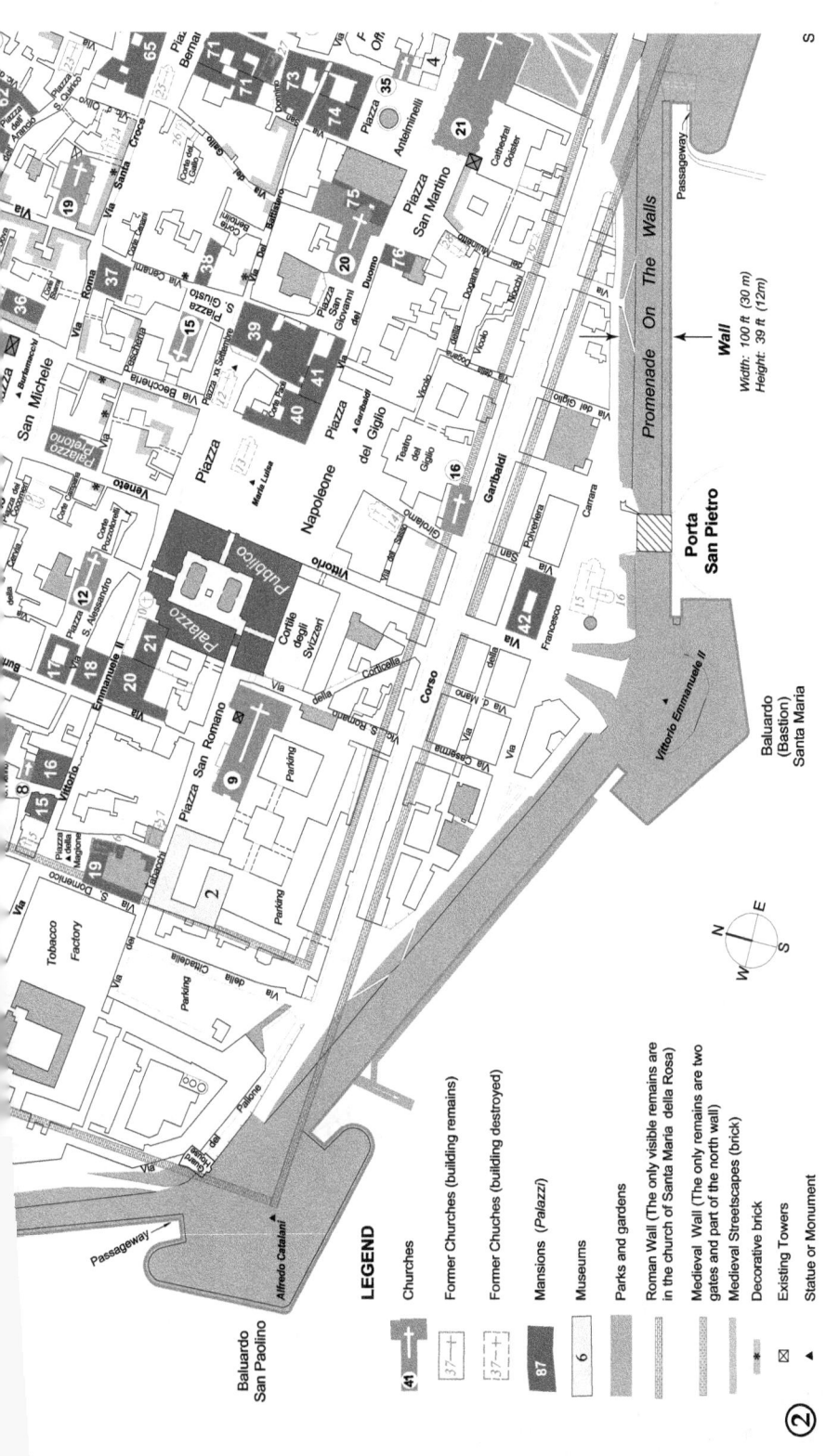

www.ingramcontent.com/pod-product-compliance
Lightning Source LLC
Chambersburg PA
CBHW052048230426
43671CB00011B/1830